Directory of the Historic Cabinet Woods

BY F. LEWIS HINCKLEY

DIRECTORY OF THE HISTORIC CABINET WOODS

THE DIRECTORY OF ANTIQUE FURNITURE

DIRECTORY
OF THE
HISTORIC
CABINET
WOODS

BY F. LEWIS HINCKLEY

CROWN PUBLISHERS, *INC.*

NEW YORK

To

J. L. STEARNS

Contributors of Illustrations

H.R.H. The Late Queen Mary
Lord James Stewart Murray
The Victoria & Albert Museum
Nordiska Museet, Stockholm, Sweden
Dansk Folkemuseum, Copenhagen, Denmark
Archives Centrales Iconographiques d'Art National, Brussels
Kunstindustrimuseet, Copenhagen, Denmark
Rijksmuseum, Amsterdam, Holland
Cooper Union Museum, New York City
Museum für Kunst und Gewerbe, Hamburg, Germany
Country Life Magazine

Joe Kindig, Jr., and Son, York, Penna.
Ginsburg & Levy, Inc., New York City
Arthur S. Vernay, Inc., New York City
Needham's Antiques, Inc., New York City
French & Company, Inc., New York City
Smith & Watson, Inc., New York City

Gaston Bensimon, New York City
J. J. Wolff Antiques Ltd., New York City

Biggs of Maidenhead
H. Blairman & Sons, Ltd., London
Hotspur, Ltd., London
Norman R. Adams Ltd., London
Morton Lee, London
Phillips of Hitchen
Ronald A. Lee, Ham Common, Surrey
Mallett & Son (Antiques) Ltd., London
Frank Partridge & Son, Ltd., London
Maple & Company, Ltd., London
A. Randolph Brett, Baldock
Charles Woolett & Son, London
Ronald Grose, London
A. Cook, London
Charles E. Thornton, Petergate, York

CONTENTS

	PAGE
Introduction	1
A Note Concerning the Illustrated Examples	6
The Growth, Structure and Properties of Hardwood Timbers	10
Color	12
Texture	12
Grain	12
Figure	13
Knurs and Buttwood	14
Burls	15
Other Extrinsic Figures	15
Luster	15
Weight	15
Hardness	15
Dimensions	16
Cutting Methods	16
Veneers	16
Seasoning and Movement	16
The Woods	19-179
Appendix	179
Bibliography	183
Index	183

ACKNOWLEDGMENTS

Aiding greatly in the preparation of this work, Mr. J. L. Stearns, Director of Research for the Timber Engineering Company, Washington, D.C., has given much time to detailed studies of photographs and wood specimens submitted for his authoritative opinions. His great help and encouragement have amounted to a collaboration in various problems resolved through an exacting knowledge in his own particular field.

Mr. John Hingston, solicitor in charge of the affairs of the venerable Leather Sellers Company, London, has signified his friendship and interest not only by obtaining a number of the important photographs of English furniture reproduced here, but also by supplying me with specimens of rare woods, and in many other ways.

Mr. Edward H. Pinto, author of the English publication *Treen*, and of various articles on antique furniture, has been helpful and stimulating in a continued correspondence especially directed toward a mutual interest in maple and mulberrywood.

Throughout the course of many years officials of the J. H. Monteath Company, New York City, have aided in this and numerous other studies of timbers through their friendly concern and the availability of their sample displays. Mr. Paul Fredericks, of Albert Constantine & Son, Inc., New York City, has been particularly affable in offering information based on more than fifty years of experience in the timber business.

Courtesies extended by Her Late Majesty Queen Mary, Lord James Stewart Murray, *Country Life*, and by leading museums and prominent business firms in England and America in making available many of the photographs reproduced here, are acknowledged beneath illustrations made possible by a most gratifying response to the present subject matter. Examples of furniture owned by English firms are represented in many instances by the excellent camera skills of Messrs. E. and D. Gibbs, London. Other illustrations are from photographs in my own working files which have been constantly augmented during the past twenty years. Those recently taken for my special requirements, and others of pieces sold through the former American Art Association, or through Parke-Bernet Galleries, Inc., New York City, were supplied by Messrs. Taylor & Dull, also of this city.

Canaan, N. Y.
January, 1960

F. Lewis Hinckley

INTRODUCTION

THE PURPOSE of this book is twofold. First, by means of an illustrated commentary of masterpieces, to provide a carefully authenticated stylebook of designs. Second, to describe and discuss at length the historic cabinet woods of which these masterpieces and other furniture have been made during past centuries. The period covered extends from *circa* 1500 in the Age of Oak, until *circa* 1860 in the Machine Age, the majority of illustrated examples representing the eighteenth century, the era in which design and the skill of the craftsman reached an excellence that has never before or since been surpassed. They were inspired to a great degree by the wide variety of materials then available in Europe and America.

The term *masterpiece* when applied to fine furniture has more than an arbitrary aesthetic connotation. In most cases, particularly with regard to French furniture since the fifteenth century, it denotes the production of an acknowledged master's mind or hand. The statutes of the Paris *Communauté des Maîtres Menuisiers et Ébénistes*, registered with the French parliament in 1751, laid down conditions that governed the production of such masterpieces. Similar though less precise rules of conduct were observed in the British Isles and America.

An applicant for admission into this Paris corporation was bound to serve for six years or more as an apprentice to a recognized master craftsman. The principal and a committee of jurors or wardens elected by working members of the guild in which entrance was sought then judged him upon his general ability and the skill with which he had executed a piece to prove his merit, known as a *chef-d'oeuvre* or masterpiece. With the acceptance of this proof piece he was enjoined to work for two years or more as a journeyman, after which he was permitted to establish himself as a full-fledged master.

A skilled handling of tools was not in itself sufficient evidence of a prospective master's ability, or that of a master "free" of his company or guild and thus permitted to carry on his own business. It was specified that an initiatory masterpiece was to be made "with great art" according to prescribed "design, composition, contour, form and profile." It was the duty of jurors, with the aid of a constable or guardsmen if necessary, to confiscate pieces which later might be judged as "misshapen," whether produced by "foreigners"—those working without communal sanction, or by masters accepted into the community.

Hence it will be seen that correctness of design, a quality synonymous with or dependent upon "composition, contour, form and profile," was of major importance in the making of a proof piece or *pièce de maîtrice*, and also in those later masterworks produced with increased experience for judgment by public favor. In these efforts the majority of craftsmen depended upon their own skills for improving and diversifying the models which they, and in many instances their fathers before them had followed with success. When more drastic changes were undertaken these were often based upon the completed projects of their more imaginative colleagues. Adding to these the fact that craftsmen not only moved from one workshop to another but also from country to country, for instance from England and Ireland to America, it will be seen how easily the origin and therefore the value of a given piece may be mistaken. An event of recent occurrence will serve to illustrate this.

At a dispersal of property from the estate of a famous collector of American furniture an Irish three-tier dumbwaiter of ordinary quality was sold for the astounding price of $3,100. Some forty years ago the same collector had catalogued this very piece for another auction sale, without any knowledge of its real provenance, and had apparently bought it himself at that sale for only $125. Evidently through association with his name, certainly without any regard for a design which, although eventually ascribed to Philadelphia, was never produced in this country, the price attained was just about one thousand per cent higher than the piece would be worth in the present retail market.

The paw-foot side chair shown here as illustration 113 is another of the innumerable examples which from design alone clearly bespeak their true origins. Yet several chairs exactly matching it in all respects have been claimed as American, and also an armchair *en suite* that has been declared in print "one of the finest New England chairs known," its slightly projected and whorled arm terminals being described as "probably unique." As in this instance, when experts specializing in single fields of antique furniture comment upon forms or lesser orna-

2

mental features as unusual, rare or unique, the use of these terms often betrays an insular point of view occasioned by a lack of concern over, and therefore a dearth of knowledge about the work commonly produced in areas outside their single fields of interest.

Similar instances which in one way or another come to the attention of collectors should stress the importance of design, not only as an aid to the aesthetic appreciation of antique furniture, but as a principal factor in guarding their decisions and their pocketbooks. The advisability of studying all related schools of design cannot be too strongly recommended as a necessity for those who wish to limit their collecting activities to acquiring only examples of English, American or French furniture.

Thomas Chippendale and Thomas Sheraton gave their names to the better known design books of the eighteenth century; that they did so does not mean that they were themselves the authors or creators of these designs in their entirety. Those issued by Chippendale in *The Gentleman and Cabinet-Maker's Director* (London, 1754, 1755 and 1762), were obtained not only through the talents of his contemporaries in London, but also through plagiary of complete designs formerly introduced by Juste Aurèle Meissonnier, a principal creator of the rococo style in France; only a few years later he came under the influence of Robert Adam, a leader in the classic movement.

With the prestige which he gained through the *Director* and by his own abilities in the management of his business, Chippendale was able to maintain three houses in St. Martin's Lane where, aside from designers and draftsmen performing their usual duties, he employed a host of joiners, cabinetmakers, carvers, inlayers and other skilled technicians, while he himself apparently devoted most of his time to waiting upon his important if not royal customers, the normal task of any proprietor in his position whether in England or elsewhere.

Ackermann's *Repository of the Arts* shows us a picture of the showrooms maintained by one such firm. In a colored aquatint engraving of the August 1809 issue of this London periodical, we can see the spacious, handsomely decorated and well appointed gallery in which patrons were received at the premises of Morgan and Saunders, Catherine Street, The Strand.

A larger and more famous establishment, that of

George Seddon in Aldersgate Street, was visited in 1786 by the German diarist, Sophie von Roch, who has left a lengthy account* of what she saw there. Mentioning Seddon himself as "a man of genius" who was "for ever creating new forms," she refers to his premises as "a building with six wings" occupied—according to her belief and terminology—by "four hundred apprentices." As joiners, carvers, gilders, upholsterers, glass workers, metalists and seamstresses, these employees were engaged "on any work connected with the making of household furniture." One department contained "nothing but chairs, sofas and stools of every description, some quite simple, others exquisitely carved and made of all varieties of wood," and one large room was "full up with all the finished articles in this line," while others were "occupied by writing-tables, cupboards, chests of drawers, charmingly fashioned desks, chests, both large and small, work- and toilet-tables in all manner of woods and patterns, from the simple and cheapest to the most elegant and expensive." As in showrooms of today a separate space was given over to the "scheme of a dining-room designed both for practical use and for ornament."

From the immense quantity of furniture produced by this firm and others in which many associate workers carried out the projects of a proprietor or of the staff of designers and draftsmen under his control, it will be realized that there is little possibility of correctly attributing any single unmarked piece to the shop in which it originated, unless at least one other piece definitely resembling it in some important respect has been so identified through some form of documentary evidence.

The important West Indian satinwood cabinet shown here as illustration 35 has been identified as the work of a particular shop on the basis of its distinctive inlaid decorations, especially through the treatment of the laurel festoons, each centering a cluster of berries. These festoons are duplicated in a "commode" for which there still exists a bill made out in 1782 by William Moore of Dublin to the third Duke of Portland. Other separate inlaid treatments of that particular "commode" have served to identify additional pieces in which they appear, and these in turn through their complementary effects in the same medium have given further confirmation of the cabinet illustrated here, serving also to identify as the work of William Moore several "commodes" that published commentary has called superior examples of English craftsmanship.

Some other observations of Sophie von Roch, the traveler from Germany, are more specifically appropriate to the subject of principal interest in the

* *Sophie in London, 1786.* Translated from the German by Clare Williams; Jonathan Cape, London, 1933.

present text. Mentioning "numerous articles of straw-coloured service wood charmingly finished with all the cabinet-maker's skill," she writes of her visit to Seddon's saw-house where "many blocks of fine foreign woods lie piled, as firs and oaks are seen at our saw-mills. The entire story of the wood, as used for both inexpensive and costly furniture and the method of treating it, can be traced in this establishment" whose owner is "intimate with the quality of woods from all parts of the earth, with the chemical knowledge of how to colour them or combine their own tints with taste." These were apparently well deserved words of praise at the time; nevertheless during the next half century cabinetmakers and botanists alike admitted to many cabinet woods "whose nature and qualities are imperfectly known," regretting "that, especially respecting many tropical woods, so little precise information exists." It will thus be understood why the bibliography here is made up so largely of works by present-day authors who have more recent scientific knowledge of woods from all parts of the earth.

A strict supervision over the selection of woods in regard to quality and strength, and in their finishing, is expressed in the regulations previously mentioned as governing the work of Parisian masters, in which are named many if not all of the domestic and imported timbers approved for use by joiners, cabinetmakers, carvers and other members of their guild. Today these woods and many others appearing in antique furniture of various countries are admired for their beauty of color or figure and for other qualities, yet apart from those which have remained constantly in fashion up to the present time the majority are seldom recognized. There is no real reason for this since both the common and rarer types of woods are in most instances easily identified on sight. They continue to go unrecognized mainly because pieces other than those made of the more popular timbers are seldom illustrated in books and magazine articles on antique furniture, and therefore illustrations are not easily available for study; nor has there so far been an attempt to describe these woods in a way that will really permit their identification.

The uncertainty that exists in regard to many of the lighter colored cabinet woods may be pointed out by mentioning only a few of those so often mislabeled satinwood, when this name can only strictly designate either of the two satinwoods obtained from the West Indies, and from Ceylon or neighboring areas. Errors of this nature may result from a lack of acquaintance with the true properties distinguishing these two satinwoods, because many unrecognized woods happen to approach them in color, or simply because these other woods appear in pieces made during the so-called "age of satinwood." This age may be accepted as dating from *circa* 1780 until the early years of the nineteenth century; however, it will be found here that West Indian satinwood was shipped to England as early as 1612, in the period when oak was the most popular timber.

A collector may find that a piece believed to be of satinwood is actually constructed of or veneered in birch, fine and inferior qualities of which were often utilized during the eighteenth and nineteenth centuries. Similarly without knowing the differences between true satinwood and citronnier or any of the amarillos, he may accept these other woods as satinwood. Believing that holly was restricted to smaller uses he will admire the plain or quietly figured surfaces of pieces substantially veneered in this wood, wondering why they do not exhibit the flashier effects of the satinwoods. He can be forgiven, however, for overlooking the opportunity of owning a piece veneered in one of the finest timbers discovered during the late eighteenth century, avodire, from the Gold and Ivory Coasts of West Africa, which has now been authenticated as a cabinet wood of this period and is illustrated here for the first time.

Among the darker woods, which in some instances require more than superficial examinations to permit accurate identification, coralwood, narra, sabicu, padauk, Botany Bay oak of a plain quality, and many others, including various types of walnut, especially Virginia walnut, are at times incorrectly designated as mahogany. But the possibilities for, and common occurrences of these and similar mistakes in regard to still others of the cabinet woods are apparently limitless, sometimes drastically affecting the value of certain pieces offered to or owned by the more exacting collectors, or even influencing the decisions of those who shop with rule in hand and an eye only to decorative value.

In compiling the present information on the histories and descriptions of the cabinet woods I have drawn upon all of the authoritative sources listed in the bibliography. Some have been quoted at length, as *The Cabinet-Maker's Assistant* (London, 1853), while entire sections of others have been condensed, combined and reworded for easier assimilation by the layman. The more informative books on world timbers treat of many that do not fall within the scope of this project, and in make-up, alphabetical or otherwise, they are not especially planned to aid in the identification of unrecognized woods. Therefore a new order has

4

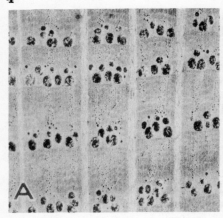

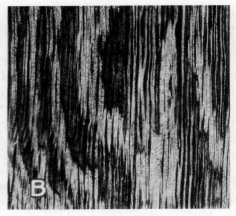

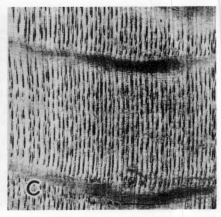

AMERICAN WHITE OAK

A ring-porous wood with coarse and uneven texture. Larger pores prominent. Pronounced growth-ring figures and large rays.

A. Magnified view of end surface.

B. Plain-sawed surface showing growth-ring figure.

C. Quarter-sawed surface showing broad and long rays.

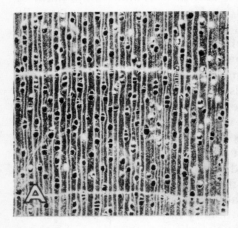

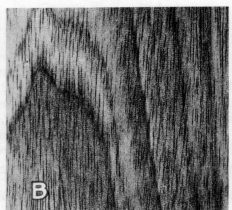

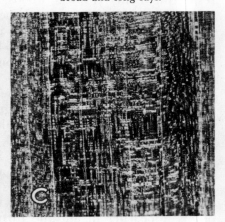

TROPICAL AMERICAN MAHOGANY

A diffuse-porous wood with medium-fine and uniform texture. Pores visible. Numerous varieties of figures occur in both plain-sawed and quartered material. Very fine but distinct rays.

A. Magnified view of end surface.

B. Plain-sawed surface showing growth-ring figure.

C. Quarter-sawed surface showing small rays.

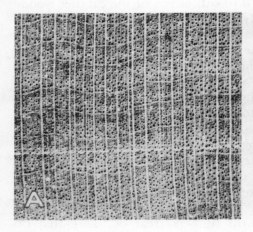

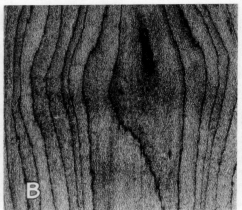

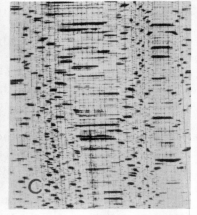

AMERICAN SUGAR MAPLE

A diffuse-porous wood with fine and uniform texture. Pores invisible without magnification. Growth-ring, curly and wavy figures; and bird's-eye markings. Very fine rays, some distinct.

A. Magnified view of end surface.

B. Plain-sawed surface showing growth-ring figure.

C. Quarter-sawed surface showing larger of rays.

Photomicrographs and photographs used for these plates were obtained from the United States Department of Agriculture, Forest Products Laboratory, Madison, Wisconsin.

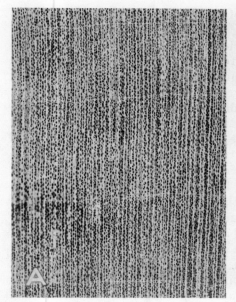 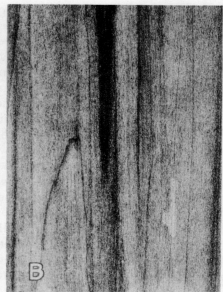 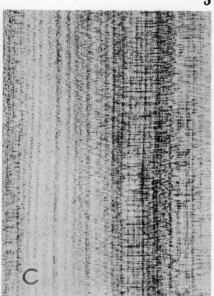

AMERICAN RED GUM

A diffuse-porous wood with very fine and uniform texture. Pores invisible without magnification.
Figures resulting principally from pigment streaks. Very fine but distinct rays.

A. Magnified view of end surface.
B. Plain-sawed surface showing pigment figure.
C. Quarter-sawed surface showing small rays.

been introduced here which has already proven to be of service in this respect while building up my own working notes.

All of the cabinet woods are considered separately and wherever possible illustrated by examples of antique furniture in which they are featured. These examples serve to carry on discussions of design and other matters, especially in sections where larger numbers of illustrations are devoted to the more popular woods such as walnut and mahogany. While it is not suggested that the sections of this book follow each other in an unalterable succession of color values generally associated with the various timbers, they are arranged according to the color or combined color value of each particular wood, ranging from the lightest to the darkest. Interpretations of these values will vary in individual reactions to certain colors. Also, terms used by one authority in specifying the colors of certain woods may apply but roughly to their tones as they appear in specimens examined and described by another.

The present system will permit the identification of an unrecognized cabinet wood within a limited number of sections devoted to those generally possessing about the same depth of color or a similar average value in this respect where striped or otherwise contrastingly marked woods are concerned. Unusual effects appearing in certain timbers must of course be described under their general head-

ings. Thus bog or black oak is mentioned in connection with the European oaks as this blackish coloring is accidental, and maple knurlwood or buttwood is described along with other cuttings of maple not characterized by such unusually dark and widespread markings.

With this arrangement the general sections are easily referred to with or without consulting the headings listed in the contents pages. Where a particular wood or special type of wood is known by any of its vernacular names, information on that wood may be more readily obtained by using the index, where all scientific names mentioned in the text also appear.

Superior figures in the text refer to notes in the appendix.

In sections devoted to the more popular woods, illustrated examples of furniture are shown. For reference purposes remarks on the designs, dates, materials or other matters concerning the illustrated pieces may be located under the heading "The Illustrated Examples." Where comments are unnecessary regarding forms and clearly defined ornamental treatments the illustrations are permitted to speak for themselves.

Contrasting with the few illustrations that show plainer woods in their less elegant uses, it will be recognized that the more finished examples of the woodworking arts were achieved only through the great skill displayed by their makers in selecting and employing the finest timbers. This skill entailed a knowledge of the properties to be recognized in available timbers, any faults to be guarded against, and the methods to be followed in cutting and handling them in other respects to assure their most attractive effects. In the final analysis it is these fine and rare woods that lend quality and distinction to the designs of furniture in which they appear. Their distinguishing characteristics will be more easily recognized, and a greater interest will be imparted to the study of old furniture through the knowledge available here in respect to the growth, structure and properties of the hardwood timbers from which these cabinet woods were obtained, their individual histories in commercial undertakings of the past and the ways in which they were handled on their journeys from forests and wood lots to their final use in the hands of master craftsmen.

A NOTE CONCERNING
THE ILLUSTRATED EXAMPLES
BRITISH *VERSUS* "OLD ENGLISH"

While the present work is primarily intended to supply a long needed professional approach to the study of woods found in antique furniture from all parts of the world, the illustrations will emphasize a fairly wide coverage of the furniture of the British Isles, America and France. Today, our explicit knowledge of American and French furniture contrasts sharply with the confusion over the furniture of the British Isles. Within the limitations imposed by the principal purpose of this book, it is of course impossible here to make any great contribution toward dispelling such confusion. Furthermore, it would be false courtesy indeed to repay the contributors of important illustrations of notable pieces, displaying the world's finest and rarest woods, by designating these in any manner contrary to former opinions made in keeping with the methods established during the past fifty years by museum authorities and other writers of note.

In view of these required restrictions and courtesies it has been decided to introduce in the present title the term *British*, in a departure from universal acceptance of the term *English* as covering any and all types of furniture such as those represented here under the more inclusive designation. This innovation is offered in favor of greater accuracy in dealing with such pieces, and in order to dispel as far as possible the current belief that nearly all furniture originating within the different countries of the British Isles must be English. This error long fostered by carelessly, unsystematically, and therefore unscientifically based "studies" published in great profusion throughout the past half century, must be subjected to intense review and undergo great revision before there can be any real understanding of what is truly English furniture, and what must be assigned instead to other countries of the British Isles.

To future writers, collectors and interested laymen it must be made known that much of the oak furniture, now looked upon as English, was made throughout the period when that wood was generally popular, and even much later, within the relatively small area comprising the principality of Wales. Also, it should be known that during the great and long continued vogues of walnut and mahogany, during the periods when other woods enjoyed favor, and in productions with lacquered, painted and decorated, or gilded finishings, furniture consonant with the fashion, even pieces representing the highest and most refined skills of the joiner, cabinetmaker, carver, inlayer and other artificers was most abundantly produced in Ireland, especially in Dublin. And work of real sophistication and refinement, in some instances fashioned after designs which originated in Dublin or London, was eventually developed in Wales and Scotland.

Current misinformation and a general lack of knowledge about these areas is therefore, of necessity, paralleled by an equal misunderstanding of English furniture as a whole, for which most, if not indeed all writers on that subject must be held responsible. Of these, Herbert Cescinsky and R. W. Symonds, principal contenders for the title actually applied to the first, "the greatest living authority on antique furniture," must be held guilty of misinforming the layman, and each other, through frequent publications extending over a period of five decades.

Cescinsky assured his readers, private supporters and museum officials that Welsh furniture was not made in that country but in the west of England, and that furniture of any interest to a collector was never produced in Ireland, but only the simplest and crudest articles of furniture—apparently to complement the beauty and delicacy of Irish table settings, silver and glass. To this expert even the grotesque designs of the commonly recognized Irish side tables carved with lion or satyr masks were not made in that country, but in England, as the Metropolitan Museum is still convinced.

Symonds recognized these eccentric examples as Irish, offering their features to the collector so that

"He should, therefore, make himself familiar with the peculiarities of Irish design, so that the recognition of examples will be easy." This expert went on to say that the amount of Irish furniture of fine quality that has survived from the walnut period "is so negligible that it demands no consideration from the collector." In contradiction, a number of such examples accompanied this intelligence, labeled as "English," including one which, as a feature of its ornamentation, actually bears an inscription in documentation of its Dublin origin.

After many years of showing Irish furniture (as "English") in all its mediums Symonds eventually must have felt called upon to make the rather weak admission that if a piece of antique furniture is known to have come from Ireland it is presumed to have been made there. It would have been too late by then for him, if indeed he ever could have entertained any such thought, to have undertaken the lengthy reviews and numerous retractions that might have been based on some knowledge of the sources from which many of the pieces he illustrated had been directly received in London. These origins are given in statements to dealers and other buyers, according to British law, as every purchaser knows, but in his glorified position Symonds apparently did not seek much information from dealers supplying him with much of the material for his illustrations. Furthermore, revisions of such magnitude might well have lost him the esteem he so persistently sought, and his influence in publicizing and arranging for the acquisition of individual pieces or groups of furniture by collectors of note might have been severely curtailed.

Among the examples chosen for Symonds' "English Furniture from Charles II to George II," the feature piece, a walnut secretary, is shown in a full-page photographic illustration, a smaller cut to display the boldly carved details, and two full-page illustrations reproducing line drawings prepared by John C. Rogers, A.R.I.B.A. These drawings represented a culmination of Symonds' observations as an expert on the construction of English furniture. Their use was intended to impart to his less informed patrons and followers in general the knowledge that he had acquired by that time through diligent study of this technical subject. This secretary was apparently of the greatest value and importance to Symonds, for he illustrated it many times over, finally describing it, for the gratification of the collector who had been permitted to acquire it, as a "scrutoir to end all scrutoirs."

When, as a part of the Untermyer Collection, this particular secretary eventually passes into possession of the Metropolitan Museum of Art it will, if properly labeled, serve, along with many other examples in the Untermyer Collection, and still others already in the Museum, for study of the design and structure techniques of *Irish* furniture—in the case of the secretary for such furniture as Ireland abundantly produced a decade to a generation or more after the date to which it has been assigned.

The recently published catalogue of the Untermyer Collection has given rise to a reaction which evidences another misunderstanding that has been permitted to exist among experts of long standing. In a review of this book signed "R. E.," apparently indicating the now retired museum authority long associated with these initials, the reviewer states that a walnut and burl walnut twin-chair-back settee, "Fig. 100, also singled out for favourable notice, suggests a Dutch origin both in line and ornament." Despite the timidity of this wording, the opinion above states that the settee originated in Holland. This designation shows a real lack of professed knowledge in the furniture of that country, for neither the "line" nor the "ornament" can be entertained as Dutch. To speak in plainer terms, the design of this settee, including the readily identifiable structural features of the back, as well as the arms, rails and legs, is not to be found in Dutch furniture, nor are the three varying types of shells and the other carved details characteristic of Dutch carving. In every respect the settee is typical of Irish craftsmanship.

It is remarkable that this collection and many others of private or institutional ownership contain numerous examples of equally typical Irish furniture which are unhesitatingly accepted as English, while at the same time others which are no less typical will raise some doubt as to their fitting into the same forced classification, and these are invariably either called "Dutch," as in the instance cited above, or turned down as not antique since they do not quite fit into specifications which are considered as representing the more restrained, and less imaginative, English furniture of the eighteenth century.

From these necessarily few and brief remarks it may be seen that the more conventional and refined Irish furniture of good, fine, or exceptionally fine quality, in varying respects sometimes more or less approaching or paralleling English designs, may easily be, and thus often has been, accepted as typical of, and originating in England. Such errors have occurred despite the fact that these Irish designs and resultant working techniques have for the most part been separately developed within Ireland itself although it is true that English design books, from the earliest on, were received and studied and sometimes served partially or rather completely in the execution of Dublin pieces.

With the possible exceptions of unheard from indigenous sources, knowledge of Irish furniture representing these more refined conventional or classic developments is held by few today, so great have been the shipments and transhipments of Ireland's masterpieces of furniture from the eighteenth century to the present day. These deliveries of specially ordered furniture and later removals of household effects included looking glasses, girandoles, chandeliers, mural paintings, interior woodwork and paneling, mantels, fireplace equipment and many other furnishings.

To throw real light upon this great abundance of seat furniture and cabinetwork, correcting all that has thus far occurred to obscure present day understanding, will require literature almost equal in amount to that which has so befogged the issue, and in this it would be well to correct former writers by reprinting their illustrated material with properly authenticated sources attesting Irish origins or, wherever this is clearly indicated, in Dublin itself.

This perception raises another enigma of our time, for in the tremendous amount of so-called "English" furniture remaining today it will be noticed that very few pieces have actually been documented as originating in London, the only English city of any real furniture-manufacturing importance. Features of design that have been presented as originating in London have been of little use in determining other London work. In fact, there is a question as to whether London was indeed so active in her furniture industries as is commonly believed.

The answer will become clearer when it is understood that in those instances where London origin has seemed necessary, the pieces so assigned have indeed reflected the superior output of a great capital city, the rival seaport and third greatest city in all Europe at the time when population statistics were first collected. This was just a few years prior to the date, 1802, when the title page of Thomas Sheraton's "Drawing Book" prominently featured its sale there by "J. ARCHER, DUBLIN."

For many years both before and after that time this great metropolis and shipping center, one of the largest furniture manufacturing cities of Europe, supplied its products to all of the western counties of England, to her southern counties, to all of Wales, and to Scotland, especially in her western counties; all this indeed with little competition from London, which in those times in terms of shipping was located far away. And apparently manufacturing and handling costs made trading with London impractical to all but a very few. English visitors, such as those whose interests passed from the London to the Dublin season of social activity, may have found it economically and otherwise more attractive to make acquisitions there; and English owners may have preferred to supply their Irish seats with furnishings that might remain more settled rather than those sometimes described as traveling about with their owners. Irish furniture is also known to have been shipped eastward as far as the West Indies, and Ireland's long history in the manufacture and exportation of looking glasses can be studied in American collections of long standing.

Later trade with Ireland can best be vouched for in the words of the traders themselves, whose buying trips started during the latter part of the nineteenth century. One of the first to engage in this latter-day trade in household effects, removed or obtained directly through local dealers, built up annual shipments of Caroline, Queen Anne, Early Georgian, Chippendale, Adam-Hepplewhite, Sheraton, Regency and even Early Victorian types of furniture that ran into hundreds of thousands of dollars. When queried on these purchases he replied: "What *imagination* those fellows had! And what skills! Since Irish furniture was not popularly recognized we called everything English." This dealer of great taste was especially attracted to the work carried out by Angelica Kauffmann (1741-1807) in Dublin and the vicinity, and always added to his shipments any pieces with painting (or murals) attributable to her hand.

Another dealer of that time, whose purchases were divided between the British Isles and the United States, said: "We all went there (to Ireland) for many years before the first World War, after which some of us dropped out as the finer things became increasingly hard to come by unless you had access to the larger homes. Everything of good design and quality we called English, and anything that didn't come up to the mark we called Irish." Still another, whose fine stock thus built up of Georgian and Regency furniture which was known for commanding the very highest prices, replied that he had stopped buying in Ireland by 1905, from then on he was able to obtain the same high quality merchandise in London without the inconvenience of traveling to Ireland.

Reference to the English art magazines of this time, including of course the still most valuable contents of these periodicals, advertisements of the most prominent dealers, will serve as further verification that by then there was an abundance of Irish furniture located in homes and shops throughout the length and breadth of England; not only specimens representative of the finest work, but also those displaying the more grotesque features easily recognized by the informed layman.

The foregoing remarks may shed some faint light on the confusion so long promulgated by the incompetence of misinformed writers, and even museum officials who never could have properly investigated the subject of old English furniture. If some recognition of the truth occurs through thus stating the simple facts of life in the profession, and if some discerning approval is gained in regard to the broader term of assignment introduced here, the secondary purpose of the present publication will have been achieved.

Lest the derogatory comments it has been necessary to make, lend credence to any belief of infallibility on my own part, it is most readily admitted, as shown by a note in connection with a still problematical piece illustrated in my own former publication, "A Directory of Antique Furniture," that I was not by that time fully cognizant of many original designs produced by the highly skilled Irish craftsmen. In that covering note I indicated my belief that the piece shown above it (621) was "still open to proof as an additional Irish model . . . in common with certain other examples" included in the book. Through persistent research throughout the intervening years this warning has proved only too true. The improper showing of these pieces has been one of my most regretted mistakes. At the time, I just could not bring myself to believe and recognize such proficiency, imagination and productivity as Irish.

In conclusion here, as a most gratifying and even somewhat surprising result of the present concentrated study of cabinet woods, when the photographs of various pieces were grouped together according to the various woods, both local and exotic, from their already proven and therefore easily recognizable designs, carved or inlaid ornamental techniques, ormolu mountings, handles, escutcheons, etc., some woods gradually emerged as selections favored by Irish joiners and cabinetmakers. Virginia walnut is one of these favorites, which may sometimes be found employed in conjunction with secondary woods such as the soft

and hard pines of the same general vicinity. Yewwood is another which attained great popularity; and generally it will be found that Ireland is the origin of pieces that appear from time to time in padauk, a wood which is invariably misspelled and mispronounced. In such a combined study these examples must suffice to bring out one particular facet of interest. There are other woods which have been partially proven to be Irish favorites, it may be mentioned, and which tempt emphasis here, but there has already been enough of mere opinion without positive proof.

Another way in which any possibility of accuracy in the study of old English furniture was doomed from the very start was brought out while investigating possible Irish connections of the furniture of certain owners whose properties appear in numerous books on the subject. As almost anyone following the subject must realize, whenever during the past fifty years a prominent owner of antique furniture has ventured out into the open market and bought himself an additional piece, from that minute on such a piece has always been published as constituting a part of the already existing collection, hence its real origin is supposedly not open to review. When piece after piece of Irish furniture in one collection has appeared as belonging to other owners, it becomes evident that such a collection, as a whole, has been recently formed. In the instance of one of the best known owners of "Old English" furniture, however, it did not seem that similar exchanges had occurred.

Over fifty years ago there started appearing in print examples of "Old English" furniture in the possession of Sir Spencer Ponsonby Fane, and certain of these have continued to be published. Since I had to realize finally that either all or most of these pieces were Irish, or that I could no longer consider myself qualified to carry on what I had considered really scientific research, I was forced to give Sir Spencer a real looking into, not in the peerage tables showing Irish seats, etc., but a full genealogical study. It turned out that the Fane (and Ponsonby) family was most prominently Irish, Sir Spencer's mother, as well as his father, was Irish, and as a good Irishman, himself, he married an Irish lady before packing up several generations of family effects which were then headed for England and fame . . . as "Old English."

THE GROWTH, STRUCTURE AND PROPERTIES OF HARDWOOD TIMBERS

Progress in the more intellectual processes associated with the designing and manufacture of classic furniture has been ever attended by increasing interest in fine and rare timbers,[1] according to their working qualities, serviceability and beauty in color and figure. As furniture-making gained in importance with each renaissance of artistic force the nature and handsome appearance of certain timbers became widely recognized and appreciated, until eventually they appeared as exotics among local supplies in ancient cities located far from their places of growth.

Native forests or smaller stands of timbers furnished the wood products of Romanesque and Gothic joiners during these incipient periods of our present civilization. Local supply continued throughout ensuing epochs, sometimes interrupted by shortages or changing demands, and with increasing facilities for travel and commerce such timbers were augmented by importations.

With the rise of Europe's great world-trading companies during the sixteenth century these importations gradually became an important part of the cargoes returned from factories and lesser points of supply in America and the East, while European timbers were exchanged within that sphere. Thus the repertory of native and exotic woods increased with the succeeding years, particularly during the eighteenth century and the beginning of the machine age.

The more common of these woods are often recognized today through their general appearances. Similar method may also serve if a clear remembrance of a rarer but authoritatively designated specimen of wood is retained when the species is again seen in one form or another. However, the proper identification of cabinet woods requires some knowledge of their structure and essential properties, as it is through these characterizing features, and the variations occurring between species, that they are determined and classified. In order to recognize these features some familiarity with the terms employed in describing woods is desirable, at least in so far as they apply in the ordinary visual examinations which are of concern here.

Throughout the past centuries *hardwood timbers* have always provided the majority of cabinet woods selected for strength and appearance. In former times *softwood timbers* might be imported when local supplies were not plentiful, but they were generally employed for utilitarian purposes or concealed beneath various applied finishes.

Timber trees growing throughout the world come under the broad heading of *Spermatophyta*. They are further classified as *Angiospermae* and *Gymnospermae*, which yield the hardwoods and softwoods of commerce. Angiosperms are trees whose seeds are carried in a seed case or fruit, whereas the seed of the gymnosperms are not enclosed in an ovary.

Angiosperms are divided into two groups, the *Dicotyledones*, in which growth rings are formed within the ascending axis or stem, and the *Monocotyledones* or *Endogenae*. The latter group consists largely of the palm (Arecaceae) family, and, except for the bamboos, or the palms furnishing minor cabinet woods, is seldom of value in the production of furniture.

Dicotyledonous trees therefore yield the principal decorative woods to be seen in antique as well as modern furniture. These hardwoods may be regarded simply as products of broad-leaved, deciduous trees, in contrast to the softwoods associated with conifer trees—keeping in mind that hardwoods and softwoods are differentiated through variations in structure, not relative hardness and softness, as occasional species in both classifications may contradict such descriptions.

All trees are fed and protected by various tissues comprising a double layer of bark. As the tree develops, a diminution of food supply causes the outer portion of the bark to dry out and die, after which the cracks and furrows seen in tough exposed barks result from the growth of the stem or from freezing temperatures. Within this protecting encirclement is the vital *phloem, bast tissue* or *underbark*. It is the function of this tissue to feed the tree. Water and mineral salts are conducted from the roots through vessels in the *sapwood* portion of the trunk to the leaves. There they are converted into sugars and salts which are conveyed down the phloem and into the roots. From the phloem they are distributed throughout the trunk by means of long narrow *rays* passing through the *growth rings* to the perimetral tissues.

Trees of the hardwood group follow patterns of growth which may be observed at the ends of sawn logs or prepared timbers. Around a central group of pith[2] cells, which are of use only during the early life of a tree, sets of wood tissues are formed. These are the *growth rings* which indicate a tree's span of life. Each ring is composed of wood substance formed at the beginning of the growing season, which is called *primary, early* or *spring wood*, and that formed later in the same season, known as *secondary, late* or *summer wood*. Early wood generally contains cells with thinner walls than those of cells developed in late wood, as a greater amount of moisture has to pass up through these vessels during the months of more active growth. Late wood is therefore the denser, harder, heavier and stronger layer.

Growth ring is the term often favored in preference to *annual ring*, for the growing season is not so sharply divided in tropical regions as in temperate or cold climes, and therefore some tropical woods do not display definite indications of each annual change in growth. Generally, the demarcation is perceptible in cross sections, while the variations between early and late growths may also form an important part of the surface figures brought out by plain sawing.

As growth rings increase in number within the stem of a very young sapling the wood substance that has been built up is composed of living tissues, and therefore at this stage of development only *sapwood* has formed. When the stem increases further in diameter the cells of inner growth layers lose their protoplasmic content and die, thus turning these layers into *heartwood*.[3] This is the darker, harder and heavier wood comprising the core or heart of a tree trunk, which in general is also more durable than the surrounding sapwood. As succeeding growth rings are added to the perimeter of the sapwood, the inner boundary of this *alburnum* continues to form heartwood or *duramen*, and thus to increase the diameter of the central, commercially valuable portion of the trunk.

Elements of sustenance and growth appearing in the wood substance of dicotyledonous trees are made up principally of vertically elongated cells known as *vessels* and *fibers*, and transversely elongated cells or *rays*.

Vessels are actually tubes comprised of open cells through which moisture ascends to the branches and leaves. When they are cut through and displayed as fine grooves or hatchings in longitudinal surfaces such markings are often referred to as *vessel lines*.

Pores are cross sections of vessels. When they are scattered or diffused throughout the annual rings, without any marked difference between those of early or late development, this constitutes a *diffuse-porous wood*. When they are evident without magnification, as relatively large openings in the early wood of growth rings, contrasting to the smaller size of those formed in the late wood, this is determinative of a *ring-porous wood*. The majority of timbers do not show these decided contrasts, which occur in a few species indigenous to the

Temperate Zone, such as oak, chestnut, ash, elm and locust, and in a small proportion of those growing in tropical forests.

Fibers are slender, spindle-shaped cells with thick walls, present in the dicotyledons, though often so minute as to be unimportant in their identification. They occur most abundantly in the median portion of growth rings, generally interspersed among the vessels and rising parallel to one another. A large proportion of the wood substance is made up of these cells, which give support to the vessels and affect the general character of hardwood timbers.

Wood rays or *vascular rays* are cells composed of storage tissues (parenchyma[4]) which develop in the stems of all dicotyledons. They usually appear as small or microscopic flecks, though in some timbers they are quite large, as in the pronounced rays of true oaks and those of the so-called Australian "oaks." They may be colorless, as in poplar, lighter in tone than the ground tissue, as in oak, or darkened by pigmentation, as in elm, birch and beech. Primary rays originate from the cambium tissues[5] of the earliest growth rings, (rather than from the pith or *medulla* with which they have formerly been associated), extending outward to the bark. Other separate rays may develop in the cambium tissues of later growth rings, therefore forming shorter or *secondary rays* of a similar nature, which also continue radially to the bark crossing the ensuing rings at right angles.

Ripple marks are produced by very thin rays that appear in more or less uniform and finely spaced rows running across the grain in plain-sawed wood surfaces. Individually these rays are indistinct to the unaided eye, but through their storied arrangements they appear as fine horizontal striations or ripplelike markings in true mahogany and certain other tropical timbers.

Pith flecks are small brownish, often corklike specks or streaks resulting from injuries produced by boring larvae of certain insects. At times they appear rather pronouncedly in longitudinal surfaces of birch, alder, willow and fruitwood timbers, and less frequently in those cut from holly, hornbeam, horse chestnut, hazel, poplar and sycamore trees. Like the characteristic markings of bird's-eye maple, they may be thickly dotted throughout a portion or portions of a timber, while the balance of the same log remains untouched. The term "pith fleck" is perhaps as confusing as "pith ray" or "medullary ray" for these flecks are also associated with the cambium tissues of a growing tree rather than its true pith. The phenomenon is generally described under considerations of parenchyma.

In connection with the preceding descriptions relative to the principal organic elements of hardwood timbers, and before taking up further structural features and properties which result in their decorative qualities and serviceability, some mention might be made of tracheids[6] and tyloses.[7] Nevertheless these elements and parenchyma are mainly important in microscopic examinations of timbers and therefore they are defined in the Appendix.

The character and disposition of structural elements, and other features of growth influenced by soil and climatic conditions result in properties which are important in determining the identity of cabinet woods and in judging them according to quality. These properties are *color, texture, grain, figure, luster, density, weight, strength* and *hardness.*

COLOR

The natural *color* developed in wood tissues results from infiltrations of chemical products by which the cell walls are impregnated. Since the heartwood contains these substances in the greater ratio it is therefore the darker portion of most timbers. Wood colors are often quite variable, particularly in the highly pigmented timbers which tend to fade and lose their brilliant tones after exposure to light and air. However, most woods darken with exposure, due to oxidization of the coloring matter contained in their cell walls, and also if subjected to heat or to prolonged contact with moisture. The natural depth of color frequently serves as a criterion by which experts judge a timber for durability and resistance to decay. As the heartwood of most timbers is the commercially valuable portion, unless otherwise stipulated in the following descriptions *color* refers to this wood rather than the lighter-toned, less important sapwood.

When the vernacular name of a timber is qualified by a color this may refer to various peculiarities of the growing tree rather than to the color of its wood. With certain birches and oaks it will apply only to the outer or inner bark of the tree. In this same respect color may also refer to the principal tone appearing in the leaves or blossoms of a tree. Therefore in lieu of undertaking a complete arborical study it is well to keep these possibilities in mind. Where names of this type are accorded common usage they will be included in the following accounts of cabinet woods, which, in giving colors proper to the woods themselves, will indicate these inconsistencies without further comments.

TEXTURE

Texture is defined according to the relative degrees of porosity and uniformity in the wood tissues. Where the wood substance is entirely composed of small elements the texture is *fine*; where numerous vessels with relatively large cell cavities appear the texture is *coarse*. When these elements exhibit little variation in size the texture is *even* or *uniform*; when there is a wide variation in size, as in ring-porous woods such as oak and ash, the texture is *uneven* or *nonuniform*.

GRAIN

Grain refers specifically to the quality and arrangement of wood elements[8] in longitudinal surfaces of prepared timbers. The natural development of pores, fibers, etc., in relation to the axis of growth results in the following types of grain:

When the general direction of the elements parallels the axis of growth this represents a *straight grain*. If, through the presence of knots, or from other causes, pronounced deflections occur in the development of the wood tissues, this lack of uniformity results in an *irregular grain*.

Wavy grain is often produced in the limb area, where compression occurs as the tree trunk and branches expand in their seasonal growths. This compressive force is represented by "wrinkles" or fine and fairly regular horizontal waves in the tissues of timbers that are known for their "fiddleback" markings.

Curly grain is properly applied where the grain is irregularly distorted or appears in bold linked formations on the face of pine boards or similar flat cuttings of certain hardwoods, such as ash and American "poplar." Similar contortions are found in a number of burlwoods, including those obtained from ash and elm timbers. (The term *curly grain* should not be confused with *curly figure*.)

Spiral grain occurs when the elements of a growing tree twist and ascend in spiry formations, a development which may result in warping when solid material of this description is employed for structural purposes.

An *interlocked grain* is produced when the elements of successive growth rings twist in alternate directions as they ascend. These undulations produce changing reflections of light in quartered surfaces of mahogany and other tropical woods, causing varied effects which will be mentioned under stripe figures.

Silver grain is the term used in reference to the flecks or broader and longer markings produced by wood rays in quarter-sawed* material. The smaller specklings appear characteristically in *silver-grained* cuttings of beech and sycamore, the bolder and often quite irregular rays occur in similarly cut (quartered) surfaces of oak. This silvered effect is also described as a *flake figure*.

Varying types of grains are also associated with the manner in which timbers are cut and surfaced. In a tangential, plain-sawed or flat-sawed surface the grain revealed is referred to as a *flat grain* or *flower grain*. When material is quartered, or radially sawed, the normal grain thus presented is known as *quarter grain, rift grain* or *comb grain*. In addition, the character and direction of the elements may result in a *smooth grain,* or in a *rough grain,* according to whether the fibers have remained flat and unbroken in the surfacing of a wood, or whether they have lifted and frayed during this operation.

FIGURE

Figure is brought out by cutting timbers so that veneers or solid surfaces display various types of irregularities in the grain, variations in color and a number of other internally developed or adventitious effects.

Growth-ring figures are produced by cutting through the annual layers of timbers in which marked differences occur in the wood substance developed during the early and late periods of each growing season. They are revealed as stripes, parabolas, ellipses and more erratic patterns appearing prominently in plain-sawed surfaces of such timbers as oak, chestnut, elm and ash, and less conspicuously in walnut, mahogany, sycamore, maple, beech, birch and many other woods.

Pigment figure results from variations in the coloring of a wood other than the contrasts appearing in normal grain figures or differences in normal color zones. Depositions of this nature are characteristic of walnut, particularly Circassian walnut, and figured red gum, timbers displaying irregular blackish pigment streaks or figures, and also of some darker timbers, such as rosewood, in which these abnormal markings are comparatively inconspicuous.

Fiddle-back figure is caused by an arrangement of wood elements as described under "wavy grain." These markings are brought out by cutting through the crests of successive undulations in the grain of

_____
* At this point, before further mention of cutting methods, it may be well for some readers to consult the descriptions of plain- and quarter-sawing, which follow immediately after these considerations of wood properties.

mahogany, maple and sycamore timbers. They appear to best advantage in surfaces that have been cut along truly radial paths, but also quite effectively in some flat cuttings.

Curly figure, differing from curly grain, is produced by irregular contortions in the wood elements, which occur chiefly at the bases of large branches and are displayed in wavy surface markings or *curls*. These horizontal figures are less delicate and regular than fiddle-back patterns, often appearing in erratic or even fantastic forms that are called *landscape figures*. Curly figure is associated particularly with maple, birch and mahogany timbers.

Other wavy figures may be described according to their size and effects, as *finger roll, ocean wave,* etc., while all figures that extend directly across the grain may be classified as *cross* figures.

Mottle figures occur where local irregularities in the arrangement of wood elements are displayed as horizontal striations in quartered surfaces of mahogany and various other tropical woods. These cloudy markings appear in ever varying distributions, either scattered, disposed in blocks, or closely grouped in striped formations. They are frequently combined with fiddle-back, and very often with stripe figures.

Raindrop figure is a type of mottling developed when single or multiple waves in the elements extend obliquely across the grain, often separated by considerable intervals of plain wood. Surface effects of this nature recall the slanting splash of raindrops on a vertical plane.

Blister figure is produced by irregularities in the wood elements due to a lack of uniformity in the development of successive growth rings. Crinkled patterns are brought out by cutting through these irregularities, emphasized by light-toned threadlike lines distributed in vermicular arrangements, and presenting an effect such as may be seen in a very unevenly quilted satin. This rare *quilted figure* is found in plain-sawed surfaces of mahogany (or in those which are today cut with a rotary saw), and it may also occur in certain other woods.

Stripe figure is a term that may be applied to vertical striations appearing in radially—or tangentially—cut surfaces as a result of variations in the tonal values of growth rings. At times this term is also used in reference to the vertical color zones of bicolored woods. As a rule, however, *stripe figures* are understood to designate flashier types of vertical markings produced by interlocked grain and displayed in radially-cut surfaces. The undulating character of this grain results in alternating reflections, and varying intensities of light as finished surfaces are viewed from different angles. These variable striated effects occur in many tropical woods, though they are particularly characteristic of mahogany.

Plain stripe is the term used in reference to fairly narrow and lengthy striations which, by their shaded effects, are set off against the even graining of a wood surface.

Ribbon stripe is broader than the usual plain stripe.

Broken stripe is produced when the striations are interrupted by even graining after running for a foot or more in length.

Roe figure applies to striped effects in which the striations are broken up into short segments, when they may present a rather dappled appearance.

Rope stripe refers to a twisted or cabled effect in the striations as they take a slanting course, usually parallel to one another, in unbroken or broken lines.

A number of wood figures are also produced by cutting timbers through elaborately marked sections adjacent to points where large branches or roots have developed. The point where a limb emerges from a tree trunk is actually a *knot*, although this term is more frequently employed in reference to a cross section of an embryonic or broken branch which has become imbedded in a tree as the trunk continued to expand in its normal growth. An incipient, broken and imbedded, or completed branch contains growth rings that are similar to, but more eccentric than those formed in the tree trunk. Thus developed knots and cross sections of completed branches are always characterized by these concentric markings.

Oyster figure or *oyster-shell figure* describes the circular or elliptical patterns displayed by the concentric growth rings in thin cross sections, or diagonally-cut sections of branches. These sections are known as *oyster pieces*, and surfaces of tables, commodes, cabinet, mirror frames, etc., with this type of veneering laid as parquetry panels or borders are said to be *oystered* or decorated with *oystering*.

Crotchwood is formed below the point where a tree trunk forks into two large branches, resulting from distortions in the elements of growth when they are diverted in approaching the bifurcation. This development may continue for six feet or more in large growths of mahogany, and it is plainly indicated in the figuring of tangentially-cut veneers. The spreading direction of the elements is revealed in catenary curves, or inverted arcs, forming what is commonly accepted as a *swirl figure*. In addition, when cutting reaches the centermost portion of a crotch log, where the greatest stress and compression has occurred, a *feather* or plumelike formation penetrates or divides the swirl figure. This feathering distinguishes veneers with a *full crotch figure* from those obtained before it has been reached, though swirl-figured veneers may also be classed as *crotchwood*. It will be noticed in the illustrations that *feather-crotch* and *crotch-swirl* veneers, as well as those with simple swirl figures, were almost invariably laid upon vertical surfaces with the grain running in an opposite direction to that which it takes in the tree.

KNURS and BUTTWOOD

Timbers cut from trees in which branches grow thick from the stem, with pronounced excrescences or *knurs* forming at the emerging points or elsewhere on the trunk, are sometimes deeply penetrated by strongly marked and greatly variegated figures, often accompanied by small curls or other maculations, and occasionally by burl eyes in the perimetrical sections. This type of figuring is discussed at some length in the consideration of maple timbers. For lack of a more definite classification wood displaying such figures has been designated as "buttwood," and even as "burlwood." It would perhaps be more appropriate to apply the term *knurlwood*, or *knurled wood*, to such cuttings since the grain is knurled or gnarled, i.e., twisted or contorted, while both *knur* and *gnarl* refer to a large *knot* or a trunk protuberance with twisted graining.

Stumpwood is formed in the lower portion of a tree trunk when the development of large roots produces effects similar to those resulting from the formations mentioned in the preceding paragraph. Walnut stumps in particularly are highly valued for this intricately figured wood, which is contained in both the exposed and underground portions. A stump may also be referred to as a *butt*, a term often used in reference to the lower and thicker portion of a standing timber that is not commercially valuable beneath stump level—or the point at which the greatest diameter of the usable trunkwood is reckoned.

Although *buttwood* is synonymous with *stumpwood* the former term is sometimes used when a veneer cannot be determined as coming from an upper portion of a timber or from the vicinity of its roots. Both types of veneers display some flashy figures that are reminiscent of the effects produced by ripples of light on satins disposed in crinkled arrangements. When such figures are penetrated by arcs that indicate crotchlike formations it may be difficult to discern whether these have been caused by the development of branches or large roots.

BURLS

A *burl* is an excrescence found growing on the trunks of various trees. The term *burr* is commonly employed in England, while *knot* is also proper for this type of rounded protuberance, or others caused by fungus diseases. Abnormal growths of this nature often assume warty, flattened hemispherical forms, appearing at various heights from the ground or close to the roots, and sometimes extending to a greater diameter than that of the trunk itself. These excrescences contain myriads of tiny knotlike markings or *eyes*, which are usually considered to be undeveloped buds of branches, and it is also believed that they are caused by insects or bacteria. Generally, a pronounced curly grain appears in veneers cut from these burls, often forming loops around the knotty eyes. Burl veneers of walnut, yew, elm, ash, birch, poplar, amboina and thuja are those most frequently seen in antique furniture.

A similar curly-grained effect, without burl eyes, appears in veneers cut from portions of trees where barrel-shaped swellings have developed in the trunk.

OTHER EXTRINSIC FIGURES

Bird's-eye figure is apparently caused by a fungus that attacks a limited proportion of North American and European maple trees, causing brownish specks to appear in the wood which extend through a considerable number of growth rings. The surrounding structural elements are directed in encircling paths, but they are not affected to the same pronounced degree as in burlwoods. These markings may appear throughout an entire tree trunk, at the core or perimeter, or they may alternate with zones of untouched wood. Bird's-eye maple is tangentially sawed to bring out this type of figuring, with the blade thus passing directly through these immersive specks which are displayed in irregular circular or oval outlines, or as tiny craterlike markings with shadowed interiors.

Plum pudding figure appears in a relatively small number of West Indian mahogany timbers, as a result of some external agency through which the wood is marked by chemical deposits. These spottings are larger and more decidedly lenticular in form than those associated with bird's-eye maple. As they are darker than the wood itself, or even blackish in tone, and usually set off by high lights in the surrounding tissues, the lenticular effects are often quite pronounced. Fairly uniform markings of this nature have been more imaginatively described as *peacock feather*, or *peacock-spotted figure*, in allusion to the ocellate spots of the male peacock's upper tail coverts.

LUSTER

Luster or gloss refers to the capacity of surfaced woods to reflect light, a quality which is largely imparted by fibers, rays and various infiltrations. Woods that are dense and hard often possess high lusters and therefore take relatively high polishes. The opposite of *high luster* is designated as *dull luster*, while other qualifications are *frosted, dappled, oily, greasy*, etc. Luster may serve the timberman as a sign of soundness, for incipient decay causes the wood in a tree to become dull and lifeless.

WEIGHT

A timber's *density* is measured with reference to the presence of elements with thick cell walls, such as appear in the late wood of growth rings. Wood floats only because of the buoyancy supplied by air imprisoned in or between these elements, and therefore the greater the amount of wood substance present, the greater will be the density of a particular timber, and the greater, also, will be its *weight*. Moisture content is of course another principal factor of weight, and certain timbers which are not particularly dense will not float until their moisture contents are reduced by girdling or by allowing them to dry out after felling. Other factors of density and weight are the amounts of mineral or nonmineral matter taken in by a growing tree. Timbers are subject to variations in weight according to structural differences arising from growing conditions, soil, age, etc., conditions which may effect variations within a species or a particular tree, as well as between related species.

The specific gravity of a wood is figured at its weight per cubic foot in relation to a similar measure of water, i.e., 62.5 pounds. Thus a wood with a specific gravity of .56 weighs 35 pounds per cubic foot. Timber weighing less than this pound figure is considered *light*, that which weighs over 50 pounds per cubic foot is considered *heavy*. Weights are generally given in pounds per cubic foot—a procedure which is followed here.

HARDNESS

As a rule greater density and weight will indicate relative *strength* and *hardness* in a timber.

This latter quality is the ability to resist indentations, and is therefore largely dependent upon the thickness of cell walls and the narrowness of cell cavities. Hardness is of course an important quality in timbers selected for the manufacture of furniture.

DIMENSIONS

The extreme dimensions of a tree, particularly in regard to its *diameter* in the trunk, or the *butt diameter*, indicating the greatest thickness of a log next above the stump, and also the measurements of round or square logs, or the billets into which some timbers are cut, are often of considerable importance in determining whether or not a manufactured wood can be properly identified within these limitations of a certain timber. This applies mainly to the *width* of solid wood or veneer panels, as few structural or surfacing problems arise in regard to vertical measurements. Allowances must be made for waste in trimming away perimetrical material, and it should be remembered that in quartering timbers the heartwood is divided into segments which halve this remaining diameter.

CUTTING METHODS

Methods followed in the cutting of timbers, and subsequent procedures in their utilization, are important factors in the appearance and stability of furniture woods after their final manufacture. The two distinctive methods of sawing timbers into boards and veneers have been employed throughout the world for centuries. They are generally undertaken to obtain a maximum of usable or specially figured material with a minimum of waste, and to secure the highest quality cuttings for required purposes of strength, durability and appearance. The simpler method is *plain sawing*, while the second, *quarter sawing*, may be carried out in variously contrived cuts once a log has been divided into four vertical segments.

Plain-sawed, or *flat-cut* timber is sawed tangentially along the log, and thus in this same relation to the growth rings, while the blade passes at right angles to the wood rays. This method is more economical than quartering, both in cost and waste. It reveals a natural figure with contrasts between the early and late wood of growth rings, a figure which is readily seen in timbers of coarse texture such as ash, chestnut and oak.

Quarter-sawed timber is obtained from a log which has first been cut into four horizontal sections or *quarters*. Each section is then radially sawed into boards or veneers, though some cuts will vary from a truly radial path. By this method wood rays are revealed in more pronounced fashion depending upon how closely cutting follows the natural direction of these tissues. In addition to this silvering, and the other figures already mentioned as obtained through quarter sawing, surfaces thus presented are harder, less subject to shrinking, and less apt to splinter than those obtained through plain sawing.

VENEERS

Veneers are thin sheets or leaves of a finer or more handsomely figured wood, that are glued to a plainer but often sounder or less refractory wood. In general they are radially sawed to bring out the decorative surface effects obtained through this cutting method, but they may also be sawed tangentially or along intermediate planes. (Today they are also mechanically sliced to scant thicknesses through a use of the machine knife, or peeled off in a continuous layer from a rotating log.) A *flitch* is a series of veneer sheets, laid together according to the sequence in which they were cut, and therefore displaying almost identical figures. From the second half of the eighteenth century successive cuttings of this type have been employed as matched facings of drawer fronts.

SEASONING AND MOVEMENT

When wood is cut and ready for *seasoning* the chief requisite is to remove such moisture as might prove detrimental in fabrication and subsequent use. The moisture present in timbers is almost entirely water, with some sugars in the sapwood, and tannins, coloring matter, etc. in the heartwood. Seasoning actually begins with the felling of a tree, as its moisture content then starts to evaporate. In drying, moisture first leaves the cell cavities and then the cell walls, a process which has been aptly compared to that which takes place when a wooden bucket of water is spilled—with the moisture absorbed by the walls of the bucket still remaining to evaporate.

Through contraction of the cell walls during evaporation, shrinkage takes place, affecting the late wood, because of the greater substance in the thicker cell walls, more than the early wood of growth rings. Contraction of the cell walls also results in a general hardening of the entire wood substance.

Shrinkage in timbers which are heavy (dense) and hard is greater than in those which are light and soft, although the reverse is often believed. Contraction is usually twice as great in plain-sawed material as in that which has been radially cut. It also occurs more readily in lateral directions than along the axis of growth, where shrinking is imperceptible.

Irregularities in the rate or direction of shrinkage, often caused by uneven reception of air or heat, may result in warping, twisting or cracking. The tendency toward *warping* is always present, for shrinkage is not entirely uniform throughout any specimen of wood, especially in woods of uneven density. Those with a straight grain and uniform texture have less tendency in this direction than others with interlocked, cross, or spiral grains, as all such growths are prone to shrink unevenly.

Unequal movement of wood is also caused by *expansion*, resulting from the absorption of moisture to an excessive degree. This swelling may take place even though a wood has been carefully seasoned. Some woods are prone to such movement, while others are less likely to be seriously affected and are known as *stable woods*. Sudden exposure to extreme humidity often results in an unequal absorption of moisture, which is as detrimental to timber and to manufactured furniture as the effects which produce warping through unequal contraction. The addition of extra moisture to the content remaining in all properly seasoned woods may occur through varnished or painted surfaces, though a harmful excess is more readily absorbed where only partial finishing has been carried out, as in a table top with the reverse side left unfinished.

Seasoning was effected in the past through *air-drying*, and *oven-drying*, somewhat in the manners employed today. Various periods of time were allotted to drying by air, extending to seven years or more. During this process boards might be stored in barns or stables, exposed to the ammoniacal fumes which were present. With oven-drying they were placed in specially constructed ovens, though these would not approach the efficiency of the closely regulated drying kilns that are operated today.

The different varieties of hardwoods appearing in antique furniture are usually determinable through simple visual examination, concentrated upon the features of identification which have now been described. These characteristics are therefore generally of greater service, in examinations accorded by the majority of persons, as well as in practical use by the lumber inspector, than are more technical features of identification.[9] However, woods that have been manufactured, finished by various methods and then undergone different vicissitudes may be modified to considerable extents in regard to their original appearances.

If agents free of coloring materials were employed to fill the pores and grain, or to provide a surface polish and any further rubbed dressing, the original color and figure would be unaffected except by atmospheric conditions, sunlight and subsequent methods of care. Such agents might be supplied in beeswax, beeswax and turpentine, plain oil[10] (where the wood treated did not darken materially through this use), plain varnish,[11] and an untinted final rubbed dressing.

Discrepancies in color or figure were often disregarded in cabinetwork executed prior to the middle of the eighteenth century, but where toning was considered desirable in these instances, or to enrich an evenly marked surface, staining[12] was introduced. This might be incorporated in the first dressing, with a spirit or oil base, and be applied as often as required. Additional toning could be secured when a tinted varnish provided succeeding coatings, and also when a final rubbing material was impregnated with coloring matter.

The extent to which even those agents which were nonpenetrating might affect a basic wood tone may be illustrated through a comparative effect when a yellow varnish is applied to a silvered surface. This process, often carried out in carved and silvered furniture of the German states, cleverly simulated a more costly gilded finish. Similarly, finishing grayish, pinkish or very light tan[13] woods, such as hickory, ash, birch, beech or maple, with a yellow or orange varnish,[14] will also result in yellowish surface tones.

The basic colors of most timbers are not only darkened by months or years of seasoning, but when made up into furniture this darkening process may continue, despite the sealing effects of finishing materials. In contrast, the natural action of light and air over long periods of time, after either uncolored or pigmented materials have been applied, may sometimes produce varying effects on exposed surfaces. Aided by the greater transparency of clear dressings, sunlight will often bleach the wood immediately beneath these agents, or stained surfaces may be faded back to their original colorings, or beyond these tones. Then, too, the varnish above an untreated or stained surface may become bleached, with or without the wood being proportionately affected.

These applied and naturally caused surface changes will, in some instances, require examination of the natural wood. An inspection of this nature may, in regard to veneers, require removal of the outer "skin," which will usually entail only a minute and temporary impairment in obtaining determinative evidence through normal coloring and texture. If advisable these identifying qualities may then be directly compared with unfinished specimens of wood such as those displayed and offered by laboratories and timber merchants.

Dependence solely upon such labeled wood samples, however, has in some instances been found ineffectual in making identifying comparisons where mutations have occurred. One attempt to classify the various woods appearing in a collection of English and French furniture was made with such dependence, and given up. It was abandoned as comparison of the unfinished samples with finished and patinated surfaces of the pieces under appraisement caused greater confusion than aid.

However, since basic coloring, figure and texture are of primary importance in the more general identification of woods, these specimens are of great value, and should have rendered service on the occasion referred to if proper allowances had been made. Wetting a small area of an unfinished sample will induce a closer though momentary approximation of a finished surface, finishing material may be applied, or a small bit of the surface to be identified may be stripped to be more readily compared with an unfinished sample.

Further problems of identification may arise when a cabinet wood must be determined within a range of two or more species yielding timbers that are somewhat similar in general aspect, which may approximate each other even more closely in certain growths, or which are difficult to distinguish in certain prepared surfaces. For instance, when a plain-sawed oaklike surface reveals no identifying rays a question will arise as to whether the wood may be chestnut—often quite similar to oak in appearance but lacking its rayed markings. Similar confusions may arise between certain growths and cuts of ash and elm, walnut and mahogany, mahogany and cherrywood, satinwood and birch, birch and maple, sycamore and planewood, etc.

Under the most perplexing circumstances identification may be obtained through microscopic examination of cellular structures, a method which usually offers positive results in regard to the hardwoods, but is not so accurate in respect to the softwoods as a class. The cell patterns formed by vessels or pores, tracheids, fibers, parenchyma and tyloses may be observed through this means in cross sections of timbers or the solid members contained in a piece of furniture. However, as the various structural configurations must be clearly revealed for such determination, a fresh cut is necessary to secure a smooth, well-defined transverse surface. This may be accomplished readily enough by paring or shaving away the bottom surface of a chair or table leg, with no appreciable damage to such members. However, similar treatment accorded to other parts of seat furniture or cabinetwork may result in greater damage to showing surfaces, or may necessitate disassembly if they must be sent away for detailed reports.

Microscopic examination of manufactured wood articles is therefore, in general, infeasible; although in problematical cases it may be of help if the most positive form of identification is considered necessary. It may be of help *only* if a cellular pattern can be definitely identified through studying published descriptions of such structures, or photomicrographs illustrating them. However, verbal descriptions can easily be misconstrued, and microphotographic studies do not cover all of the woods utilized in antique furniture.

During the course of the present investigations two of the foremost technological laboratories were unable to offer any corroborative opinions whatsoever, based on surface views of cabinet woods submitted in photographic form. Not even a single differentiation between West Indian satinwood and the botanically varying East Indian satinwood could be arrived at through excellent, ample-sized photographs which could be clearly studied under a magnification of ten diameters. Similar examination of small section blocks from the illustrated specimens would be necessary for these specializing experts to form their opinions, contrasting to the more practical approach of a timber authority such as Mr. J. L. Stearns. The importance of such practicality is thus further emphasized to the student of antique furniture, and to the collector who does not wish to part, even for a time, with small sections of his prized possessions. Furthermore, the more technical identifications are sometimes open to doubt when veneers, rather than solid cuttings of wood, are submitted for inspection.

The following descriptions and illustrations have been compiled and selected to provide a guide for ready use by those interested in antique furniture, or in the buying or manufacturing of modern furniture. Therefore its aim does not extend beyond such interests, with the possible exception of timbermen—who generally prefer a similar practical approach to the subject without reliance upon microscopic views of end surfaces. An ordinary reading lens may prove serviceable in studying the illustrations, just as a greater magnification has been used to good effect in connection with some of the photographs they represent. Excellence of quality in the photographs provided for this project will enable a more substantial understanding of the woods they portray than can be obtained through either simplified or highly technical descriptions.

1. HORSE CHESTNUT

The horse chestnut, *Aesculus hippocastanum* Linn.,[15] was introduced from the East into various parts of Europe during the sixteenth and seventeenth centuries. Its large nutlike seeds are inedible in any form, despite such beliefs as that held by Evelyn concerning their usefulness as medicine for "horses or other cattel." The tree is seldom cultivated in Britain as it is unsuited to the climate there, but under favorable conditions it attains a height of about one hundred feet and a butt circumference of about sixteen feet.

Chestnut and horse chestnut timbers have been loosely described under headings of the single common name, an incongruous association which has resulted in some confusion over these two widely varying woods. Such timber as the latter species yields is not generally available in large dimensions, and while it has been utilized for the manufacture of small decorative articles and as an inlay material the wood is of insignficant economic importance.

The heartwood and sapwood are not sharply defined, the general color ranging from very white to a yellowish tan, according to the time and manner in which the tree is felled and the timber handled. Proper methods in these respects may result in a bone-white hue. Classed as a soft hardwood, the wood is soft and perishable according to the usual standards as it is highly absorbent and prone to twist or warp. In texture it is very fine and uniform, and a delicate wavy grain figure is often present in finished surfaces which display a rich satinlike luster. The weight varies from 30 to 40 pounds per cubic foot. It is possible for horse chestnut. (Fr., *marronnier de l'Inde*) to be confused with certain cuttings of European poplar, linden or willow.

2. HORNBEAM

The Hornbeam, *Carpinus betulus* Linn., is indigenous to Continental Europe, and to Great Britain, where it is known in some localities as the "yoke elm," apparently from a long use of its wood in fashioning yokes for draft animals. The tree reaches an extreme height of about eighty feet and a butt diameter of about four feet.

There is no distinct variation between the alburnum and the central portion of the tree trunk, hence the color of the wood is uniformly of a whitish or yellowish-white hue, sometimes marked by a light tan figuring. It is a hard and tough wood, with very small pores and a fine, uniform texture. Rays are faintly visible in the usual plain-sawed surfaces, appearing as fine lines of a slightly deeper tone than the ground color and often extending for an inch or more in length. Hornbeam is difficult to work, except in turning, but it is capable of taking a smooth finish and a good polish. The weight varies from 43 to 55 pounds, averaging around 51 pounds per cubic foot.

Hornbeam was employed to a limited extent for inlaid decorations of cabinetwork produced in northern and central Europe during the eighteenth century. It was also adopted as the *Bois de Charme* of *marqueteurs* working in France. At times the wood may have been ebonized, as in current practice, a process possibly resulting from the fact that the central portion of the tree trunk becomes blackish after it has been pollarded.[18]

3. HOLLY

European holly, *Ilex aquifolium* Linn., is an evergreen species in the hardwood group, growing either as a shrub[16] or tree. The plant is widely distributed on the Continent, and in the British Isles where it attains a height of sixty feet and a butt diameter of four feet. Especially large growths are found in Ireland. To secure its lightest color the timber must be converted for use immediately after felling and stored in a dry, shaded place. In the British Isles a lengthy process was evolved through which the wood was boiled and then carefully dried to assure this light tone.

Holly is normally of a chalky or ivory-white color, though at times it takes on a slight greenish tinge. In common with other very light-toned woods its varnished surfaces display pale yellowish effects. The wood is very fine and uniform in texture, sometimes appearing with mild growth-ring figures. Delicate rays develop in clustered arrangements that are characteristic of radially-cut veneers. Holly offers a firm, smooth surface and takes a good polish. Veneers of old furniture may be marked by fine cracks, which occur with some frequency in this material. It is said that in rare instances burls are found in dimensions suitable for use in cabinetwork. Weights of the usual trunkwood cuttings vary from 45 to 55 pounds per cubic foot.

During the sixteenth century this holly was utilized in intarsia work, later being employed as a medium of parquetry and marquetry decorations, as a panel or border veneer and as a banding material. It was also ebonized to serve as a substitute for ebony, and Evelyn mentioned its use under thin plates of ivory to render this material more conspicuous. In the eighteenth century holly was treated with various penetrating stains, or tinted with water colors to increase the palette of colors then employed in marquetry work. It continued to be valued for its natural coloring, however, and in this capacity was considered the whitest and most costly wood appearing in the wares produced at Tunbridge Wells[17] in England. Holly was also employed for frieze panels and larger surfaces of tables, commodes and cabinets, eventually appearing in the case work of pianos and other musical instruments.

In considerations of old furniture produced within the British Isles, holly is often mistaken for boxwood, or even for satinwood; while the various light-toned woods, other than *bois de houx*, employed in France and in other Continental countries, are more greatly confused.

American holly, *Ilex opaca*, is closely similar to the European timber in color and structure. The American wood was utilized as a veneer in later colonial cabinetwork, and particularly in productions of the Early Federal period. It was then employed for panels, decorative inlays, bandings and keyhole escutcheons. Local timbers were also exported to Europe during the eighteenth century.

THE ILLUSTRATED EXAMPLES

The semicircular table displays holly veneers in

1. A George III inlaid mahogany and holly console table Courtesy of Biggs of Maidenhead.

2. An Early Federal inlaid mahogany and holly sideboard

its frieze panels, and in its smaller inlaid details. Patterns offered by Hepplewhite's *Guide* are reflected in the plain and tinted inlays of this console table, *circa* 1780-1785. A more extensive use of holly veneers is seen in the American sideboard, apparently made in or near Baltimore, *circa* 1790. Here these veneers indicate sawing along a more or less tangential plane, and they have developed the very fine cracks often found in applied surfaces of this wood. Holly also appears in various other pieces illustrated in this book, particularly in those inlaid with oval or segmental fan paterae.

Fig. 1

Fig. 2

4. SPINDLE TREE

The spindle tree, *Euonymus europeae* Linn., supplied French *marqueteurs* with their *bois de fusain* of eighteenth-century cabinetwork. This wood is almost white in color, with a fine, uniform texture that provides a very smooth finished surface. These qualities, and the fact that a rich yellowish cast is assumed after varnishing, result in a close similarity of appearance between *bois de fusain* and boxwood.

5. WHITEBEAM

The whitebeam (literally white *tree*), *Sorbus aria* Linn., is an ornamental fruit tree of Europe and the British Isles which may develop to a height of fifty feet. On the Continent the timber was formerly utilized for various fine and common purposes, including marquetry work. In the latter capacity it appears as the *bois d'alisier* of French eighteenth-century furniture. It is almost white in color if properly handled, failing which it turns to a yellowish or yellowish-tan hue. The texture is fine and close, enabling the wood to be finished with a hard and smooth surface. Radially-cut material is distinguished by numerous fine rays which are clearly visible. The weight is 39 pounds per cubic foot.

6. LAUREL

The laurel, bay tree or bay laurel, (Fr., *laurier*), *Laurus nobilis* Linn., is best known for its foliage, used by the ancient Greeks to crown victors in the Pythian games or for other marks of distinction, and handed down as a favorite motif of classic ornament. The tree reaches a height of about fifty feet in Mediterranean regions, whence it was introduced into England during the sixteenth century. As a timber it is not particularly durable, being suitable only for inlays or other small uses, though even in work of this character it was never employed to any considerable extent. The wood is whitish in color, often tinged with pink, possessing a fine to moderately fine texture, and a straight or occasionally interlocked grain.

Howard quotes a Philadelphia advertisement of Benjamin Randolph, 1770, who was then making wooden buttons for the patriotic citizens who refused to wear imported ones: "I should be glad if the people of the country would furnish me with different kinds of stuffs, as it falls in their way, such as the best apple tree, holly, laurel, &c. that is hard and clear grained, &c. &c. &c." It is likely that *laurel* here would be acceptable as a product of the laurel bay, the cucumber or another magnolia of our eastern states. Both of these woods are creamy-white to tan in color, medium hard and lustrous, and often marked by purple or black streaks.

7. HICKORY

Hickory is obtained from numerous varieties of the American genus *Hicoria* (or *Carya*) growing throughout the eastern half of the country, the principal species being *H. alba*, *H. glabra* and *H. ovata*. The common name is derived from *pawchohiccora*, a liquor made from the nut kernels by the Indians of Virginia. In shortened form this name was applied by English settlers to the tree itself. The genus is not found in Europe, where it is believed to have become extinct at the close of the Ice Age.

The hickory tree attains an extreme height of about one hundred and twenty feet and a butt diameter of about four feet. It is of slow growth, producing the hardest and strongest of our native timbers, with unequaled wearing qualities. While the tough and springy wood is serviceable for straight and bent members of seat furniture it is difficult to nail or to work in the requirements of cabinetwork.

It was formerly believed that the white sapwood was preferable in quality to the less pliant, light pinkish-tan heartwood. Whether this belief extended back to colonial times is not recorded, but most of the hickory appearing in the simple framed seat furniture of this time, or of Early Federal production, is very white in color, thus indicating the possibility of an extended prejudice.

This ring-porous wood has a straight, open grain, presenting a coarse, uneven texture with pores showing as distinct grooves in longitudinal surfaces. In tangential surfaces this furrowed texture

3. A colonial turned hickory side chair with Franklin fly whisk

is accompanied by darker hatchings, and by thin, indistinct rays. The weight is 45-55 pounds per cubic foot.

While hickory is sometimes mistaken for ash, the structure and hardness of the former wood results in the distinctive graining just mentioned, which is straighter and more evenly parallel than that of ash. The hickory found in both old and new furniture is also lighter in color than the latter wood, while growth-ring figures appear in shorter and more strongly marked hatchings.

Hickory is distinct among the woods of American furniture, being employed here for the purposes mentioned above, and in connection with the considerations of ash. It was generally combined with this other wood or finer varieties of native timbers, though infrequently it will be found in all members of seat furniture.

THE ILLUSTRATED EXAMPLE

Fig. 3   This was made with all stationary chair members of hickory. As it is remembered, Virginia walnut—in the purple tone varying from northern selections of walnut, was combined in the treadle mechanism. This would indicate an origin in Pennsylvania or southward. The design of the chair is not particularly characteristic, nor is it one to be repeatedly associated with "Pilgrim" dates as this particular frame, along with many others of the same class, was made during the second half of the eighteenth century. A fan was to be attached to the horizontal arm and made to swing by operating the treadle, an invention attributed to Benjamin Franklin.

8. ASH

The European ash (Fr., *frêne*), *Fraxinus excelsior* Linn., is native to most of the Continent and Great Britain, growing best in moist soil and reaching an extreme height of over one hundred feet and a butt circumference of thirty feet or more. The wood is grayish- or creamy-white in color, characterized by a rather coarse texture and a straight grain, the contrast between porous springwood and dense summerwood producing a decorative growth-ring figure in plain-sawed material. It is moderately hard and tough but may be readily bent when heated or steamed. Heartwood and sapwood are not always sharply defined, growths of this nature being utilized to the full diameter of the tree. Ash is one of the timbers that are subject to serious attack by larvae of the furniture beetle. The weight averages 45 pounds per cubic foot.

Some ash timbers contain an irregular dark brown or blackish heartwood of perfectly sound nature. This is said to be "prevalent in trees grown in badly drained soils, but the connection between the two conditions is not yet definitely established." It is also likely that pollarding[18] may result in a darkening effect.

Normally developed burls appear at almost any height of the tree trunk as well as at the base or in the roots. Veneers obtained from such growths may present either delicate or pronounced markings. The eyes are of about pinhead size, grouped amid curly grainings, separated by areas of plainer wood, or in an all-over distribution accompanied by curly encirclements. A fungus that attacks the living tree often penetrates these markings, causing fine black streaks to appear in or around them.

Some burl growths occur as large mushroom formations entirely encircling the tree trunk, composed of two different organisms of wood and fungi growing together. These may be symbiotic, living together in beneficial or unharmed association, or parasitic, when the organism of the tree is harmed.

Green ebony, in the application of this name to ash, refers to dark and strongly marked wood such as that which was utilized for many years in England prior to its adoption as a Tunbridge veneer. This variation was described by Evelyn in his *Sylva* as "curiously camleted and vein'd, I say, so differently from other timber, that our skilful cabinet-makers prize it equal with ebony, and give it the name of green ebony, which the customer pays well for; and when our wood-men light upon it, they make what money they will of it." Although this abnormality is attributed to a rare growth of ash it is possible that it may be produced in fallen timbers that have been colored by fungus action—a phenomenon that occurs in oak timbers that have lain in damp ground for long periods of time.

Ash has been utilized for many centuries by European joiners and cabinetmakers. The timber might be selected either by rural craftsmen, or by those of principal furniture centers where burl ash was favored as a principal surfacing veneer or, as an inlay material, in combination with costlier woods. Green ash (*frêne vert*) was also widely favored for its effect in marquetry work. In England the solid wood was commonly used for the fashioning of Windsor chair seats, in Ireland and Wales it served in similar and finer purposes, and in Scotland it was frequently chosen as a concealed structural material. During the nineteenth century burl ash, or *loupe de frêne*, became popular in Parisian *ébénisterie* of Empire and Restoration designs.

Hungarian ash develops a bold twisted graining which is displayed with a watered or wavy lustrous effect in plain-sawed veneers. Such veneers were employed in Thomas Chippendale's premises on St. Martin's Lane by about 1770, though they appear to have become popular in Austrian furniture at no earlier date, a popularity which was revived between 1800 and 1830. Other cuttings of the Hungarian wood are characterized by rich and lively flamelike figures, thus also contrasting with the figurings of timbers grown in western Europe, and in particular to those of a very mild character which are distinctive of some French furniture.

Oriental species of ash, generally varieties of *F. mandshurica*, were utilized in the production of eastern furniture. These timbers are frequently lighter in weight, and of deeper brown or reddish-brown tones, than any European varieties of ash. During recent times one of the lighter-colored species, cut to show a strong "peanut-shell" graining, has been favored in furniture of modern designs. Veneers of this nature have been sold in Europe and America under the Japanese name of *tamo*.

American white ash, *F. americana* Linn., appears in the eastern half of this country and in New Brunswick, growing to an extreme height of about eighty feet and a butt diameter of four to six feet. The wood is grayish-white to light tan in color, generally possessing a straight grain and displaying the same type of growth-ring figures seen in European ash. Timbers from old slow-growing trees show a distinctive type of cross figuring and are therefore designated as curly ash. Weights are given as both lighter and heavier than those associated with the European species, averaging around 40 pounds per cubic foot—despite the fact that twice as many growth rings per inch develop in the American tree.

A less important timber, American black ash, *F. nigra*, is alternatively known as northern brown ash, hoop ash and basket ash. This is a tall but slender tree in which the trunk develops to an extreme diameter of eighteen inches. It is found in New England, New York and Pennsylvania. The heartwood varies from light or medium tan shades to a fairly deep brown color. In structure this wood is closely similar to white ash, its weight being slightly lighter—34 to 39 pounds per cubic foot. While the longwood obtained from this tree is not particularly sought after, veneers are obtained from burls that form on the narrow trunk.

Colonial chairs of spindle-, banister- and slat-back types were produced here in white ash, generally combined with maple and hickory, a combination that was maintained in later Windsor forms. The wood was also used for concealed structural purposes in seat furniture and cabinetwork turned out in northern states. Black ash was selected occasionally for veneer bandings of Early Federal tables, chests of drawers or cabinets. It is possible that burl ash was used for surfacing early case pieces, but where this name has been applied to the wood of various lowboys and highboys, in the William and Mary or Queen Anne styles, all of those examined during the present study have turned out to be maple knurlwood. Burl ash was employed for turning into bowls and trays of various sizes. These Early American utensils display a typical compact arrangement of swirl graining which usually extends throughout an entire surface, though at times the characteristic straighter graining is revealed in some areas of the wood.

During the first half of the nineteenth century Canadian white ash was exported to the British Isles, where it was especially favored for drawer sides, bottoms and *mounters*; the latter term referring to the center bearer dividing the drawer bottom and helping to support the longitudinal stress. From the time of the first importations white ash, as mentioned in *The Cabinet-Maker's Assistant* (1853), "gradually and to a considerable extent superceded the other woods used for the interior fittings of chests of drawers, wardrobes, and similar articles of furniture." For this preference two reasons are given, "the entire absence of smell which distinguishes ash, and the ease with which it is wrought as compared with the cedars, etc., formerly in use for the purposes to which ash is now applied."

THE ILLUSTRATED EXAMPLES

All solid members of the armchair, tripod stand, Fig. 4 and side table are made of ash; the curved seat rails Fig. 5 of the chair being surfaced in burl ash. British tables of the type shown here, and similarly designed stands for Late Stuart cabinets, were fre- Fig. 11 quently supplied with turned legs and feet of ash, an odd choice of material since walnut was readily available in more ample dimensions than those required for such narrow turned supports, and this wood is equal or superior to ash in resisting vertical stress.

The chest-on-chest displays boldly marked burl Fig. 6 veneers inlaid with a herringbone banding, and its base is finished with a quarter-round molding rather than the more usual cavetto-type edging of

4. An Early Georgian ash and burl ash armchair

6. A George II inlaid burl ash chest-on-chest Courtesy of Arthur S. Vernay, Inc., New York City.

5. An old British turned ash tripod stand Courtesy of Arthur S. Vernay, Inc., New York City.

7. A George III inlaid burl ash secretary

9. A Viennese "Empire" commode in Hungarian watered ash and plain ash

8. A New England bird's-eye maple, black ash and mahogany chest of drawers

10. A Korean red ash cabinet

11. A Late Stuart inlaid walnut and ash side table Courtesy of Arthur S. Vernay, Inc., New York City.

Fig. 7 English practice. In contrast, both sections of the secretary are inlaid with a more delicate, intricately checkered chain banding. A scrolled and fret-pierced pediment formerly accompanied this example.

Fig. 8 An effect somewhat reminiscent of Brazilian tulipwood has been achieved by a use of black ash* for the borders of the American swell-front chest of drawers, *circa* 1810. In this piece the panel surfaces of maple have been arranged in an unusual manner, so that more pronounced bird's-eye markings appear at either side of the drawer handles, and only lightly figured wood in between. The Fig. 9 design of the Austrian commode actually represents a retention of Empire features in a Biedermeier production of 1820-1830. This piece also indicates the extensive use of long drawer locks on the Continent, in which the keyhole occupies a central position rather than one close to the top edge of the drawer, as in some European work, and

---

* Cf. *Baltimore Furniture*, The Baltimore Museum of Art, 1947, fig. 4: a card table with similar frieze veneers (described as "imported zebra wood").

in customary English and American practices.

The deeper coloring of Oriental ash sometimes permits a more decided resemblance to *moiré* effects than is found in the finest Hungarian timbers. These watered markings are most plainly seen in the small doors and the intervening panels Fig. 10 of the Korean cabinet, a piece dating from the early years of the eighteenth century.

9. BIRCH

Various species of birch are widely distributed throughout Europe and North America, with vernacular names indicating certain similarities among species appearing in widely separated areas. In common with other timbers these names are frequently derived from outer features of the tree, such as the color of its bark, rather than through characteristics associated with its wood. European growths seldom attain heights of more than seventy feet or butt diameters of more than two feet, while American trees develop to extreme heights of one hundred feet and diameters up to five feet.

The common, white or silver birch, (*Fr. bouleau*), *Betula alba* Linn., is found throughout most of Europe. In southern regions the tree grows only at considerable elevations, while as one of the hardiest timbers flourishing in poor soil and exposed situations, it appears as a rare growth existing above the Arctic Circle.

The wood is of a light creamy-tan color, with a fine, uniform texture, and in general possesses a straight grain, though quartering may bring out handsome curl figures. Growth-ring figures and rays are indistinct. The weight is 35-48 pounds per cubic foot. Some cuttings of this European birch resemble satinwood in texture and grain, with Russian timbers attaining the fullest yellow tones.

In northern areas of the Continent highly figured cuts of birch were employed in the production of both seat furniture and cabinetwork, particularly during the late eighteenth and early nineteenth centuries. Burl veneers were also favored by the most skilled craftsmen, including no less an *ébéniste* than David Roentgen of Neuwied.

Trees growing in Scandinavia and Russia are often attacked by larvae producing cavities that are filled in with cells of a deep brown color. These small markings are formed in V-shapes, set amid swirled graining in the light-toned grounds of finished surfaces. Wood figured in such a manner is now designated as Karelian burl, after the Finnish province where considerable quantities of this timber have been obtained. Similarly marked timbers were utilized by Scandinavian craftsmen during the eighteenth century, later becoming popular in Russian furniture.

The common birch also grows in the British Isles, appearing as one of the few trees that thrive among the heather of the Scottish highlands. It is joined there by the species *B. pubescens*, which varies mainly in outward appearance, with some hybrids produced by the two growths. In outlying sections of the British Isles, especially in the north of England and in Scotland, birch was employed for the making of seat furniture, cabinetwork and turnery. During the Early Victorian period it became so popular that certain rooms of contemporary mansions were entirely furnished in this medium, either in native or imported material. Around the turn of the eighteenth century birch was also substituted for, or used in conjunction with satinwood, later being stained to imitate mahogany or walnut.

In America, birch has never been popular as a primary furniture wood, although *The Cabinet-Maker's Assistant* considered the timber growing on this continent to be superior to that of Europe:

For a long period it has furnished the staple commodity in use, for almost all the purposes for which hardwood is required; and more recently, the finer specimens of it have been employed in the manufacture of bed-room, hall, and even drawing-room furniture.

Of American birch, there are seven varieties; but of these we shall mention only the three which are commonly imported to Britain, namely, the *Betula lenta*, or mahogany birch, the *Betula excelsa* [sic], or yellow birch, the *Betula nigra*, or black birch. The *Betula lenta*, or mountain mahogany of America, called also mahogany birch, and sweet birch, is, on account of the excellence of its wood, the most valued. We have seen many specimens, which, in a finished state, rivalled in beauty the finest mahogany. These were of the kind familiarly called *curled*; a descriptive designation warranted by its resemblance to curled mahogany, in having the plane surface variegated by a series of semicular shades of color, alternately light and dark, occasioned by the different angles at which the light falls upon the grain of the wood.... It is difficult to convey by mere description an idea of the rare beauty of such specimens as we have mentioned: for when finished in French polish, they possess a transparent appearance, suggestive of colored crystals or precious stones, having the light reflected from a surface polished at different angles, rather than a plane surface of wood.... We do not approve the practice of coloring birch, with the view of making it resemble mahogany. To use coloring matter, whether in the form of vegetable juice, or gum in solution with the polish, is, we apprehend, only to spoil good birch when applied to it; inasmuch as the stain or gum has the effect of destroying that transparent lustre which we regard as its principal beauty.

Birch logs of the quality of which we have been speaking, bear but a small proportion to the whole amount imported from Quebec, the port from which this variety is shipped for Britain. It is to be found growing not only in Canada, but also in the middle states of Pennsylvania, New York, the Jerseys; but from these localities the cost of transmission forbids its being sent to this country.

In 1839 the imports of these birch timbers into England had reached a figure of 336,151 cubic feet, with a consumption of 307,450 feet.

Betula lenta Linn., native to Canada and to our eastern states from Maine to Delaware, is still known in some sections as mahogany birch or mountain mahogany, though American timbers are generally classified as sweet, or cherry birch. The heartwood varies from a light yellowish-red to a reddish-tan hue—often of quite a dark tone. The sapwood is a dingy white color. This birch is moderately hard and close in texture, and is characterized by rays that appear distinctly as deep-toned flecks in quartered surfaces. The weight averages around 47 pounds per cubic foot.

Betula lutea or yellow birch also grows in Canada and through the northeastern section of the United States. This species is known alternatively as Quebec birch or Canadian yellow birch, and as red, gray, or silver birch; while northern selected curly-grained wood is now referred to as Canadian silkywood. The heartwood is generally somewhat lighter in color than in sweet birch, while the usable sapwood is almost white in hue. This wood is fine and even in texture, usually with a straight grain but at times displaying curly markings. The weight is 40-48 pounds per cubic foot.

Betula nigra Linn., which is black, red, or river birch, ranges in this country from Massachusetts to Florida, growing best in the southern states. *The Cabinet-Maker's Assistant* states that timbers from New Brunswick, Nova Scotia and Cape Breton Island were exported in large quantities, "this variety having been much earlier introduced to Britain than the others." The wood is of a light or medium tan color, with a close, rather crooked grain and less figure than other birches. The weight is 37 pounds per cubic foot.

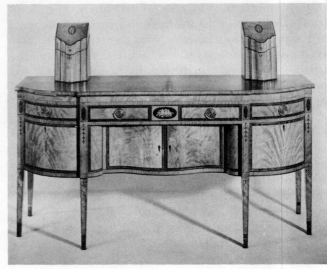

13. An Early Federal inlaid curly birch sideboard

Birch was used to a limited extent in American furniture of the early colonial period, and in later Windsor- or tavern-type pieces. Occasionally it appears as the principal medium of more sophisticated, or even fine productions. It is also found in veneers of our "branch satinwood period," dating around the close of the eighteenth century. When the wood is not stained to a cherry- or mahogany-red color it is apt to present a rather muddied appearance, particularly in the softer, unfigured surfaces.

THE ILLUSTRATED EXAMPLES

The fall-front writing cabinet is by the famous Stockholm master, George Haupt, 1741-1784, who trained in Paris and London. Marshal Lagerquist of the Nordiska Museet has been kind enough to sketch this piece in order to indicate the principal veneers. The central panel of the *abattant* is of ("undyed") birch, with dyed hornbeam, and citronnier, forming the imbricated leafage, and the entwined ribbons, of the inlaid festoon. Citronnier appears again in the minor inlays, and the dark panel borders are of amaranth. Fig.

Dating from about 1800, the sideboard is recorded as formerly owned by Charles Carollton, of Carollton, Maryland. Here carefully selected, highly figured birch veneers have been combined with narrow strips of satinwood. In a cursory examination of the illustration a less careful use of the larger veneers may be overlooked. One of the deep drawers, which has been repaired, shows the figure of the birch veneer running in an opposite direction to that of the balancing panel. While working errors are not too common, they have Fig

12. A Swedish Louis XVI inlaid birch, citronnier and amaranth *secrétaire à abattant* Courtesy of the Nordiska Museet, Stockholm.

occurred with some frequency in the various mediums of chair- and cabinet-making, and in repairs carried out by careless workmen. Mistakes of this nature are more often unnoticed in looking at a piece of furniture from various angles, than in the more entire view offered by a photographic reproduction.

10. MAPLE

In medieval times the European maple was known as the *Mazer* tree. *Maser, Manscin, Masar* and *Mösurr*, in Middle English, Old Welsh, Old German and Old Norse, also referred to the maple, and to Gothic or Renaissance drinking vessels fashioned from the burls that develop on its trunk. The maples of Continental Europe are represented chiefly by the species *Acer campestre* Linn. and *A. platanoides* Linn. The former species is the common maple; the latter is a faster growing tree known as the Norwegian maple, which appears in Scandinavia, Russia, Germany, and parts of France and Switzerland, yielding a softer but handsomely veined timber.

The English field maple is a variety of *A. campestre,* one that has been introduced in Scotland. This variety is not common as a tree, although it may develop to about half the size of the more important Continental growths. English authorities do not consider it worthy of mention as a timber.

There is little variation between the wood of the European common maple and that of our own sugar maple. Therefore the properties of Continental timbers will in general coincide with those of the more important North American species; *vide infra.*

Maple (*Ahorn* in German) has been utilized in the construction of Central European furniture ever since the Gothic period, first in the solid wood and later as highly decorative veneer panels, bandings and other inlays. Fiddle-back cuttings have also furnished violin-makers with one of the finest materials for the back and side surfaces of their instruments. When bird's-eye maple became a fashionable medium of Continental furniture ample supplies were obtained in Poland, Germany and Russia.

The richly figured maple timbers of Italy, Germany and Austria were well known and highly regarded in England at the turn of the seventeenth century. Their merits were described at length by Evelyn, whose random notes, repeated in the fourth edition of *Sylva*, 1706, contain no direct reference to the native English Maple as supplying a fine cabinet wood.

After mentioning "the delicateness of the grain, when the knurs and nodosities are rarely diapered, which does much advance its price," the diarist stipulated "that especially, which grows in Friuli, Carniola, and Saltzburglandt." This is followed by quotations from Pliny, referring to "the elegancy and fineness of the wood . . . especially the white, which is wonderfully beautiful; this is call'd the French-maple, and grows in that part of Italy, that is on the other side of Po beyond the Alps: The other has a curl'd grain, so curiously maculated, that from a near resemblance, it was usually call'd the Peacock's-tail, &c. . . . The *bruscum*, or Knur is wonderfully fair, but the *molluscum* is counted most precious; both of them knobs and swellings out of the tree. The *bruscum* is more intricately crisp'd; the *molluscum* not so much. . . . The *bruscum* is of a blackish kind."

Evelyn also noted that "The knot of the [maple] timber was the most esteem'd." After discussing the "pretty undulations and chamfers" obtained in various other timbers, which he accredited to "the rain distilling along the branches," he pointed out that "above all, notable for these extravagant damaskings and characters, is the maple; and 'tis notorious, that this tree is very full of branches from the root to its very summit. . . . These arms being frequently cut, the head is more surcharged with them, which spreading like so many rays from a centre, form that hollowness at the top of the stem whence they shoot, capable of containing a good quantity of water every time it rains; This sinking into the pores, as was before hinted, is compell'd to divert its course as it passes through the body of the tree, where-ever it encounters the knot of any of those branches which were cut off from the stem; because their roots not only deeply penetrate towards the heart, but are likewise of themselves very hard and impervious; and the frequent obliquity of this course of the subsiding moisture, by reason of these obstructions, is, as may be conceived, the cause of those curious works, which we find remarkable in this, and other woods, whose branches grow thick from the stem."

The references to "knur," "knobs," "swellings" and "knot" are plainly indicative of the excrescences from which so-called buttwood, and burlwood veneers are obtained. "Maculated" may apply to various types of spottings, but "damaskings" and "characters" indicate variegated patterns differing from those of curly, bird's-eye, or burl maple, and coinciding with those developed in knurlwood. In former usage *knurs* might be synonymous with *knots* or excrescences as defined here in connection with American sugar maple, or the term might refer to gnarls, indicating twisted grainings or cross figures. Both *knurs* and *nodosities* still remain in use as descriptive of trunk protuberances—with their definitions containing no references to formations as burl growths.

It is only logical that such handsomely marked timbers would be coveted by English cabinetmakers of Evelyn's time, and that through ordinary trade or introduction by immigrant craftsmen they would appear in English cabinetwork. Nevertheless, when veneers with these unusual markings are found in large-scale pieces of contemporary workmanship they are in general promptly identified as mulberrywood. The principal difference between most of these veneers, and those obtained from American trees, is that their figures are at times more delicately curled, or "crisp'd."

There are numerous species of maple to be found in North America, some yielding timbers of excellent quality while others have little commercial value. The principal species since colonial times has been the rock, or sugar maple, *A. saccharinum* Linn., important even then as a source of maple sugar, as well as for its timber. This tree grows throughout the eastern half of the United States and in lower Canada, attaining an extreme height of one hundred and twenty feet and a butt diameter of four feet.

In pursuing his investigations Evelyn found that: "The savages in Canada, when the sap rises in the maple, by an incision in the tree, extract the liquor; and having evaporated a reasonable quantity thereof (as suppose 7 or 8 pound), there will remain one pound, as sweet and perfect sugar, as that which is gotten out of the cane; part of which sugar has been for many years constantly sent to Rouen in Normandy, to be refin'd."

The timber varies in color from a light creamy-tan, to a deeper, pinkish-tan hue; with the application of a plain varnish finishing to a light or medium yellowish-tan surface tone. It is hard and strong, with a fine, even texture, and displays rather delicate deep-toned lines that heighten the effects of very mild growth-ring figures. The grain is generally straight, though decorative material is common in old furniture where the careful selection and matching of such wood is frequently apparent. The more usual grain figures include fiddle-back, curly or "tiger stripe," and bird's-eye markings. Landscape and blister figures appear in a limited proportion of timbers. Rays are visible as exceedingly fine flecks running parallel with the grain in plain-sawed material. The weight averages around 45 pounds per cubic foot.

Sugar maple is difficult to work, even in straight-grained timber, while figured cuts presented further hindrances to the tools of Early American craftsmen. The wood is also subject to warping, and to splitting if nailed. It is one of the few woods in which vertical shrinkage may occur to a noticeable extent. Maple that is evenly figured and free from dark specks or discolorations is difficult to obtain in present supplies.

> *Whoever has got any curious*
> *Maple Tree knots to sell may hear*
> *of a Purchaser from the Publisher.*
> Boston Gazette, *April 30–May 6, 1739*

The use of the word *knots* in this advertisement[19] may refer to those portions of the maple tree where knurlwood is developed, or where buttwood is formed.

Despite the timetables offered in regard to American furniture, highboys and other case pieces following William and Mary and Queen Anne designs were produced in Massachusetts at the time of this notice. Veneers obtained from *maple tree knots*, displaying flamboyant dark-brown or blackish figures were currently selected for surfacing these examples. Therefore the advertisement may well have been directed toward securing such material for use in cabinetwork, rather than for more common purposes.

These dark markings of maple knurlwood are brought out by a plain varnish finish, without any staining, just as this same polish affects curly maple—in which the grain often appears to take on dark-brown or charcoal-black tones. In England similar effects are frequently believed to result from a long-lost method of ebonizing, with some magical power enabling a deep penetration through the unusually hard substance of very densely grouped tissues. This supposition is easily disproved if investigation is not confined to simple visual examination.

Veneers of maple knurlwood or buttwood have often been identified as "burl ash" in America, and as "burr elm" in England, despite the fact that they present larger, more flamboyant and blacker markings than occur in these other timbers or their burlwoods. These markings and their ground tissues are very dense and solid, presenting hard, exceptionally smooth surface textures, in contrast to the coarse textures of veneers obtained from ash and elm burls.

In addition to the use of maple in central and northern areas of Europe, and in the British Isles, the wood was also employed by cabinetmakers working in France, especially from 1820 to the middle of the nineteenth century. There it is known as *bois d'érable,* burl maple as *broussin d'érable,* and bird's-eye maple as *érable moucheté.* When bird's-eye maple came into vogue in Great Britain, during the Late Georgian period, timbers displaying this phenomenon were imported from Canada, where they were obtained in New Brunswick, Prince Edward Island and Nova Scotia. Veneers with bird's-eye markings were favored for exterior surfaces of the smaller cabinet pieces, and for the lining of writing interiors. The latter utility was continued during the Victorian period, when the clean appearance of the wood was appreciated as much as its ability to reflect light into enclosed spaces. Maple was also esteemed for its contrasting effect when combined with exterior surfaces of mahogany, rosewood or walnut.

American craftsmen selected maple as one of the principal materials employed during the colonial period. This popularity was continued in many sections throughout the eighteenth century, often in productions retaining earlier features of design, but also in those fashioned along contemporary lines. The wood received its highest approbation in New England, but it is also found in seat furniture and cabinetwork produced in New York, New Jersey and Pennsylvania, and to a far lesser extent in the work of more southerly states. Curly-

figured maple received the greatest approval, following a rather brief use of knurlwood veneers, apparently in the vicinity of Ipswich, Massachusetts. Bird's-eye maple came into demand at the close of the century. The plainest wood was often used for concealed structural purposes, a utility practiced by some of the finest shops flourishing in Salem, Boston and Providence.

THE ILLUSTRATED EXAMPLES

A high regard for this cabinet wood is manifest in the finished design and execution of the Pennsylvania highboy. Here a Queen Anne design is Fig. 16 modified by cable-fluted stiles supporting a dentiled cornice. This example was produced during the middle decades of the eighteenth century.

Recessed panels with scallop-shell headings are featured in the secretary with wood-paneled doors, *circa* 1775, and in the example below with arched Fig. 18 and inlaid crest, *circa* 1810. These panels are characteristic features of American block-front furniture, but it is not generally recognized that such

14. An Early Federal bird's-eye maple, black ash and cherrywood chest of drawers

15. A New England curly maple secretary Courtesy of Ginsburg & Levy, Inc., New York City.

16. A Pennsylvania curly maple high-boy Courtesy of Joe Kindig, Jr., & Son, York, Pennsylvania.

17. A Regency inlaid bird's-eye maple sofa table Courtesy of Biggs of Maiden-head.

18. A New England maple secretary Courtesy of Ginsburg & Levy, Inc.,
New York City.

20. A maple knurlwood cabinet on Carolean carved and gilded stand Courtesy of Frank Partridge & Sons, Ltd., London.

21. A Thomas Tompion barometer with maple knurlwood case At Hampton Court Palace. Reproduced by gracious permission of Her Britannic Majesty the Queen.

19. A George III inlaid bird's-eye maple cylinder desk Courtesy of H. Blairman & Sons Ltd., London.

22. A New England inlaid maple knurl-wood highboy

forms were frequently repeated around the close of the eighteenth century. The writing interior of the "Sheraton" secretary has been treated in a manner typical of this school.

Panels of bird's-eye maple are combined with cherrywood in the piece with boldly scrolled apron, *circa* 1820, featuring a careful use of highly marked veneers as favored in New York as well as in New England. The example displays cross-banded borders of black ash.

Decorative inlays and stringing lines of ebony appear in the sofa table showing a British use of maple *circa* 1810, in the solid wood and in bird's-eye veneers, serving as an interesting change from the more usual satinwood furniture. A few years earlier in date, the cylinder-front desk is remark-

able for an even more brilliant selection and employment of these veneers in flat and rounded surfaces, giving attractively scintillant effects.

The example veneered in maple knurlwood, or buttwood, is a New England highboy in which the form and structural details have been derived from British designs of *circa* 1700, translated here in a production of *circa* 1710-30. Hence, the use of maple knurlwood veneers in this country may, according to the designs of this example, be conservatively estimated as occurring between 1710 and the middle of the century, possibly until about 1760 or a decade or so later than the date of the *Boston Gazette* advertisement for maple tree knots.

Continental skills are represented in the British example with intricately chased mounts and elab-

Fig. 15

Fig. 14

Fig. 17

Fig. 19

Fig. 22

Fig. 20

23. A Late Stuart inlaid maple knurl-wood secretary Courtesy of Hotspur Ltd., London.

orate stand. When a varnish coating is removed from veneers of this type the darker areas appear in natural medium-brown tones, or where blacker effects are presented the natural tones may be somewhat darker but not actually verging on black.

Fig. 23   In choice of materials as well as design the following secretary indicates probable origin in the workshop of Coxed and Woster,* a partnership apparently existing for at least twenty years after

the close of the seventeenth century. A darker figuring in the veneers has induced some conjecture as to whether these are of mulberrywood but the ground is much lighter in tone than that of mulberry heartwood. As in the other knurlwood examples shown here, facings of the long drawers are composed of at least four or five veneer strips butted together. The case of the barometer made by Thomas Tompion, *circa* 1695, was recognized Fig. 21 by John C. Rogers as of "stained burr-maple," this description appearing under his remarks on cabinet woods in *The Dictionary of English Furniture*, London, 1924.

---

* Pieces made by Coxed and Woster also serve to document the use of rosewood, as a border and molding material, in London during the early years of the eighteenth century.

11. SAVANNAWOOD

The Federal Society of Philadelphia Cabinet Makers, emulating London practice, published books of prices at the turn of the eighteenth century. In these listings extra prices were given for work to be carried out in kingwood, snakewood, zebrawood, yewwood and other rarities. "Savannah" is one of these—still undetermined in actual use.

This may be savanna wattle, *Citharexylum fruticosum* or *C. quadrangulare* of the West Indies, or a related variety of the genus as it appears in these islands and in southern Florida. The hard, durable wood produced by any member of the genus is also known as fiddlewood or *bois côtelet*. Descriptions of such timbers are not available though an unspecified variety is mentioned under a general heading of "Negrito." This is described as "one of the most ornamental of all tropical trees in Florida," yielding wood of "a whitish-straw color, with a soft, close grain, but taking a very smooth surface from the tool."

12. SOUTH AFRICAN YELLOWWOOD
(A softwood)

South African yellowwood is produced by various species of *Podocarpus*, particularly *P. elongata* and *P. thunbergia*. The latter species, known as upright yellowwood, was formerly considered superior in quality to, and more abundant than the former, which has become the more important timber in modern commerce.

The *Podocarpus'* species are evergreen trees of the yew family (Taxaceae), and are classified as softwoods. However, while South African yellowwood may possibly be likened to a pine of exceptionally fine quality, just as yew bears a superficial resemblance to cedar, it differs from the typical softwoods in having no clearly defined growth rings, and, in general appearance, more closely approaches the aspect of a hardwood.

This material appears in old furniture produced in the Cape Colony for Dutch and English residents. The heartwood and sapwood are not sharply defined, presenting an even, light yellow, or straw-yellow color. The texture is fine and uniform, and the wood generally straight-grained, with no figuring. Weights vary from 25 to 35 pounds per cubic foot.

13. BITTER ORANGE

The bitter orange tree, *Citrus aurantium* Linn., is indigenous to Southern Europe, but has been propagated in northern Continental regions and in the British Isles. Its wood is of a light yellowish color, possessing a compact texture with very small scattered pores and rays. The weight is recorded at 49 pounds per cubic foot.

This has been used for small inlaid or turned articles and for carvings. In the British Isles it was used as an inlay material of furniture produced during the seventeenth and eighteenth centuries, and, as *bois d'oranger*, it appears in French marquetry work of the latter period. At this time the wood was also employed for principal surfaces or inlaid decorations of German and Scandinavian furniture.

14. BAMBOO

The bamboos are woody or arborescent grasses of the genus *Bambusa* or other related genera, as *Arundinaria* and *Dendrocalamus*, which are distributed in the tropics and subtropics of both hemispheres. They are monocotyledons related to the palms, and angiospermous plants co-ordinate with the dicotyledons producing hardwoods. However, they do not form growth rings, and they are not true timbers—although they often serve in similar capacities.

The more typical bamboos are represented in the first named genus, in which *B. arundinaria* is the most important species. This plant grows in clumps and may attain a height of one hundred and twenty feet. The hollow stems reach diameters of five or six inches, and are so hard and durable that they are used in the East for building, for furniture of all sorts, palanquin poles, cooking utensils, and to serve many other purposes. The smaller stalks are also utilized for parts of furniture, and for musical instruments, walking sticks, etc.; while the shoots are used for food.

European importations of bamboo furniture and other articles, particularly from China, were responsible for adding the form of this wood to designs of western furniture produced during the latter decades of the eighteenth century. It became popular at this time to fashion seat furniture and cabinet pieces with uprights, moldings and other rounded members carried out in imitation of bamboo—simulating the divided and grooved stem, and occasionally with a partial use of real bamboo. The light and soft yellow color of this wood might also be imitated, but painted or japanned effects were usually preferred. Work of this type came into vogue throughout most of Europe. In England, chair designs were generally executed in beech-wood, though holly and other woods were also utilized. The London firm of Elward, Marsh and Tatham specialized in such designs around the turn of the century, and in 1802 supplied seat furniture of this description for the Royal Pavilion at Brighton. These pieces blended admirably with other chairs of real bamboo received at about the same time from China.

THE ILLUSTRATED EXAMPLE

Fig. 24 This is very similar in form to those mentioned above, which may be seen in H. Clifford Smith, *Buckingham Palace*, Figs. 320-322, along with other chairs in imitation bamboo. While the bamboo has supplied a favorite theme of Eastern art for many

24. A Chinese bamboo armchair

centuries, and furniture made of this wood has been used in China over an equally long period of time, it is apparent that designs of this type were largely produced through demands of European merchants visiting China during the reign of the Emperor Ch'ien Lung and that of his successor.

15. SYCAMORE

The European sycamore, *Acer pseudo-platanus* Linn., is native to southern and central areas of the Continent, being introduced in Britain during late Gothic times. The tree grows to heights of over one hundred feet, developing to a butt diameter as great as six feet. The wood varies in color from yellowish-white to light tan with a yellow cast. It is comparatively hard, with a fine, even texture and a lustrous surface. A decorative fiddle-back figure is characteristic, though occasionally this is replaced by more pronounced curly markings. Rays appear distinctively in the usual quartered veneers. The weight is 39 pounds per cubic foot.

Solid cuttings of sycamore, employed in either principal or secondary capacities, are found in Continental furniture of designs more generally executed in oak or walnut. After the middle of the eighteenth century the wood was cut with more complete attention to its fiddle-back figure. Selections of this type were then utilized as veneers in furniture of the highest quality, particularly in France where the wood is known as *bois de sycomore*. Of the German cabinetmakers, David Roentgen was especially partial to the qualities and stripy effects of this wood, employing it with the grain running in contrary directions on the faces of numerous writing tables and cabinets.

In England, sycamore was frequently used as an inlay material prior to its adoption as a principal cabinet wood at the time that Robert Adam's influence first became apparent. This popularity soon extended to Ireland, where some of the finest pieces of Dublin origin were veneered and inlaid in sycamore.

Frequently, but not "generally," the natural color of the wood was altered by staining it to a soft, clear green tone, which appears in old furniture as a pleasant gray-green hue, contrasting to the overly brilliant or harsh shades seen in fraudulent works. This stained wood, distinguished as harewood, was used as veneers for plain or inlaid panels, as a medium of parquetry or marquetry decorations, or as a banding material.

THE ILLUSTRATED EXAMPLES

Fig. All of the inlaid surfaces in the oval occasional table are of sycamore. The treatment of this piece is strongly suggestive of work performed by Charles Topino, *M.E.*, 1773-1789. Had the table passed through unethical trade channels it would surely have been stamped with a forged *pontil* mark in

25. A Louis XVI sycamore marquetry and tulipwood occasional table

the name of this *maître ébéniste*. From a rather wide use of the same, and closely similar parquetry and marquetry patterns in French furniture of the period, it is apparent that of the many German craftsmen working in that country during the later decades of the eighteenth century, some were specially engaged in supplying these inlays to the more important cabinetmakers of native and foreign lineages.

The writing table is representative of the loose foliage patterns that were developed by British designers of about 1780, soon to be followed by those of a more conventionalized or fixed nature. A vertical use of sycamore veneers permitting the fiddle-back figure to run in the opposite direction together with a contrasting lower arrangement is often found in Continental furniture, particularly where there is a recessed superstructure. Still, there was no definitely established procedure, and in a number of French cabinets this more effective method has been entirely disregarded.

Fig. 26

26. A George III inlaid sycamore writing table Courtesy of J. J. Wolff Antiques Ltd., London.

16. ELDER

The elder, *Sambucus nigra* Linn., grows as a shrub or small tree appearing over a wide portion of the European continent and in Britain. Its wood varies in color from a light yellowish shade to a yellowish-tan hue. Sparse and very minute pores are characteristic of this species, and pronounced rays which are displayed prominently in quartered surfaces. The timber is soft when freshly cut, becoming quite hard after drying, in which state it weighs 44 pounds per cubic foot. Known in France as *bois de sureau*, elder was occasionally employed there as an inlay material, with a limited use also occurring elsewhere in Europe.

17. BARBERRY

The common barberry, *Berberis vulgaris*, appears as a shrub thriving in the North Temperate Zone of Europe. In the more sizable growths stems measure as much as four inches in diameter. The heartwood is of a yellowish color, sometimes streaked in lighter and darker tones. It possesses a hard, dense texture, with growth rings and rays showing distinctly in longitudinal surfaces. The lighter-toned sapwood, which is also serviceable, is of a bright yellow color when freshly cut, generally darkening to a considerable extent on exposure to sunlight.

This species supplied one of the yellow woods of inlaid decorations and turned work executed in Europe during the seventeenth century, uses which were continued in some areas after the increase of such supplies through importations of more valuable timbers. In later manufactures barberry appears as a medium of Tunbridge wares. A specimen of English barberry, cut from a slender branch, displays an even greenish-yellow or citron-green coloring, thus being darker than the usual descriptions but otherwise conforming with the properties mentioned above.

18. LIME

The lime or linden tree of Europe, *Tilia europaea* Linn., is common to Russia, Austria, Germany, France, the Netherlands, and to England, where it was probably introduced during the Elizabethan period. Heights of eighty to ninety feet are reached in the fullest growth of the tree. When freshly cut the wood is of an ivory-white or very light yellow color, but this turns to buff or leather-brown tones with long exposures. Limewood possesses a fine, close texture, though it is soft enough to be marked by the pressure of a finger nail. The pores are very small and obscure, but fine parallel rays are fairly distinct in the fresh timber. After an unusually high degree of moisture content has been removed the weight (air-dried) is 35 pounds per cubic foot.

Because of its even texture, capacity for sharp outlines, freedom from knots, and general facility in carving, limewood was recognized as an excellent material to provide the sculptured effects so popular during the Renaissance and baroque periods. It was especially favored in architectural work, in the relief ornament of cabinets designed along similar lines, and for the elaborate frames of mirrors and paintings. The naturalistic themes introduced by the Dutch school were particularly suited to a rendition in this material.

Today limewood is largely associated with the work carried out by Grinling Gibbons in England, *circa* 1670-1710, and by his followers who continued to practice in that country for some years after his death in 1720. As Gibbons' sponsor, Evelyn mentions his talents in *Sylva*: "The trophies, festoons, fruitages, encarpa, and other sculpture in the frontoons, friezes, capitals, pedestals, and other ornaments and decorations, (or admirable invention and performance) to be seen about the choir in St. Paul's and other churches; royal palaces, and noble houses in the city and countrey. All of them, the works and invention of our Lysippus, Mr. Gibbons; comparable, and for ought appears, equal to any thing of the antients; having had the honour (for so I account it) to be the first who recommended this great artist to his Majesty Charles the II. I mention it on this occasion, with much satisfaction."

As a medium for elaborate ornament in full relief, limewood would be unexcelled except for its delicate nature in such use. This is mitigated to a large extent by the positions such works were generally intended to occupy—though cleaning often presents a difficult problem. Carving was executed with little danger of splitting or warping, but very sharp, thin-edged tools were necessary, due to the soft nature of the wood and the resulting liability to roughen under a dull or coarse blade.

Later uses extended to other requirements in the production of furniture, and in the making of musical instruments. *The Cabinet-Maker's Assistant* observed that limewood "From its inert character . . . makes an excellent ground for japanned and inlaid work, and [it] is used for the frames of the best japanned chairs, inlaid with mother of pearl."

27. A Grinling Gibbons carved lime-wood wall mirror

THE ILLUSTRATED EXAMPLE

The mirror frame is one of the most important of its type, and may well be attributed to the hand of Grinling Gibbons. Aside from the intricate and naturalistic rendering of animal and plant forms, a net and its contents, centered amid the pendant of shells and fishes, has been executed with almost Oriental dexterity. After two and a half centuries of aging the limewood has toned to a soft walnut-brown color.

19. LARCH
(A softwood)

The larch is a conifer that differs from most trees of this class in being of a deciduous nature. As a timber it has been highly valued since Greek and Roman times in southern Europe where many of the Venetian Byzantine buildings were con-structed on larch piles. The tree is found in moun-tainous sections of Italy, Switzerland, France, and as far north as Siberia. Heights of over one hundred and twenty feet, and butt diameters of about five feet are attained. Serviceable timber is produced within a few decades of growth, while the life of the tree may extend to over five hundred years. This timber is one of the hardest of those appear-ing under the classification of European softwoods, and is especially valued because of its freedom from knots.

The principal species is the common, or Euro-pean larch, *Larix europoea* or *L. decidua*, which was introduced into England during the seven-teenth century. The resinous heartwood, as seen in the usual flat cuttings, is of a light creamy-tan color with thin orange veinings, generally presenting an appearance midway between that of the more deli-cately barred Danzig pine, and European spruce with its heavier parallel markings. These tones may vary in depth according to the soil and situation in which the tree has grown. Larch is moderately fine and uniform in texture, and generally straight and even in the grain. The fibers are closely interwoven, while growth-ring markings are spaced according to variations in the nature and rate of development. Weights range between 31 and 47 pounds per cubic foot.

As a Continental timber, known in France as *bois de mélèze*, the wide range of this species permits its appearance in furniture of many different localities. Although it was more frequently utilized for solidly constructed pieces, it also appears as a veneer in examples of the highest quality. It is said that in several of the Swiss cantons larch was so highly valued in the past that it was purchased at twice the price given for oak of similar dimensions.

From about 1725 cultivation of the larch was carried out extensively in Britain, particularly by Scottish landowners in Peebleshire, Argyleshire, in the neighborhood of Dunkel, and at Blair Athol. Between 1805 and 1830 natively grown timbers had reached a point in this cultivation where they could serve a large demand for various purposes, including those connected with cabinetmaking. Despite

an earlier introduction in England, it is probable that the finest furniture in this medium was then executed in Scotland.

The fourth Duke of Athol was responsible for the greatest propagation of the larch in Scotland, continuing the interests of his father and grandfather. At Blair Castle, the family seat, is a pair of dwarf cabinets or commodes in this favored wood, ordered by the "planting duke" from a local designer, one Bullock, and furnished at the time of their execution in 1817 with slabs of Glen Tilt marble.

THE ILLUSTRATED EXAMPLE

We show one of these larch commodes at Blair Castle. Some indication of the soft tone acquired by the wood and the character of its markings may be seen in the doors and the solid colonettes. Each center panel of the doors is composed of four balance-matched oyster pieces, showing about forty concentric growth rings extending from the darker core to the outer angles. The wide mitered borders display the usual grain stripes and simple figures found in plain-sawed surfaces.

Fig. 2

28. A Regency brass-inlaid larchwood dwarf cabinet Courtesy of Lord James Stewart Murray, Blair Castle, Perthshire. Copyright *Country Life.*

20. POPLAR

The European poplar, *Populus canescens*, is a common species appearing throughout the Temperate Zone of the Continent. The tree reaches a height of one hundred feet or more and a butt diameter of four feet, yielding "a very fine timber, of much more value than it is popularly supposed to possess." This timber is distinguished by a light yellowish-tan color, very fine and obscure pores and rays, and a close texture that is comparable to that of rock maple. It presents a hard surface capable of taking a very smooth finish. The weight is 35-40 pounds per cubic foot.

In northern areas of the Continent, particularly in Germany, poplar was utilized for the production of furniture executed in the solid wood, and for veneer panels or inlaid decorations of cabinetwork. Poplar burl veneers were especially favored during the late classic and Biedermeier vogues. These veneers might be entirely or partially marked with a very mild and delicate "peanutshell" graining, which is distinctive though it is often mistaken for the stronger figure of amboinawood. Mistaken identifications are quite general in respect to the use of burl poplar in British furniture of Sheraton and Regency designs.

The English poplar, *P. alba* Linn., is a smaller tree which is not actually indigenous to England but was probably introduced from Holland, where the species is still common today. The wood is somewhat similar to that of *P. canescens* in its plainer growths, though softer and a little lighter in color. It is recorded as an inlay material of the sixteenth century, though no extensive use of natively grown timbers has ever occurred in England.

Italian poplar, *P. serotina*, attains a great size with the bole measuring six feet or more in diameter. A rapid growth rate accounts for a much greater softness in the timber than is found in northern growths. This wood is almost white in color, with little figure, and it is as soft and light in weight as certain mild growths of pine. Italian poplar was largely used for secondary purposes in cabinetwork of this Mediterranean country and adjoining areas. It has appeared in the drawer linings and other interior parts of commodes and cabinets which, without proper consideration of designs and materials, have been attributed to origins in Westphalia, Flanders, and other northerly regions.

THE ILLUSTRATED EXAMPLE

The writing and backgammon table with trestle supports dates from *circa* 1810-1820. An attractive foil for the ebony inlays is provided by the light tone of the burl poplar veneers, which are additionally enhanced by brass bandings, and, according to memory aided by lenticular examination, a narrow border of calamander. Fig. 29

29. A Regency inlaid burl poplar backgammon and work table

21. WILLOW

The willow, *Salix alba* Linn., (*S. coerulea, S. triandra,* etc.), appears in many varieties that are indigenous to Continental Europe and the British Isles. Osiers or withies—the small branches, twigs or shoots of willow trees and shrubs—have been employed for centuries in making cribs, trugs, creels, paniers, and other wicker wares of European use. *Twiggen* chairs, resembling the archaic *halmstol* of Scandinavian countries, were also produced in England and elsewhere in Europe from willow twigs, or surfaced with wickerwork.

Trees of this genus often maintain shrublike forms, the more erect growths attaining a height of well over one hundred feet and a butt diameter of five feet or more. The wood varies in color from pinkish-white to reddish-tan hues. It is tough and elastic, but rather soft, with minute pores and rays, a fine, uniform texture and a straight grain. The weight averages around 30 pounds per cubic foot. Willow may be mistaken for horse chestnut, lime, or European poplar—to which it is related.

During the seventeenth and eighteenth centuries this wood was utilized in the construction of rural furniture and accorded a limited use as an inlay material. In the latter capacity it may appear as the *bois d'ozier* or French marquetry work, or as one of the stained woods used to imitate ebony.

The weeping willow, *S. babylonica*, was introduced from China and the Near East, its pendulous habit having been associated for many centuries with the quality of sorrow. This association was revived in the West, where a wide admiration of the ornamental tree developed at the turn of the eighteenth century. Then the "weeping willow growing beside a cenotaph" became a favorite commemorative motif of European paintings, prints and needlework.

22. HAZEL

The hazel, in various species of the *Corylus* genus, appears as a shrub or small tree growing throughout most of Europe. Of these species the common hazel, *C. avellana* Linn., more often assumes the former proportions, though trees may develop to a height of about thirty feet if they are not selected for coppicing.[18] The demand of this plant for a moist soil has been associated with the choice of a flexible hazel twig as the indicating rod of the water-diviner.

Also known as nutwood or *Nussholz*, and *bois de coudrier* or *noisetier*, hazelwood is of a pinkish-white to reddish-tan color, with no distinct variation between heartwood and sapwood. The texture is usually close and uniform, and the grain straight, although these properties are variable. Rays may appear as light-toned lines or flakes in longitudinal surfaces. Occasionally veneers are cut from stumps or roots of the larger trees. The weight of the long-wood (trunkwood) is 35-45 pounds per cubic foot.

This timber was generally utilized in European furniture of rural districts, although it also appears in more elaborate veneered and inlaid examples produced in the larger towns and cities of Austria and Germany. Cabinetmakers of these countries often combined hazelwood with other local materials, or with those received from Hungarian forests.

23. AMERICAN "POPLAR"

"Poplar" and "yellow poplar" are names that have come to be associated with the American tulip tree, *Liriodendron tulipifera* Linn., and with its wood, despite the fact that this species does not belong to the poplar, but to the magnolia family. Alternative names are whitewood, cucumber wood, "popple," and, in England today, canary yellow wood. The Onondaga Indians of New York called the tree *Ko-yen-ta-ka-ah-ta*, or white tree, while an additional name, canoewood, refers to a use of the wood by certain of the aboriginal tribes in fashioning their primitive dugouts.

Record heights of about two hundred feet, and butt diameters of about twelve feet, have been attained by this tree. The heartwood is usually bi-colored, as a rule appearing in light yellowish-tan or -brown, and soft light- to medium-green tones; the sapwood is of a creamy-white hue. The timber is further distinguished by a fine, uniform texture, a straight grain, and numerous tiny rays appearing distinctly in radial sections. It is soft, easy to work, and light in weight—26 to 29 pounds per cubic foot.

This wood was widely used for structural purposes in American cabinetwork of colonial and Early Federal times. Original selections of "poplar" for these purposes often provide bases of identifica-

30. A New England "poplar" and birch child's bedstead Courtesy of Ginsburg & Levy, Inc., New York City.

tion for American work in the consideration of pieces displaying strong foreign influences. On the other hand, in numerous instances a prompt acceptance of this popular structural material has resulted in substitutions of drawer linings or other elements, taken from inferior native productions, to replace other woods, or worm-holed material, appearing in fine Irish or English examples which have then been offered as of American provenance.

During the greater part of the eighteenth century poplar was heavily stocked by cabinet shops operating in the northern states and southward through Pennsylvania. At times individual craftsmen employed the wood for all, or the major solid parts of furniture designed in rather simple fashions, though in such instances it was generally painted, grained or stained to simulate the color of a finer wood.

THE ILLUSTRATED EXAMPLE

Fig. 30 Simple staining has been used in the instance of the child's field bed, in which the earlier details are canceled by the turned members of the posts, indicating a late eighteenth-century production.

24. MAGNOLIA

The genus *Magnolia,* named after the French botanist Pierre Magnol (1638-1715), includes many species of trees and shrubs, a large number of which are native to North America. The most important as American timbers are the cucumber tree, cucumber magnolia or mountain magnolia, *M. acuminata* Linn., and the evergreen magnolia, laurel bay or laurel magnolia, *M. grandiflora.* The mountain variety has a range of growth extending from western New York diagonally southward to Louisiana, while the evergreen magnolia is a coastal variety appearing from North Carolina to Florida.

These two hardwood timbers are quite similar in appearance. Varying from a creamy-white color to straw-yellow and yellowish-tan hues, the heartwoods are frequently marked by purplish streaks. They are fine and uniform in texture, and straight-grained, displaying mild types of growth-ring figures in tangential surfaces, and numerous rays in the radial sections. Both timbers resemble American "poplar" in general appearance, though magnolia is a harder wood, and somewhat heavier—weighing about 35 pounds per cubic foot.

Despite the greater range of the cucumber tree, magnolia is usually considered a southern timber. The evergreen magnolia was utilized in the construction of simple furniture used by the less prosperous of southern planters and smaller land-owners. From these same states the trees was introduced into England during the first half of the eighteenth century, and also the sweet bay magnolia, *M. virginiana*, which John Bannister took over with him in 1688.

25. BOXWOOD

The box tree, *Buxus sempervirens* Linn., of Mediterranean regions attains a height of fifty feet and a butt diameter of twelve inches, but the species appears as a smaller evergreen tree or shrub in northern areas of the Continent, and in the British Isles. This common box grows wild, but it is also cultivated, being planted for centuries in England where it has been used for hedges, borders and topiary figures. Great numbers of these plants are known to have been cut down in that country during the early years of the eighteenth century. Evelyn wrote of ladies and gentlemen resorting to box gardens "in the heat of Summer to walk, collation, and divert themselves in those antilex natural alleys and shady recesses."

Boxwood possesses a light, soft yellow color, and a silky luster. Very thin bands of a deeper yellow tone are developed in the narrow growth rings. These lines may be displayed in longitudinal surfaces, or the wood may be quite plain in character. A hard and dense structure, resulting from the slow growth habit of the plant, is generally accompanied by a straight grain. In contrast to the appearance of rays in holly, these cells in boxwood are so minute as to be invisible, even through an ordinary magnifying glass. The weight is quite variable, ranging from 53 to 70 pounds per cubic foot.

Throughout Europe this wood has always been carefully handled to assure the best color and working qualities. As the *bois de buis* of French woodmen and cabinetmakers it has been given especial attention in cutting, storing and seasoning. The varying tonal effects of old waxed or varnished surfaces can be seen in the wide edge bandings of Late Stuart cabinets, where the wood usually retains a light coloring, and also in earlier sculptured work, which often displays buff or amber hues.

During the Renaissance and baroque periods boxwood was widely utilized for intarsia work and marquetry decorations, for applied carvings and plaques, and for the turned ornamentation of European furniture. It was also popular with sculptors and carvers who made statuettes, chessmen, etc. Evelyn mentioned a contemporary use of box tree roots in furnishing "the inlayer and cabinet-maker with pieces rarely undulated, and full of variety." Later in the eighteenth century the wood was largely replaced by holly, and by maple, birch and other light-toned veneers which became increasingly popular in the inlaid decorations of furniture produced on the Continent and in the British Isles.

Among the illustrations one of the most characteristic uses of boxwood may be seen in the cabinet-on-stand veneered with oyster pieces of olivewood, No. 46. In this piece boxwood was employed for the panel borders and other banding work of the drawers and writing fall.

26. CITRONNIER or CITRONWOOD

Citronnier is the French name generally used in reference to the timber of the citron tree, *Citrus medica*, which the cabinetmakers of France formerly "utilized in *ébénisterie de luxe*," although, as in its original interpretation, this name is still applied to ether the citron or the lemon tree. The genera *Citrus* and *Zanthoxylum* are both included in the family Rutaceae, thus *citronnier* is related to West Indian satinwood.

The citron tree thrives in the protected soil of Mediterranean areas, in southern France, Italy, Spain and Portugal. Its wood is of a pale yellowish or yellowish-tan color, possessing a fine, uniform texture and a medium luster. Rather mild growth-ring figures are displayed in solid or veneer cuttings, which were obtained principally in plain-sawed material. When cut more or less in a radial direction some curly or mottle figures are produced. The wood is fairly hard and close in the grain, indicating a weight of about 45 pounds per cubic foot.

Some of the leading *ébénistes* of Europe, particularly in France and Germany, produced late rococo and classic furniture designs in *citronnier*. The light-toned wood was frequently selected, in lieu of tulipwood, for panels set within surrounds of *bois violet, acajou, amarante* or other more darkly colored woods, or it was employed for all showing surfaces of fine cabinetwork. This particular fruitwood was also employed by craftsmen of suburban towns located in districts where supplies were readily available.

The favor extended to *citronnier* far exceeded Continental interests in the use of satinwood. Although the Mediterranean timber seldom rivals in quality the more famous exotics obtained by French and Dutch ships trading with the Indies, it was exported to northern countries for use by Paris-trained cabinetmakers or their equally skilled compatriots. As seen in finished surfaces of old furniture, *citronnier* often presents an effect, in graining and color, midway between a fine European birch and the plainer cuttings of West Indian satinwood. The finest selections offer a pleasant relief in their quiet figuring and mellow surface tones, contrasting to the stronger markings and tonal intensities of the satinwoods.

THE ILLUSTRATED EXAMPLE

One of the most decorative effects achieved through the use of two contrasting veneers is that obtained when a light yellow wood is combined with one of a rich purple cast. This is exemplified in the vitrine cabinet made of *citronnier*, in which

Fig. 31

31. A Directoire inlaid citronnier *cabinet-vitrine* Courtesy of M. Gaston Bensimon, New York City.

the front surfaces and the rear panels of the open shelves are inlaid with bandings of amaranth. A production of *circa* 1790-1795, this piece bears the pontil mark of Adam Weisweiller, the *ébéniste* accountable for an earlier writing cabinet shown here under amboinawood.

27. AVODIRE

Avodire, *Turraenthus africana*, is found in a limited distribution extending for some thirty miles along the Gold Coast, to the Ivory Coast of West Africa. The tree grows to an extreme height of one hundred feet, with the irregular trunk developing to a diameter of about thirty inches. Of a pale cream color when freshly cut, this so-called "African satinwood" takes on very light yellow or amber tones with continued exposure. The texture is firm and uniform, though not so fine as in the true satinwoods. A wavy or irregularly interlocked grain produces handsome roll figures that extend diagonally across quartered surfaces. Another, even more characteristic feature of this wood distinguishes it from satinwood. While growth lines appear in West Indian and East Indian varieties of satinwood, as indeed in most woods, avodire shows no growth rings, and therefore no surface lines of this nature appear in longitudinal planes. Rays are displayed as regular, pronounced flecks in radial sections. The average weight is about 35 pounds per cubic foot.

THE ILLUSTRATED EXAMPLE

Fig. 32   This piece, *circa* 1790, is the first to prove this wood was used in the British Isles during the Late Georgian period. Some time ago it was thought that avodire had been recognized in the similarly figured veneers of a fine late eighteenth-century *secrétaire à abattant* of Dutch provenance. The color matched exactly with a specimen sample of the now well-known wood. However, with more detailed examination it was found that delicate growth lines ran through these veneers, and while they were apparently obtained from a species other than those yielding the satinwoods of later eighteenth-century commerce, they could therefore not be determined as avodire. The efficacy of photographic examination has been demonstrated in regard to both examples. Both were accepted or rejected through photographs taken of them. These prints were studied under a lens of ten diameters' magnification, and the findings were confirmed by Mr. Stearns through his more specialized knowledge and equipment.

32. A George III inlaid avodire secretary *Courtesy of Needham's Antiques, Inc., New York City.*

28. WEST INDIAN SATINWOOD

West Indian satinwood was received in England more than a century before mahogany became the most popular medium of Georgian furniture. Timbers now recognized by this name were formerly known as yellowwood, and were obtained from various trees of the genus *Zanthoxylum*, especially those of the species *Z. flavum* yielding the true West Indian satinwood of commerce.

During the seventeenth century these timbers were of major importance in the Bermudas or Somers Islands, with particularly large growths appearing on Cooper's Island and Ireland Island. In 1612 the Bermuda Company wrote to Governor Moore, the first magistrate to hold office in the islands, requesting him to ship a ton of yellowwood to London, and it is said that an illicit trade resulted from the high value placed on this new timber. Twenty years later Governor Wood issued an order that no "planks or juncs" of yellowwood were to be taken on board any vessel leaving the islands. Since no effort was made to replenish the steadily decreasing forests they were nearly exhausted by the middle of the century.

The West Indian satinwood of later ventures, *Z. flavum*, was found in Puerto Rico, Santo Domingo, Jamaica, and in the smaller islands, including the Bahamas. This species develops either as a shrub or tree, and, as a member of the family Rutaceae, it is related to the species yielding citronwood and orangewood.* Trees of about forty feet in height are now common, with butt diameters extending to twenty-four inches. Howard gives the latter measurement as probably exceeding four feet in timbers of exceptional growth.

When freshly cut the wood is pale yellow or yellowish-tan in color, taking on richer or mellower tones in the lustrous surfaces of old furniture. The texture is fine and uniform, the grain either straight or irregular, in the latter instance accounting for handsome mottle and roe figures. Lines produced by growth rings appear in longitudinal surfaces, and rays in those of quartered material. A rather high oil content is present, and a scent like that of coconut oil when the timber is worked. Weights average between 52 and 56 pounds per cubic foot.

The Cabinet-Maker's Assistant emphasizes the importance of Santo Domingan timbers in British trade carried on with that island after the French Revolution and expulsion of the white population:

The black population, disinclined to the continuous labour of the plantations, allowed these to go to waste, and had recourse to the spontaneous supply of commodities for export furnished by their almost interminable forests. Amongst the other woods thus brought into notice, satin wood was exported in large quantities into Britain, and rapidly rose into general favour. Close in the grain, of a pale yellow colour, and elegantly veined, it presented an agreeable variety to the more sombre coloured woods, of which drawing-room furniture had been commonly manufactured, and for a number of years it was extensively used in preference.

That it did not retain this eminence is to be accounted for partly from the caprice of fashionable taste, and partly from the fact that when polished

with bees' wax, the mode then in use, it speedily gave off its colour and presented a pale blanched appearance. This defect has been remedied by the introduction of French polish, which preserves the colour; but the wood had fallen into disfavour before the remedy had been discovered, or rather, before it had found its way to Britain.

Another cause of the comparative neglect into which satin wood has fallen, is its greasy nature, which renders it liable to part from the bed on which it is glued in veneer, or at joints where it is framed or wrought solid. This oily matter, held in the cellular tissue of the wood, gives it a highly aromatic odour, and renders it very inflammable. Although fallen into disrepute as a material for entire suites of drawing-room furniture, it is still employed for articles of ornament, interior finishings, picture and mirror frames, and such purposes as maple is used for....

A fuller account of the natural appearance and habits of this wood would have been desirable, but hitherto there has not appeared any full account of the botany of the West Indies from which such information could be drawn.

Yellow wood appears in an account of work carried out in 1772 by Chippendale, Haig & Company, for David Garrick, while three years later this firm supplied Edwin Lascelles with a "large Circular Table of fine yellow Sattin wood . . . inlaid with various fine woods." It was not until about 1780, however, that West Indian satinwood was popularly employed in the production of British furniture, a use which extended into the early years of the following century, and which was revived toward the close of that period.

While the West Indian timber was often employed for all showing surfaces of this furniture, it was seldom accorded such extensive use in America, except in a few Baltimore and New York productions. Instead, West Indian satinwood was utilized in rather sparing fashion when it was received here around the close of the eighteenth century, following occasional earlier shipments of "Sattin wood" and "yellow wood" at about the same time that these terms appear in the Chippendale accounts. Favor here was extended to "branch" satinwood, cut in oblong feather-crotch veneers, and laid as separate or balanced panels that lend considerable interest to the mahogany examples in which they appear.

Continental craftsmen selected citronwood as a principal surface veneer in their departures from the customary uses of mahogany and other deep-toned woods. This material approximated most of the effects offered by West Indian satinwood and therefore their selections were not compelled to-

---

* Orangewood has been noted as an inlay material of antique furniture, in which capacity ordinary visual identification is impractical; a lack of distinguishing characteristics other than color will be seen in the ordinary orangewood sticks used in manicuring and dental work.

34. Regency inlaid West Indian satinwood cabinet Courtesy of H. Blairman & Sons, Ltd., London.

33. A George III inlaid West Indian satinwood and thujawood dwarf cabinet Courtesy of Biggs of Maidenhead.

35. A George III inlaid West Indian satinwood break-front cabinet Courtesy of French & Co., Inc., New York City.

36. A Phyfe carved and inlaid West Indian satinwood card table Courtesy of Ginsburg & Levy, Inc., New York City.

37. A New England carved and inlaid mahogany and West Indian satinwood work table Courtesy of Joe Kindig, Jr., & Son, York, Pennsylvania.

ward a use of the exotic timber. The occasional reception of *bois satiné* in France, just prior to the Revolution there, is apparently due to the prosperous trade then existing between the southern ports of that country and her West Indian colonies.

THE ILLUSTRATED EXAMPLES

Fig. 33   A second view of the dwarf cabinet in West Indian satinwood (141) appears in the section devoted to thuja, as the contrasting panels are of this other wood and the double doors enclose a nested arrangement of drawers that are faced in thuja. This piece, dates from around 1790.

Fig. 34   In the cabinet surmounted by a striking clock, *circa* 1800, the darker panels are apparently of sabicu rather than rosewood, and tulipwood has been employed for the wider bandings. This piece has an interesting association with one of London's early scientific institutions, Weeke's Museum in Tichborne Street, the name and address inscribed on the clock face. Tichborne Street, connecting Coventry Street and Regent Street, was in 1795 still known as Shug Lane, a thoroughfare "but meanly built," where "a variety of figures which exhibited the powers of mechanism" were contained in the grand room of the museum.

A diversity of other fine woods are combined with West Indian satinwood in the carved and inlaid break-front cabinet, including mahogany, tulipwood, holly, and green-stained holly—not harewood in the usual sense of the word. It is remarkable that in such an elaborate production the two lower banks of drawers are not finished with inlaid bandings to correspond with those immediately above, and with the multiple borders of both the glazed and paneled doors. The inlaid fan segments, garlanded urn supported by palm fronds, and festoons are marquetry motifs developed *circa* 1785 and employed by William Moore of Dublin.   Fig. 35

In its design, the pedestal card table resembles a number of examples by Duncan Phyfe, who is now believed to have executed some work in West Indian satinwood. This master is also credited with a mechanism, appearing in the present piece, which causes a pair of fly brackets to swing out when the   Fig. 36

38. *(Left).* A New England inlaid mahogany and West Indian satinwood writing cabinet Courtesy of Ginsburg & Levy, Inc., New York City. 39. *(Right).* A New England inlaid mahogany and West Indian satinwood chest of drawers

two rear legs are similarly moved, to support the folding portion of the top. Assuming both of these suppositions to be correct, should further investigations prove that any other New York craftsman, such as Michael Allison, is responsible for the present example, this would indicate that Phyfe's working methods as well as his designs were appropriated by his less renowned competitors.

Fig. 37

Fig. 38   The three following pieces exemplify a distinc-

Fig. 39 tively American practice, wherein crotch veneers

of West Indian satinwood were employed in narrow oblong panels, generally in balanced arrangements, and in combination with mahogany. All are representative of cabinetmaking skills exercised in the principal New England towns between 1800 Fig. 37 and 1820. The small table, and the chest of drawers Fig. 39 supporting a matching dressing mirror, are both inlaid with narrow bandings along their top edges, a refinement also associated with work performed in Baltimore and in Dublin.

29. EAST INDIAN SATINWOOD

East Indian satinwood is a product of the species *Chloroxylon swietenia*, belonging to the Meliaceae or mahogany family. This timber has been obtained principally from Ceylon, but it is also found in southern India. The tree may be girdled[25] long before it is felled, at which time the trunk is cut into logs measuring up to twenty-five feet in length and to about forty-two inches in diameter.

The wood varies in color from light to dark golden-yellow tones. It is fine and uniform in texture, with obscure pores and rays. Longitudinal surfaces display the usual vertical lines resulting from tonal variations in the growth rings. The grain is narrowly interlocked, producing plain contrasting stripes, or broken stripes, in quartered ma-

41. A George III inlaid East Indian satinwood secretary

40. A Regency inlaid East Indian satinwood and amboinawood specimen cabinet Courtesy of Frank Partridge & Sons, Ltd., London.

terial, usually accompanied by delicate cross mottles. Most of the timber is characterized by these rather set figures, with a plain log considered as exceptional. Weights average between 58 and 62 pounds per cubic foot.

The hard, compact and brittle nature of East Indian satinwood renders it fairly difficult to work, but it is remarkably lustrous and takes a high finish. Its figures are generally unsuited to large-scale furniture designs, or for panels of large sizes. Sheraton noted that the East Indian wood "is used in general only for cross bandings," basing this remark on his observations that it "runs narrow," and that the West Indian wood was "often more valuable . . . because of its breadth and general utility." No doubt timbers received in England during Sheraton's time did run narrow, as they are often no more than twelve inches in width today. Still, cabinetwork of ample proportions might have been veneered with diamond-matched, or otherwise contrived panels and borders—if the East Indian wood had possessed the decorative appeal of West Indian satinwood.

At about the same time that East Indian satinwood was introduced into the British Isles, during the close of the eighteenth century, it also appeared in Dutch cabinetwork. However, some use in Holland may have occurred before this time, as the wood had been utilized in Dutch colonial possessions at an earlier date. Dutch ships supplied a number of the woods employed by Continental craftsmen, and it is probable that a limited use of this particular timber in the Baltic countries may be accredited to the same source of supply.

Inlaid decorative motifs and bandings are of great interest to students of design, but for the greater part are too delicate to reproduce with any particular degree of clarity. Details such as mock glyphs or prisms, narrow slantingly-diced ("barber-pole") bandings, etc., also appear in projects of various French and German cities, while others are more often associated with furniture produced in the British Isles, and in America. These details include the oval fan patera, bowknots, cords with tassels, an arrow-feather banding, and a linked checker banding with block units composed of nine alternate light and dark squares or dies, which are joined by matching triple links.

THE ILLUSTRATED EXAMPLES

Fig. 40 Rosewood compartments and small drawers are contained in the upper section of the small collector's cabinet, *circa* 1810-1830. The coved lid is painted with borders of conventional ornament, and contains the mortised section of a lever lock, operated from a keyhole in the hinged front panel. All principal surfaces of this piece display the typical fine, and somewhat heavier, ribbon-striped markings of East Indian satinwood. An unusually heavy burl figure in the amboina veneers is penetrated by areas of wavy configurations. Striped and lightly mottled veneers in the upper section and sides of the secretary, *circa* 1800-1810, appear in Fig. 41 contradistinction to the showy zigzagged mottles of the featured panels.

30. MANILAWOOD

All work, either solid, or Veneer'd with Sattin or Manilla wood to be extra in the pound from Mahogany Calculated with all the work on it, except banding........£0 2s 6p.

The wood mentioned in this Philadelphia cost

list, and in *The London Cabinet-Makers' Union Book of Prices*, 1811, (*vide* BOTANY BAY OAK), may refer to narra amarilla, though it is more likely that the wood referred to is molave—the most widely used timber of the Philippine Islands. The molave, *Vitex parviflora*, develops a short crooked trunk with a diameter extending to six feet or more. The wood is usually light yellow in color, sometimes appearing in straw or yellowish-tan shades. It is very hard and strong, fine to moderately fine in texture, with a slightly irregular grain producing figures that are reminiscent of those found in the plainer cuttings of satinwood. The weight is 59 pounds per cubic foot, heavier than West Indian satinwood, but about equal to the East Indian wood.

In addition to its other qualities, molave shrinks very little, even in drying, it does not split, and it is very durable. For these reasons it has been extensively used in the Philippines for heavy construction work. During the nineteenth century tests were carried out in England which proved the excellence of this material for cabinetwork and shipbuilding.

31. THE AMARILLOS

The amarillos comprise a number of tropical American timbers that vary to considerable extents in their properties, but are generally characterized by golden-yellow or red-tinted yellow colorings. Today these timbers are especially associated with the Brazilian species *Lafoensia puncifolia* and *Terminalia obovata*, and with the Venezuelan species *Aspidosperma vargasii*. They are also included among others classified under the general name of "ariba," which is usually indicative of yellow or yellow-red woods somewhat resembling gold-toned Spanish mahoganies.

Still other timbers may be known as amarillos in a particular area of transmission, as fustic is known in Bolivia. This wood is obtained from the species of *Chlorophora tinctoria*, of the mulberry family, and is important in the manufacture of dyes, though it formerly received some use as a cabinet material. A long history (and some indication of its appearance) is evidenced in the many names it bears, including fustoc, fustick, old fustic, dyers' mulberry, cubawood, yellowwood, mora, mora amarilla, palo amarillo, p'ao amarello, *bois de fustock, bois jaune, satiné jaune, bois d'orange, clairembourg, Brazilienholz, Jamaikaholz* and *citroenhout*. In mentioning the names applied by the French, M. Clouzot gives the species as *Morus tinctoria*.

Fustic is of a rich light yellow color with a sulphur cast; the sapwood ranging through cream tones to those of a light oak or chestnut. Quartered surfaces display narrow striped markings of a deeper shade than the ground color, and very delicate bee's-wing mottlings. The wood is generally hard and heavy, with a very fine, uniform, satiny texture, the pores and rays being unusually small. Some cuttings are rather coarse. The weight varies from 50 to 62 pounds per cubic foot.

Another of the names applied to certain amarillos is canarywood. This wood is mentioned in *The Cabinet-Maker's Assistant* as a timber closely resembling or identical with "vinhatica"—sometimes called amarilla. Nineteenth-century supplies are described as ranging from nine to fourteen inches in diameter, the wood being "straight and close in the grain, about the texture of American birch, but much heavier; its general colour is a golden yellow, or light orange; on end section, the annular ranges are waved and of slightly varying shades; this circumstance imparts a minutely veined expression to the wood in plank, which much enriches and beautifies it. The characteristic and finer colour, is frequently intermixed with dingy streaks of a yellowish brown, and fissures and cracks often occur, extending considerably around the heart. Were this wood uniformly coloured, and free from defects, it would be a very valuable cabinet-wood."

According to Laslett, the vinhatico of Brazil "is yellow in colour, light, open-grained, and is probably inferior in quality. It appears to be a species of Cedar, and is used by the cabinetmaker, and for many purposes in carpentry." In contrast, Howard describes amarillo vinhatico as possessing a warm nut-brown color, and as "a very valuable wood" which "might readily pass as true mahogany"; he gives the weight at 49 pounds per cubic foot.

The latter authority notes as the botanical names of the species from which amarillo vinhatico is obtained: *Pithecolobium vinhatico* Record, *Plathymenia reticulata* Benth., and *Euxylophora paraensis* Huber. The last of these designations he associates additionally with another timber to which he gives the name of p'ao amarello, a name that is also applied to fustic. Pau, or p'ao amarello is described by Howard as having "a grain like a fine Spanish mahogany, but is of a bright, rich, warm golden-yellow colour. The tint is not that of satinwood, but is more like a bright prima vera." The species *Euxylophora paraensis* is recognized by timber merchants as supplying Brazilian satinwood, widely known as canarywood, which is presently used as a substitute for San Domingan satinwood.

The two other species given by Howard, and *Plathymenia foliolosa*, are recorded by Record as supplying vinhatico timbers. All three are found in the Bahia region of Brazil and southward to Argentina, growing to heights of over one hundred feet and attaining diameters of more than three feet. They yield wood that may be as soft as Spanish cedar, or more in a class with the light grades of mahogany. In addition to the terms *vinhatico* and *amarello*, such timbers are now known as yellow mahogany, Brazilian yellowwood and Brazilian mahogany. Their weights vary from 35 to 45 pounds per cubic foot.

These "amarellos," and the amarillos in general are distinguished by medium or fairly large pores, and textures varying from rather fine to fairly coarse. Some cuttings produce wood that is straight in the grain, while in others mahoganylike figures are displayed. Certain of these timbers are more likely to retain their natural colorings to greater extents than others. In modern uses the amarillos are more readily stained and finished to imitate mahogany than are the principal varieties of satinwood. Their weights may range from 34 to 63 pounds per square foot.

Of the amarillos and canarywoods that were imported into the British Isles during the past, only fustic is documented as a material of the eighteenth-century cabinetmaker. While this wood is believed to have been recognized as an inlay of Late Stuart furniture, it is recorded as a material employed by Thomas Chippendale during his partnership with Thomas Haig.[20] Coinciding so closely with the adoption of "fine yellow Sattin wood" by this firm, and by other shops in the British Isles, it is apparent that West Indian satinwood soon replaced fustic as a "Yellow Wood" of Georgian cabinetwork. Sheraton wrote that twenty years previous to his time the use of fustic had been discontinued "as it was found to turn by air and the heat of the sun to a dead brownish hue."

From the number of Late Georgian cabinet pieces appearing in yellow woods that do not resemble either true satinwood or very pale mahogany, it is apparent that the more typical varieties of amarillos or canarywoods were employed in their manufacture; probably more often than fustic. For want of more accurate identification they are generally referred to as "satinwood," although they differ considerably from West Indian satinwood, and to a greater extent from East Indian satinwood. Where they are more reminiscent of a blond mahogany, a modern primavera, or a fine birch, provisional names are less readily supplied.

42. A George III inlaid amarillo and yewwood dwarf cabinet
Courtesy of M. Comer of London Inc.

When the properties of such woods are reasonably similar to those mentioned as characteristic of the amarillo–canarywood group, it is quite likely that their identification has been established within this group. It would seem that in such instances, without further technological proof, either of these long-standing and widely accepted terms might be employed as appropriate to, and quite fully descriptive of such woods. Due to the great disparities

43. A George III inlaid amarillo break-front bookcase

in color, texture, grain and weight, it is unlikely that further proofs will be available in specimen cuttings of currently available timbers, although they may serve to some extent in corroboratory capacities.

Several little-known South American timbers are obtained from trees of the *Canella* genus, their descriptions often coinciding with those applying to the amarillos. Howard describes *Canella batalha* as "a close-grained wood with a bright lustrous sheen, of a rather pale colour resembling satinwood, for which it would form a good substitute."

THE ILLUSTRATED EXAMPLES

These indicate various diversifications occurring in the grain and figures of yellowwoods that may be included in the amarillo–canarywood group. Authoritative opinions that have been based on serious concerns over the specific origins of the principal woods appearing in these particular examples, agree that none are representative of the usual mahoganies and satinwoods of commerce.

The yellowish veneers featured in the marquetry dwarf cupboard, *circa* 1790-1810, are believed to be of Brazilian satinwood, known also as an amarillo, and as a canarywood. Digressing from a customary treatment which might be expected in London work, the balancing crossetted top panel is of yew rather than the same light yellowwood featured in the double doors. Fig. 42

Grainings and figures presented in the bookcase with scrolled pediment are also characteristic of certain amarillos, while the more pronounced diagonal roe stripes are reminiscent of avodire. The flat-grained wood of the door panels and pediment has a birchlike appearance. In design this piece is similar to a bookcase made for Queen Charlotte *circa* 1780-1790. With the exception of the base, all framing members, panels and larger moldings are inlaid with delicately checkered bandings. The terminals of the pedimental scrolls are inlaid with eight-pointed stars. Fig. 43

32. MADEIRA or CANARYWOOD

Joseph Armitt, a Philadelphia cabinetmaker who died in 1747, owned at about this date 721 board feet of "Maderah." This timber was reckoned at less than half the value per foot of a much smaller stock of mahogany. Maderah, which is Madeira, Madeirawood or Madeira mahogany, is the wood of *Persea indica* or *P. canariensis*, native to Madeira and the neighboring Canary Islands. The genus *Persea* is comprised of a large number of trees and shrubs belonging to the laurel family (Lauraceae), hence this wood is not a true mahogany. Nevertheless the name *Madeirawood* is still used in reference to various mahoganylike woods, and to true mahoganies of the palest colorings.

Specifically, Madeira mahogany is the wood of the Indian Bay, *P. indica*, also known as the canarywood tree, and timbers similar to those stocked in Philadelphia were known in London as canarywood. There they have been described as "an inferior kind of mahogany, light yellow in color." As far as can be ascertained, the properties of this wood have not been recorded, and it is no longer a timber of any commercial importance. Apparently supplies were plentiful in the past, for Madeira was so called because it was well wooded. The Canary Islands were so called from the large dogs (L., *canis*, dog) found on one of these mountainous isles, while the manner in which the natives moved about is said to have suggested the *canary*, a lively old French dance mentioned by Shakespeare.

33. SAFFRONWOOD

The saffronwood, *Elaeodendron croceum*, is a South African tree found in the vicinity of the Cape Colony. There its timber served in the production of furniture used by the early Dutch settlers, and, during the latter half of the eighteenth century, as a commodity of trade with Holland. As a yellow wood that appears in various medium hues of this color, the more characterizing feature is a handsome walnutlike grain. It is hard, tough, heavy and noted for durability, properties which made it serviceable for other, heavier types of local work, and for the blocks used by wood engravers.

34. CAPE BEECH

As a material of old furniture, cape beech, *Rapanea melaophloeos*, is found only in pieces made during the eighteenth century or later for residents of Holland's Cape Colony. Very little is known about this South African timber which the Dutch know as *beukenhout*, and which was formerly valued for the contrasting effect of its yellowish-tan color when it was used in combination with other, darker woods. An account of South African furniture notes "a surface resembling satinwood." Howard mentions the wood as "moderately heavy, strong, hard and brittle, with a good figure, polishes and planes well, but is not durable when exposed. Used locally for furniture and wheelwrights' work. . . . Weight 44-45 pounds."

35. JUNIPER
(A softwood)

The common juniper, *Juniperus communis*, is a European evergreen species of shrubs and trees, growing abundantly in northern parts of the Con-

44. A Swedish inlaid juniperwood center table Courtesy of the Nordiska Museet, Stockholm.

tinent and in mountainous southern sections. When it develops as a tree the trunk provides a satisfactory timber which may be used in the production of furniture. In Britain the juniper appears more frequently as a shrub, although fairly large growths occur in the south of England and in mountainous parts of Scotland and Wales. Evelyn mentioned that "The Swedish juniper (now so frequent in our new modish gardens, and shorn into pyramids) is but a taller and somewhat brighter sort of the vulgar." It was this variety that served Scandinavian craftsmen as a cabinet wood. Juniper berries are used for flavoring gin, a name which is a contraction of *geneva*, through *genévrier*, the French name for the juniper tree.

Juniperwood possesses a yellowish or light tan color, a fine and uniform texture and a straight grain. A further characterizing feature is a mild, fragrant scent. It is a fairly brittle and somewhat knotty wood, but it is easily worked and serviceable for cutting into veneers or for use in turnery. The weight varies from 25 to 35 pounds per cubic foot.

THE ILLUSTRATED EXAMPLE

Fig. 44

This has been entirely faced in juniperwood, including the cross-grained edge veneers concealing the core upon which the top surface is laid. The slanted dicing of the border lines is as typical of southern as of northern work. Similar bandings are often found in so-called French provincial examples, produced in the principal large cities and smaller towns of that country. Apparently made between 1800 and 1820, the design of this table represents a transition from the Directoire to the Biedermeier vogue, as these modes were translated in Scandinavia.

36. SANDALWOOD

The sandalwood tree, *Santalum album* Linn., is native to India, Ceylon and Australia. Its timber has been so greatly valued in the East that the tree has seldom been permitted to develop a diameter of more than twelve to fourteen inches in the trunk. The heartwood color is a dull yellow or yellowish brown hue which darkens with exposure. The wood possesses a very close, firm texture, with exceedingly small and numerous pores, and very fine rays, both of which are invisible to the unaided eye. The grain may be either straight or wavy. A sticky feeling is noticeable on touching an unpolished surface, and a distinctive aromatic scent is present. The weight is 55 pounds per cubic foot.

Aside from its use in furniture making, carving and other ornamental work of typically Eastern designs, sandalwood was utilized to some extent in the production of furniture modeled after Western styles for use by residents of the European colonies. *Bois de santal citrin* is also listed by Clouzot among the materials employed by French *ébénistes* of the eighteenth century. During the nineteenth century a great amount of sandalwood was shipped from Australia to China where, from the appearance of a similar wood in furniture of the northern provinces, some speculation has arisen as to whether a related timber formerly thrived within the borders of that country.

37. AMYRIS or BOIS DE RHODES

The amyris tree, *Amyris balsamifera* Linn., is an important tropical American timber and a source of amyris oil or West Indian sandalwood oil, used for medical and other purposes. Alternative names are candlewood, rhodeswood, Jamaica rosewood and Venezuelan sandalwood. The wood may be of either a yellowish, or a medium-brown color. It is fine and uniform in texture, straight in the grain, and capable of taking a high polish. A distinct scent appearing in this timber has been contradictorily described as fragrant and unpleasant. A spicy taste has also been noticed. The weight is 62-68 pounds, averaging around 66 pounds per cubic foot.

Bois de Rhodes is the name given to amyriswood in France, where it was employed as an inlay material of eighteenth-century cabinetwork. Howard mentions an immense commercial interest in the timber during this period, when around 1790 substitute species were discovered in Hawaii, resulting in an important trade with China which was at its height between 1810 and 1825.

38. LILAC

The Lilac, *Syringa vulgaris* Linn., appears in the British Isles as a shrub or small tree. In former times this plant was known as the pipe tree because, after the pith had been bored out, its straight shoots were used for the stems of smoking pipes. The wood varies in color from a light yellow to a salmon-tinted hue, and is generally marked by veins or wider streaks of soft brownish tones. It is a hard and strong material, with a close, smooth texture, and rays appearing as tiny flecks in quartered surfaces. As a cabinet wood lilac is associated principally with inlaid decorations of furniture and smaller wares produced at Tunbridge Wells during the turn of the eighteenth century and later.

39. GUMWOOD

Sweet gum, *Liquidambar styraciflua* Linn., one of our most abundant hardwood species, is also known here as red gum, white gum, liquidamber and bilsted. In Europe today the timber is referred to as satin walnut. The botanical name alludes to an amberlike tone in the wood, and to the juice exuded from the tree. Sweet gum is native to the eastern portion of the United States, southward from Connecticut and the lower tip of New York. Growths of one hundred and forty feet in height are recorded, and butt diameters of five feet.

In this wood the pores and rays are so minute and uniform, and the growth rings so indistinct, that the most characteristic markings are those produced by pigmentation, apparently due to results arising from growing conditions, especially in reference to soil. The heartwood is yellowish- or reddish-tan in color, with a fine, uniform texture and a satinlike luster. Occasionally mild growth-ring figures may appear in tangential surfaces, or stripe figures in those obtained through radial cutting. Pigment markings occur in irregular gray and dark brown, smoky streaks or figures caused by natural deposits of coloring matter. Timbers marked by wispy or heavier cloudy effects of this nature are now designated as figured red gum, while an absence of such markings is noted by a classification as plain gum. The weight of this species is 37 pounds per cubic foot.

The tupelo gums, *Nyssa sylvatica* and *N. aquatica*, are quite similar to sweet gum in their properties. *N. sylvatica* grows in a more extensive range of the eastern states, reaching farther north in New England, while *N. aquatica* is confined in the East to coastal regions of the southern states, from Virginia through Georgia. Both species are known by the same, or varying names in different states, though black gum or pepperidge usually distinguishes *N. sylvatica*; and sour gum, white gum or swamp gum are applied to *N. aquatica* in southern states.

Timbers yielded by the tupelo gums are generally of a pale yellowish color, with little variation between the heartwood and sapwood. They possess a fine texture, offering a smooth surface finish. Ribbon-stripe figures may be present when the wood is quartered. The weight is 35 pounds per cubic foot. While sweet gum has been compared to walnut or a light-colored mahogany, some grades of the tupelo gums have been likened to American "poplar."

Sweet gum appears with some frequency in colonial furniture of New York, where it was also used for wall paneling. In old inventories the wood is referred to as bilsted. Designs of other examples in which this timber has been found, of colonial or Early Federal dates, indicate New Jersey or Pennsylvania origins. However, from the wide distribution of the gumwood species it is apparent that the tupelo gums, as well as sweet gum, may occur in work of more southerly states, either in primary or secondary capacities.

THE ILLUSTRATED EXAMPLE

This has a New Jersey history but is typical of New York in its design which, except for a reversal Fig. 45

45. An American gumwood chest-on-chest Courtesy of Ginsburg & Levy, Inc., New York City.

in the number of upper and lower long drawers, is similar to that of a model depicted in the label of Samuel Prince, a New York cabinetmaker whose advertisements appeared in local newspapers from 1768 to 1776. The soft yellowish tone of the wood, seen best beneath the fret meander of the cornice, and near the fluted pilaster, at one time caused it to be erroneously described as maple.

40. OLIVE

The olive, *Olea europoea* Linn., is a low, slow-growing, long-lived tree that has been cultivated for many centuries in southern Europe. Supplies of the wood are now seldom obtainable in widths of more than about eight inches, though inquiries among the timber dealers have revealed that in rare instances this measurement has extended to about seventeen inches. The wood is of a light yellowish-tan color, sometimes with a tinge of green, and it is usually marked by dark brown or blackish pigment lines. Sparse and obscure pores account for a close and even texture, and a very hard and smooth surface capable of taking either a medium or high polish. Narrow growth rings are clearly visible, but rays are obscure. In the past veneers were occasionally obtained from burl growths. The weight is 50-60 pounds per cubic foot.

46. A Late Stuart olivewood oyster parquetry fall-front writing cabinet Courtesy of Hotspur Ltd., London.

47. A George III olivewood marquetry "commode"

Cross sections of olive stems or branches, laid in borders and panels of oyster-shell parquetry, were employed in English cabinetwork produced around the close of the seventeenth century. At that time the longwood was also used as a border and molding material. During the eighteenth century olivewood, or *bois d'olivier*, was at times utilized as a veneer of fine cabinetwork executed in the British Isles, in southern France, Italy and other sections of the Continent where the tree thrives. In general, however, the use of this wood has been restricted principally to the production of small decorative articles and turnery.

THE ILLUSTRATED EXAMPLES

Fig. 46 The superiority of British cabinetwork as compared to related performances in Italy, Holland or elsewhere in Europe during the late seventeenth century, is indicated by the design and parquetry work of the cabinet-on-stand. Certain techniques displayed in other pieces of this description attest the collaboration of alien craftsmen, but even in such instances it is apparent that foreign skills were held in restraint, either through the supervision of British designers or shop foremen, or as a result of some other form of indoctrination. Hence, cabinets of this type and quality are never mistakable as to provenance. As in many of these early pieces, the light-colored borders and the narrower inlays of the writing fall are of boxwood.

Fig. 47 In the marquetry "commode" plain-sawed veneers of about seventeen inches in width surround the central cartouche of the double doors. This width is about five inches greater than the larger diameters of olive trees as suggested in consulted books on timbers. Therefore during the present study some consideration has been given to the possibility that the wood might be manchineel. However, through the aid of timber merchants, the Bureau of Agriculture, and the olive oil industry it was finally determined that very old olive trees attain diameters of seventeen, and possibly twenty-four inches—or even more. As there was no doubt at the time of examination that these particular veneers were of olivewood, and as manchineel has never, as far as it is known, been identified in a piece of this general date, *circa* 1770-1780, the original identification has been adhered to.

This "commode" and a pendant came from Castle Moyle, County Kerry, Ireland. A partially open view of the companion piece is illustrated in *A Directory of Antique Furniture*.

41. MANCHINEEL

Manchineel, *Hippomane mancinella*, is a poisonous tropical American tree, growing principally in the West Indies and in northern areas of South America. In 1762, as *manchenille*, this timber was recommended to American joiners and cabinetmakers as "a very fine ornamental wood," brought to this country from Jamaica. As *mansanille* the species also appears among a collection of wood specimens formed by Anders Berck, professor at Uppsala, Sweden, between the years 1746 and 1774.

The Cabinet-Maker's Assistant, in 1853, described the manchineel tree and its wood: "At mature growth, this tree is of vast size. . . . The fruit, foliage, and sap are highly poisonous. The whole tree abounds in a milky juice, of a most venomous description, which, when dropped upon the skin, produces a sensation of severe burning, followed by a blister. It is said that the Indians poisoned their arrows with it. The fruit is like a small apple, appearing so tempting and like the English fruit, that many strangers have been poisoned by it. The workmen who fell the trees, first kindle a fire around the stem, which causes the juice to become so thick as not to flow or disperse from the blows of the axe, otherwise they would run great risk of injury from its deadly properties.

"The wood is a most beautiful material for furniture, being finely variegated with yellowish brown and white; it is very close and hard, and susceptible of a high polish."

Professor Berck's sample varies from this account in displaying a rich, soft yellowish-tan ground color, marked with thin "smoky" veins or streaks, and closely resembles olivewood in appearance.

42. ALDER

The common alder, *Alnus glutinosa*, the Norwegian, white or gray alder, *A. incana* and other related species are indigenous to north temperate regions of the Continent and to Britain. Usually growing in moist ground and often found along rivers or canals, the tree attains an extreme height of ninety feet and a butt diameter of four feet. In dry, sandy soil, where its ramifying roots cannot reach full development, the plant assumes a shrublike form.

Although it is not an important timber today, in the past alder was highly prized for heavy structural purposes. The longwood is generally quite plain in character, though watered effects and curl figures occur, and the oldest trees develop richly knarled butts and knots. Veneers obtained from these latter sections display flashy knurled figures approximating those found in maple timbers. When the wood is first cut it appears in a pinkish-white color which soon becomes deeper and redder, changing again with continued exposure to permanent golden- or reddish-tan hues. Alder resembles European birch in its fine, smooth texture and straight grain, but it is a much softer wood. This softness is accompanied by a resiliency permitting planed surfaces to resist ordinary mars by denting. Pores and rays are indistinct in this wood. Weights vary from 26 to 41 pounds, averaging around 33 pounds per cubic foot.

Scandinavian cabinetmakers were especially partial to alder and "Alder Root" in their designs following baroque, rococo and classic style developments. As *bois d'aune* the wood also appears as a medium of French marquetry work, and it was similarly employed in some of the German states. British craftsmen utilized alder mainly for turned articles and the smaller wares of cabinetry, although it may appear in chairs and tables produced in rural sections, particularly in the north of England and in Scotland.

48. A Swedish inlaid alder knurlwood and ash cabinet Courtesy of the Nordiska Museet, Stockholm.

49. A Swedish inlaid alder writing table, in the Louis XVI taste Courtesy of the Nordiska Museet, Stockholm.

THE ILLUSTRATED EXAMPLES

These indicate a continued appreciation of alder in Sweden throughout the eighteenth century. A strong resemblance to the markings of maple knurlwood is manifest in the similarly cut veneers of the cabinet with stretchered pillar legs; *circa* 1710-1730. Some of the highly figured wood has been cut in fairly sizable dimensions, though the panels and surrounds are composed of veneers that have been butted together, or pieced out with angular insets differing from the cursive patchwork more common as a Continental technique. Ash has been combined with alder as a border and molding material. The flat-arched and ressauted cornice, and intricately mitred breaks in the door moldings are representative of treatments fostered in all northern areas of the Continent during the late baroque period.

The slant-front writing table, *circa* 1780, presents a well-balanced composition in marquetry work. A book, quill pens and an inkholder are more accurately rendered than in many French examples of the Louis XVI period. At this time Swedish cabinetmakers adopted the architectural gutta as a favorite decorative motif, appearing here in the bands of three guttae, or drops, employed as capitals of the legs. The die mounts, directly above, are of an angularly-lobed leaf pattern that was repeated as an inlay device in some examples

50. A Swedish alder buttwood chest of drawers Courtesy of the Nordiska Museet, Stockholm.

Fig. 50 of Late Georgian furniture. Bowknotted and festooned escutcheons, and garlanded ring handles in the Louis XVI taste have been retained in the chest of drawers, *circa* 1810. Displaying the most typical buttwood markings of these alder pieces, the veneers of this example are dotted through with small circular insets and larger rounded patches, replacing imperfections developed in the growing timber.

43. DOGWOOD

The dogwood or cornel, *Cornus sanguinea*, growing as a small tree or shrub in the British Isles, produces a wood that was formerly used in making goads, dags, skewers and other sharply pointed instruments. It is also recorded as an inlay material of old English furniture. Evelyn considered this particular dogwood to rank among the hardest species of timbers "which are best to receive politure, and for this purpose linseed oyl or the sweetest nut oyl does the effect best."

The heartwood varies in color from a yellowish-tan hue to a brilliant yellowish red, generally possessing a firm and uniform texture and developing with a straight grain. It may be likened to American dogwood, *C. florida*, a substitute timber in English use today with the alternative name of false boxwood. The weight is about 50 pounds per cubic foot.

Other dogwoods are found in tropical America and Australia but their use in old furniture has not been determined. However, assagai wood or *assegaihout*, produced by a member of the dogwood family, *Curtisia faginea*, was employed in producing furniture for Dutch settlers in the Cape Colony of South Africa. The name is derived from an earlier use in making the native spear or *assagai*. In color, the wood varies from a bright red to a dull plum tone. It is hard, tough and close-grained, and has been compared to a plain but heavy mahogany. The weight is 60 pounds per cubic foot.

44. DEODAR
(A softwood)

Deodar, *Cedrus deodara*, native to India and the Himalayas, is also designated as Indian cedar or Himalayan cedar. This timber is one of the most important softwoods of India. It possesses the necessary qualifications of a cabinet wood, and has appeared in antique furniture emanating from the northwest provinces of that country. The tree grows to a height of one hundred and fifty feet, attaining a circumference of thirty feet or more. The wood is of a rich light yellowish-brown color which has been compared to that of polished brown agate. It is moderately hard, with a fine to medium-fine and uniform texture, generally accompanied by a straight grain. Finished surfaces are capable of taking particularly rich polishes. A resinous scent is either fragrant, or pungent and unpleasant, according to varying accounts. The weight is 35 pounds per cubic foot.

45. CAMPHORWOOD

The true camphor tree, *Cinnamonum camphora* Linn., is indigenous to China, Formosa and Japan. Timbers were formerly obtainable in large dimensions but supplies are now difficult to obtain. The wood varies in color from a dingy grayish-yellow tone to a browner hue, and is often marked by irregular darker streaks. It is quite variable in texture, and also in grain—frequently displaying growth-ring figures, cross mottles and occasional small knots in a single board. A strong scent of camphor persists for centuries. The weight is recorded at 41 pounds per cubic foot.

Howard points out that "The well-known seamen's trunks which have been made in China, and sold even to-day in the Eastern bazaars, are passed off as being entirely constructed of camphor-wood, but the tops, bottoms, and backs are made of . . . inferior wood (that of the Cinnamon Tree, *C. zey-lanicum*), and the remainder only is of the true camphor-wood."

Camphorwood appears principally in traveling chests and boxes brought from China to Europe during the past centuries. Furniture exhibiting a combination of Oriental and European features was also produced in this medium for use by European residents of the eastern colonies. During the nineteenth century the wood was recommended to English cabinetmakers for use in concealed structural purposes.

In the Dutch East Indian possessions, Borneo camphorwood, *Dryobalanops aromatica* or other species, was utilized for the same traveling and storage facilities as those mentioned above. This timber has a reddish-tan color, a fairly coarse but even texture, and no particularly distinctive figure to recommend it for fine uses. Its aromatic scent is apt to vary from that of camphor, and to fade with many years of exposure. The weight is 49 pounds per cubic foot.

THE ILLUSTRATED EXAMPLE

This camphorwood chest is furnished with ornamental fastenings of heavy brass. If it was made in Ceylon, as believed, or in the Danish settlement on the neighboring Coromandel Coast, the wood may be representative of either species noted here or of a lesser known variety found in India. The chest is mounted on a stand of separate origin, Fig. 51

51. An East Indian brass-mounted camphorwood chest Courtesy of the Kunstindustrimuseet, Copenhagen.

apparently fashioned by a craftsman with some knowledge of the techniques developed in northern areas of the Continent during the early years of the eighteenth century. It is made of a differing wood, possibly a product of the East Indies, which cannot be accurately determined through magnification of the photograph.

46. BROOM

In medieval English and German tongues *brom*, *brome* and *bram* referred to various thorny or berry-yielding shrubs; while *bramal* and *bremble*, akin to *bramble* and *broom*, designated any rough, prickly shrub, especially a bramble bush producing berries. Today *broom* applies more directly to the shrub *Cytisus scoparius*, the common broom of Europe.

Thus the name of this shrub has a different interpretation from that of the broom tree, a Jamaican growth with slender, densely crowded and almost leafless branches presenting a broomlike appearance. Also, the name of *broomwood* is now given to a tropical American shrub, *Moluchia tomentosa*, rather than to such wood as may be obtained from the European broom.

The European or common broom grows abundantly throughout the Continent and the British Isles, known also as the Scotch broom, Irish broom, etc., according to regional distributions. This shrub is famous as the *planta genista* (French *plante genêt*) which was the badge of the Plantagenets. Spanish broom, *Spartium junceum*, is a closely allied species, as is also the dyers' broom, *Genista tinctoria*, from which a yellow dye is obtained.

As a shrub that attains a height of only four to six feet, with the stems seldom exceeding two inches in diameter, the broom has rarely been utilized in the production of furniture. According to the Royal Botanic Gardens at Kew, there is little variation between the heartwood and sapwood, at least permitting a full use of available material without color contrasts—although such contrasts were not always considered detrimental in the use of laburnum and yew. The same authority likens this wood to the sapwood of laburnum in superficial appearance, thus indicating a soft yellowish-tan ground color with deeper lines resulting from similar contrasts in the growth rings. To this may be added a mild type of pigment figure, appearing in narrow and irregular brownish veinings, and small knots are apt to be distributed through areas of the wood. The rarity of broom as a cabinet wood is indicated by the fact that it is

not mentioned in any of the standard works on timbers, even in those by British authorities.

THE ILLUSTRATED EXAMPLE

This not only documents the use of this uncommon wood, but also gives proof of the designing and working skills achieved in Perth, Scotland, just Fig. 5 three years after Chippendale opened his premises in St. Martin's Lane. Records at Blair Castle give

52. A George II inlaid broomwood secretary Courtesy of Lord James Stewart Murray, Blair Castle, Perthshire. Copyright *Country Life*.

the date of execution as 1756. A short time later the secretary was seen by Bishop Pococke who described it as "a bureau made of wood of broom fineered, the folding doors of which are glass in Gothic figures, and the frames are most beautiful in this wood, and particularly the Urn of carved work at the top of it has a fine effect: this wood is brown in the middle and white on each side, and is much like rosewood" (!). The writing lid is inlaid with a wide herringbone banding, but except for that particular feature, the execution of this piece attests a fairly prompt reception of the designing techniques advanced by London masters.

47. LOCUST or FALSE ACACIA

The false acacia of Europe is actually the common locust of North America, *Robinia pseudacacia* Linn., known also in this country as black locust and yellow locust—from the color of the sapwood. While the tree was introduced in France and England during the seventeenth century it has never been regarded as important for its timber. European growths attain extreme heights of about eighty feet and diameters of three feet or more.

These trees develop a heartwood which is usually similar to that of the American locust. When first cut a greenish color is revealed, which soon turns to a golden-tan or browner hue. Faint greenish streaks often appear in the seasoned wood, or a slight tinge of red may occur in the pores. False acacia is hard, tough and horny, medium-fine to coarse in texture, and generally straight in the grain. Growth rings are conspicuous, and fine but distinct rays contrast with the darker tone of the ground tissues. The weight is 40-55 pounds, averaging 46 pounds per cubic foot.

An additional name, honey locust, is sometimes used in reference to this *Robinia* species, but the term correctly applies to the species *Gleditsia triacanthos* Linn. Although this timber was recognized by *The Cabinet-Maker's Assistant*, the light-tan, coarse-grained wood has never been valued as a medium of cabinetwork. The tree is found chiefly in Virginia and the Carolinas, where its seeds were used by the Indians to produce a much prized intoxicating liquor. The same authority declared that in North America locustwood was "more highly valued by the cabinet-maker and turner, than any other native timber," an interest which, if true in any portion of this continent during the nineteenth century, did not extend back into the eighteenth century.

As *bois de faux acacia*, occasional cuttings ob-

53. A Regency locustwood parquetry backgammon table

tained from locust trees growing in France were utilized in marquetry work produced there during the eighteenth century. The wood has also been identified as a veneer appearing in English cabinetwork executed during the Sheraton and Regency periods.

THE ILLUSTRATED EXAMPLE

This displays this uncommon wood in its parquetry surface, frieze and supporting frame comprised of solid members. A design published by Sheraton apparently had some effect on the partiality of British cabinetmakers for the general form of this table. The trestle frame is a Regency innovation which remained popular throughout this period, being employed in various types of gaming, writing and sofa tables, a number of which appear in calamander, and in zebrawood.

Fig. 53

48. BUTTERNUT

The butternut, *Juglans cinerea* Linn., grows in this country with a range extending from Maine to Georgia, except in coastal areas below Virginia. An alternative name for its timber, white walnut, has been known to confuse experts on furniture of our southern states. Without recognition of differences appearing in the related species, *J. nigra*, speculation has been raised as to "whether or not Black Walnut can be differentiated from White Walnut"!

Growing to an extreme height of one hundred feet, and a butt diameter of four feet, the butternut produces a timber that is paler in color than the lightest northern walnut, and is also much softer and lighter in weight than any true walnut. The heartwood is of a buff or light-tan hue, a coloring emphasized by the sapwood which is almost white. Structural properties and figures are fairly similar to those appearing in the related species, but butternut is characterized by larger pores, resulting in a coarser texture than that of black walnut. It is also a much weaker timber, splitting easily, while the other wood is far stronger, more serviceable, and generally of a quality better suited to the purposes of fine cabinetwork. The weight is only 25-27 pounds per cubic foot.

Butternut was utilized to a limited extent in Early American furniture, usually for secondary purposes rather than in prominently displayed surfaces. During the Victorian period the wood was given some greater prominence as, despite its shortcomings, it is easily worked, capable of taking a good finish, and with proper staining can be made to resemble the surface appearance of black walnut.

49. CHESTNUT

The European chestnut, *Castanea sativa*, is also known as the sweet, or Spanish chestnut, and, in France, as *le châtaignier*. This species thrives best in southern areas of the Continent, though it grows satisfactorily in the British Isles, where it was probably introduced by the Romans. The tree reaches a height of more than one hundred feet and a butt diameter of ten feet. In general appearance the wood is quite similar to that of the common oak. Howard states that it is impossible to distinguish between the two in finished work, which is certainly true where examination is so restricted that it is impossible to determine whether broad rays, characteristic of oak but not of chestnut, are present or not.

Chestnut usually has a bright, clean appearance, especially in the paler cuttings of this light tan to deeper brown timber. The wood is not quite as dense as oak, and it is inferior in hardness and strength. It is too coarse in texture for turning, but satisfactory for broad carving and other purposes where a straight-grained material is preferred. Numerous very fine rays are present but scarcely visible to the unaided eye. Weights vary from 30 to 45 pounds, averaging around 36 pounds per cubic foot.

In some chestnut trees the heartwood takes on a deep brown color, either uniformly or unevenly distributed, caused by the fungus *Fistulina hepatica*, which is responsible for a similar effect seen in brown oak. It was formerly believed that fungi, insects and boring beetles could not damage chestnut, and that in order to lend a preservative quality to the more abundant wood, chestnut was mixed with oak[21] in construction work of Gothic and Renaissance times. That this is incorrect is attested by British governmental authority in the published statement that "*C. sativa* is susceptible to attack by the Powder Post beetle, the Death-Watch beetle, and the Common Furniture beetle."

This timber was occasionally employed in the finer Renaissance and baroque furniture produced on the Continent, and imported timbers were used for similar purposes in England during the oak period there. More often it was selected by rural joiners of districts in which the tree thrived best. As the wood presents a much plainer appearance than quartered oak, selections would be largely dependent upon local supplies of the two timbers. Where wood surfaces were to be concealed beneath applied finishes, chestnut might be more acceptable than pine or other less durable timbers, and as a surface for veneering, chestnut might be considered more satisfactory than oak.

The American chestnut, *C. dentata*, is also known in this country as the sweet chestnut. While the species flourished here until the present century, the wood held little attraction in the production of Early American furniture, except for some use in concealed structural purposes. It is very similar to the European timber in appearance, though somewhat coarser in texture, lighter in weight, and never obtainable in such large dimensions. The dwarf chestnut or chinquapin, *C. pumila*, has been claimed as a species utilized in southern furniture of simple designs.

Colonial or Early Federal cabinet pieces appear from time to time with chestnut drawer linings or other interior parts channeled through by the two-lined chestnut borer, *Agrilus binineatus*. This insect bores into the standing tree and riddles it with large and lengthy holes. Affected timbers may nevertheless remain commercially valuable, and are still marketed as sound wormy chestnut.

Recent shortages of chestnut timbers resulted

54. A Louis XV chestnut armoire

from the chestnut blight which appeared here in 1904, introduced from Asia in the form of the fungus *Endothis parasitica*. This larva attacks the bark of the tree trunk, producing lesions that completely girdle and kill the tree—hence the other name for the blight, chestnut bark disease. Striking first in the northeast section of the country, this disease gradually spread to other tracts in the commercial range of the species, which extends from New England well into the southern states. Contrary to some beliefs, all stands of the timber growing within this range were not affected, and supplies have continued to come into the market up to the present time.

THE ILLUSTRATED EXAMPLE

Fig. 54 This shows a typical use of chestnut in plain-sawed material, the lower cupboard doors displaying growth-ring figures of a milder character than usually found in oak. The fact that each door panel is made in two pieces indicates that the timber was obtained from a tree of only moderate size. As armoires of this type were originally fashioned with four paneled doors, it is apparent that the wire network here was substituted to lend the effect of a *bibliothèque*.

50. ELM

The common elm, *Ulmus campestris* Linn., appears in most of Europe where the tree has been specially planted since the sixteenth century. Evelyn mentions a resolution introduced during the reign of Henry IV, "of adorning all the highways of France with elms, &c." Growths of over one hundred and twenty feet in height are recorded, and diameters of four feet or more in the trunk. This portion of the tree is free of branches to a considerable height, so that much of the timber appears without knots. The wood possesses a dull reddish-tan color, a coarse and uneven texture, and a deeply interlocked grain. The weight averages around 35 pounds per cubic foot.

A particularly characterizing feature of all elm-woods affords a principal aid in distinguishing them from the various species of ash. When the vessels of a timber are cut through in obtaining tangential material, vessel lines appear as surface grooves or hatchings, and form the irregular bands that are displayed in growth-ring figures. Large vessels in the early wood of growth rings developed in elm timbers appear as such surface bands made up of dark-toned lines. Within these principal bands, three to nine additional ones appear, composed of less pronounced hatchings. This phenomenon results from an unusual development of the late wood, and does not appear in any timber produced by species of ash.

The wych-elm or mountain elm, *U. glabra*, may appear on the Continent, although the species is more common as a natural growth in England, Scotland and Ireland. Slightly smaller than the common elm, the tree generally loses its central column at no great height from the ground. Its wood is somewhat lighter in color than that of the latter species—often with a greenish cast, and it is not so coarse in texture nor so uneven in the grain. It is also the stronger, more elastic and heavier wood, weighing 43 pounds per cubic foot. The Dutch elm, *U. hollandica major*, is a European hybrid growing to about the size of the wych-elm. Now planted for ornament, the tree was formerly valued to some extent as a timber. In color and weight the wood approximates these properties of the common elm, but it is noted for a greater strength and firmness in texture than occurs in other elms.

In Britain the common elm, now generally designated there as *U. procera*, and the wych-elm are joined by the Dutch elm and at least four other species. Evelyn noted "four or five sorts," and in listing the uses of the wood during his time included the making of "trunks, and boxes to be covered with leather; coffins, for dressers and shovelboard-tables of great length, and a lustrous colour if rightly seasoned; also for the carver, by reason of the tenor of the grain, and toughness which fits it for all those curious works of frutages, foliage, shields, statues, and most of the ornaments appertaining to the orders of architecture." Later uses extended to both fine and simple work in this material, with burlwood veneers featured in some metropolitan furniture.

The many variations in color tones and markings of elm timbers are especially noticeable in veneers obtained from burl growths. Some burlwood cuttings display small compact markings resembling these features of burl ash, while others present larger grain figures or highly erratic patterns. Such

veneers often contain defective areas which must be replaced by correspondingly shaped patches of more substantial nature. These patches will be found in old furniture of fine quality as well as in less finished work. Extreme dimensions of burlwood veneers are indicated by material recently obtained from trees growing in the neighborhood of the Carpathian Mountains. Sherwood states that "sheets of veneer five by six feet are not unusual" in these elm burls, though "defects of all kinds are common."

The recurrent use of elm by English craftsmen was attested when *The Cabinet-Maker's Assistant* made its late appearance. Then it was noted that the wood had been extensively employed "in the manufacture of furniture up to a very recent date. Although, at present, it is rarely used except for the commoner sort of Windsor chairs and similar articles, not more than twenty years have elapsed since it formed a principal material for drawing-room furniture of the best description." The main cause of this material's going out of fashion was given as perhaps due to the expense of labor necessary "by the small size, irregular form, and faulty texture, of the pieces of veneer which could be obtained. In order to cover a large surface with small pieces of veneer of an irregularly circular or

55. An Early Georgian elm burl bureau
Courtesy of Norman R. Adams Ltd.,
London.

oval shape, very much more work was needed to join them to each other, than is required in the case of mahogany or rosewood. But even when this was effected, a greater amount of time was employed in filling up the smaller or larger holes usually found in the veneers . . . work of this description is rarely called for, except for the purpose of matching suits of furniture."

Continental craftsmen also selected elm for seat furniture and cabinetwork of fine quality, not only in burl veneers but often in flat-grained material. This partiality extended from Scandinavia, through the Netherlands and Germany, to France. In the latter country elmwood, or *bois d'orme*, was especially favored during the Late Empire or Restoration period when burl elm (*loupe d'orme*) was adopted in Parisian *ébénisterie*.

Although the American Elm, *U. Americana* Linn., grows throughout the entire eastern half of this country, the timber was not utilized in furniture of colonial or Early Federal times. However, Canadian elm was exported to the British Isles in large quantities during the nineteenth century, with shipments amounting to from forty to fifty thousand feet annually by the middle of that period.

THE ILLUSTRATED EXAMPLE

A particularly fine and sizable burl has been utilized in surfacing the bureau or slant-front desk, *circa* 1730-1750. No joins appear in the two upper drawers, while only two veneers were required for each long drawer, and four for the lid. The writing interior is treated in a similar manner, with continuous veneers free of bandings or edgings other than the narrow cock beading. Little could be added to the already rich appearance of the bureau, or to its aesthetic merit, by introducing either matching or contrasting inlays.

51. OAK

Among the various species of oak that are native to Europe, the English oak is most famous through its association with the early history and literature of that country—and with the arts pertaining to architecture and furniture making. However, foreign oak timbers may share this fame, for English use of the historic material was so great, even in Gothic times, that additional supplies, classed as *wainscot*, were extensively imported from the Continent. During the reign of Henry VIII, one Harrison, of Redwinter in Essex, recommended

that the local "parke oke . . . is the finest for joiners craft," offering the comparison: "for oftentimes have I seene of their workes made of that oke so fine and faire as most of the wanescot that is brought from Danske [Denmark], for our wanescot is not made in England."

Wainscot is given by *The Cabinet-Maker's Assistant* as derived from *wandschot*: *Wandt*, a wall, and *Schot*, a defense; referring to the use of oak boards in Germany, Holland and elsewhere on the Continent as a finishing material for interior walls, prior to the introduction of plaster. The name is also believed to derive from the Middle Low German *Wagenscot*, the wooden boards used to partition wagon beds and other sleeping compartments; or from the Old Dutch *waeghe-schot*, a partition or closure of boards, as used in beds which could be partially or entirely closed.

Before the adoption of two-handled saws, boards were produced by riving or splitting timbers before they hardened. When of oak they split along the path of the rays, hence "wainscot" also gives the inference of radial or quartered material, either riven or sawed. This term was formerly applied to partially dressed oak logs that were shipped from ports in northern Europe, with their sides displaying rayed or "silvered" effects. "Clapboard," too, is derived from the early manner of riving oak into wainscoting, through the German *klaffen*, to split apart, the outer edge of such boards being of greater thickness because they divide into sectors or wedge-shaped pieces.

European Oak, *Quercus robur* Linn. (now sometimes referred to as *Q. pendunculata*), with *Q. sessiliflora*[21] and many variations, grows throughout the Continent and in the British Isles, with a southern range extending from Spain to Austria and Turkey. Heights of eighty feet and butt diameters of five feet are not uncommon, while very old trees have been recorded with these measurements extending to one hundred and thirty feet, and more than ten feet.[22]

Timbers formerly obtained from Russia, through her Baltic ports or via Danzig, varied in color—from a light tan to darker tones of brown, and also in the clarity of their silver markings. They were frequently harder and heavier than other European oaks, and almost free of knots. These qualities, combined with the finer grain and milder character of Russian oak in comparison with supplies obtainable in England, account for the long-existing demand from that country.

Prussian timbers are frequently as brown in tone as the darker of those cut in Russia, with sufficiently bright and pronounced rays to qualify for wainscot purposes. Rhenish and Dutch Oaks are closely similar, but the regular growth of trees in southern sections of Germany, particularly noticeable in Franconian oak, produces a milder, more evenly figured wood than is usually found in northern Europe. Timbers of this same mild quality are also obtainable in Austria, displaying a uniform yellowish-tan color and a bold silver grain.

Italian oaks include the species *Q. robur*, and also *Q. cerris* or Turkish Oak, producing a reddish-tinted wood of only fair quality. The former species yields a wood that is light brown in hue, hard and strong, but less elastic than most northern timbers, more difficult to work and subject to defects. Spanish and Portuguese oaks may be even darker in color, more porous and softer, and they are usually plain and even in the grain. The cork oak, *Q. suber*, also native to these three southern countries, still provides the most common source of commercial cork.

The holm, holly or evergreen oak of southern Europe, *Q. ilex* Linn., was introduced in Britain during the sixteenth century. There it has been grown largely for its ornamental appearance and seldom attains a height of more than thirty feet. Holm oak possesses a light brownish or reddish-brown color, and a close grain, resulting in the inconspicuous character of its growth rings and an unusually heavy weight of 60 pounds per cubic foot.

Despite the high quality of many Continental oak timbers they often display a spiritless uniformity in comparison with the decorative character of the best British oak. Possibly the closest resemblance is found in French oak (*bois de chêne*), especially that of northwest provinces. There the red oak is similar in color, texture and general quality to the British red or brown oak, though the color of the French wood is not developed through the conversion which occurs in British trees yielding brown oak.

In Britain the common oak is *Q. robur*, while *Q. sessiliflora* and various hybrids are also found. These varieties were at times, but not generally, specified in the requirements of builders and furniture craftsmen, and, as elsewhere in Europe, British timbers were apt to be quite variable in quality according to conditions pertaining to soil and climatic conditions. In general they range in color from a light yellowish tan to deeper and warmer shades of brown. The texture is usually coarse and the grain straight, with characteristic growth-ring figures appearing in plain-sawed material. Rays are of two descriptions, the larger appearing in tangen-

tial surfaces as dark lines, often exceeding one inch in length, while in quartered surfaces they show as lustrous, broad and irregular flecks or lengthy flakes. Weights average between 46 and 52 pounds per cubic foot.

Irish oak has been claimed as both superior and inferior to British oak, the quality of the former timber having been recognized as far back as the eleventh century, when William Rufus requested it for the building of Westminster Hall. According to tradition this wood was also utilized in English furniture, as well as in the earliest Irish productions.

British Brown, or red oak is obtained from certain trees which have been attacked by the fungus *Fistulina hepatica*, causing the heartwood to take on a darker hue—generally a reddish-brown coloring but varying from medium shades to much deeper and richer tones. This pigmentation may extend partially or entirely through the heartwood, or it may be interrupted by streakings of a lighter shade, or by the natural ground color. In rare instances blackish tones develop, producing mottled effects which resemble the markings of tortoise shell. This phenomenon may occur in trees of normal growth, in those which have been pollarded, and also in burls[23] that have formed on either type of timber.

Green Oak is produced by another fungus, known as *Cholorsplenium aeruginosum*. When sections of a standing oak have received this attack a lively green or blue-green color is developed. Wood of this type was seldom utilized except for inlay purposes, eventually becoming a medium of Tunbridge wares.

Bog oak or black oak is the black or grayed brownish-black, and often streaked wood of timbers, or their branches, that have lain submerged in peat bogs or other moist ground for lengthy periods of time. This type of coloration is associated largely with such timbers found in England and Ireland, though similar material has been uncovered in Russia. After drying out the wood may become very hard and remain serviceable, or this process may result in serious cracking or in complete disintegration.

North American oaks are comprised of many species and their variations, all of which are classified either as white oaks or red oaks. Once these timbers have been cut into lumber there is no means by which they can be identified according to their exact species. Microscopically, they may be determined only within the two classifications according to color. Without such examination even color is not a true guide, as some white oak possesses a reddish tinge and some red oak lacks this shading.

Of the two classes white oak has always been recognized as the more valuable timber, being the less porous and less brash or brittle wood. White oak is also slightly heavier than red oak, (46-50 pounds, as against 45 pounds per cubic foot), and more resistant to decay. The most important species of this class is the true white oak, *Quercus alba* Linn., growing throughout the eastern half of the country with its range extending into Ontario and Quebec. This timber reaches a height of one hundred and thirty feet, when the trunk may measure six feet in diameter. The heartwood varies in color from a yellowish-tan shade to deeper and redder tones. It is hard, compact and usually straight in the grain. Numerous light-toned rays appear in larger and bolder formations than in any other American or European oaks, and in more definitely radial dispositions. They may extend in rather straight lines, in arcs, or in irregular linear forms. Exposed lengths of five inches have been noted in descriptions published by timber authorities, but these are exceeded in some selections of white oak appearing in Early American furniture.

From Romanesque times to the baroque period oak was the most commonly used wood in Continental Europe and the British Isles. Remaining examples of oak furniture executed during the earlier style periods often exemplify the natural tendency of this wood to harden considerably with age. The color may also darken through centuries of time, though if originally selected from timber of a normal hue it is quite certain that, without the aid of oil or other darkening agents, oak does not acquire the blackness claimed as a natural toning in old English furniture. This is readily proven through certain of the earliest French and English examples which have received hardly any surfacing attention, and consequently have become almost gray with age. The strength of oak is also demonstrated in many surviving examples, and a considerable resistance to the decay caused by larvae, which are more apt to attack the sapwood of cut timber than the stouter heartwood.

Oak was continued as a structural material when use of fine surfacing veneers became popular. In this capacity, it has been said that oak was favored by northern craftsmen, in contrast to an equally preponderant use of pine by cabinetmakers of southern Europe. This is far from the truth, for Scandinavian and North German work of this description was carried out principally in pine, and

this wood was often given preference in the British Isles. The use of oak was mandatory as a foundation for veneered work executed in Holland, it was employed to a considerable extent in the finer French, English and Irish productions, and it was used to some extent in similar work of South German and Austrian furniture centers.

Material that was to be used as a foundation for veneers would be tangentially sawed, offering more absorbent and even planes than could be obtained in the harder, rayed surfaces of quartered cuttings. Tendencies toward shrinking and warping were gradually counteracted by increasing skills in structural methods. In comparison with the widespread use of pine and other softwoods for such work, the appearance of oak as a medium of concealed structural use will generally denote a greater original expense, not only in material, but in designing and working talents as well.

In various sections of the Continent, or even in cities of some importance, furniture made entirely of oak continued in popularity throughout the eighteenth century—in designs continued from earlier periods, or following the current style developments. During the Regency period in England, oak was also recommended as highly suitable for some of the more sophisticated designs then offered to British craftsmen. Veneers of burl oak, now often indiscriminately classed as pollard oak, became more fashionable at this time in comparison with an infrequent use during the earlier decorative periods. This popularity was fostered by the Lancaster firm of Gillow,[24] and no doubt received some impetus through deliveries made by this firm to their warerooms in London.

Following European practice, oak was selected by early settlers of the American colonies for producing such articles of household furniture as had not accompanied them in their travels from various areas of the Continent and the British Isles. Apparently most of these pieces were of a purely utilitarian character and not considered worthy of preservation during later times. A few examples fashioned with more than ordinary skill and taste are preserved in public and private collections, or come into the market at infrequent intervals. Some work in oak was continued during the first decades of the eighteenth century, but after this time the wood was seldom utilized in American furniture. Occasionally it was employed for concealed structural portions of later colonial and Early Federal pieces, usually in combination with other secondary woods, and serving a purpose where exceptional strength or solidity was required.

56. A Romanesque chip-carved oak chest Courtesy of the Victoria and Albert Museum, London.

57. A Flemish carved oak armoire Courtesy of the Archives Centrales Iconographiques d'Art National, Brussels.

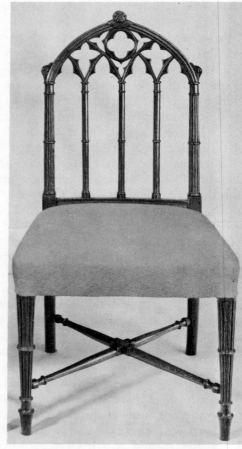

58. A Regency carved oak side chair

59. A Regency inlaid pollard oak
sofa table Courtesy of H. Blairman & Sons Ltd., London.

60. A Regency inlaid pollard oak
octagonal table Courtesy of H.
Blairman & Sons Ltd., London.

Large numbers of oak mangle boards have been received in America and England, where this primitive type of ornamentation may be referred to as "Friesland carving." Ogival tracery panels are characteristic of numerous architectural designs appropriated by the French *huchier* during the Late Gothic period, *circa* 1480-1520. Single linen folds are fairly typical of French design, and often provide a means of differentiating closely related Flemish and German examples. The finest Gothic and Renaissance productions of these other states were at times carved with restrained, though rather rigid ornamentation. More often, however, they were overwrought. German craftsmen, in particular, who were capable of performing fine work, would be inheritantly impelled to supply the ends with commensurate evidences of their skills. This propensity, and the tendency to perform various intricacies in molding and inlaid work, is also apparent in many later examples of German craftsmanship.

THE ILLUSTRATED EXAMPLES

Fig. 56   The early chest of Romanesque form is believed to have come from a church in Hampshire, and to have been made in England during the thirteenth

century. In its simple slab construction with recessed cross bracings at either end, it is more typical of Continental than of English workmanship. Exactly matching chip-carved stellate and whorl patterns, and innumerable variations of these themes have been contrived and repeated by rural craftsmen of Scandinavia, Germany and Switzerland for more than eight hundred years. Metal and wood fastenings in many of these chests also perpetuate earlier contrivances. When lighter structural forms were adopted, in the seventeenth, eighteenth and nineteenth centuries, the same ornamental devices were continued in lieu of more skilled carving, for they were easily effected with a carpenter's compass and chisel.

The quality of the carving, and the front shaping of the Flemish armoire demonstrate the suitability of this wood in finer uses than those Fig. 57 associated with oak furniture of the English school. While elaborate productions in this medium were still executed in France and elsewhere on the Continent during the middle decades of the eighteenth century, the work of Liege is outstanding. This particular example was made *circa* 1745 at Verviers, then a small town in the bishopric of Liege, situated within a short distance of the large capital city, and close to Aachen (Aix-la-Chapelle) a free imperial city of Germany where equally fine cabinetwork in oak was fashioned along similar lines.

Following the experimentations of Chippendale and his contemporaries, medieval forms were more accurately rendered in British furniture and architecture after 1800. The resulting Gothic revival is regarded as an English movement inspired by a revolt against the restrictive conventions of the eighteenth century. However, the same impulse was soon felt on the Continent where Gothic designs were revived some thirty years later. Projects following the "Gothic or old English fashion" were offered among the furniture designs published by George Smith in 1808 and 1826, including a "Drawing Room or Gothic Chair" which bears some resemblance to the example presented here. The Fig. 58 foremost material of the "old English fashion" has been employed as a veneer in the two following Fig. 59 examples. Both of these tables exhibit plain and Fig. 60 silver-grained oak surfaces of a rich golden color, and a relatively compact texture in comparison to that of normally developed timbers. A pollard burl is featured on the central drawer front of the pedestal table.

Broad and lengthy rays are presented in the Connecticut cupboard, *circa* 1690-1710 or later. Fig. 61 Here the architectural features and flat-carved foliage ornament are elaborations of English themes

61. A Connecticut carved oak press cupboard

as developed in Hartford county, and employed in a number of these so-called tulip-and-sunflower cupboards.

52. TEAK

Teak, *Tectona grandis* Linn., is native to India, Burma, Siam and Java. This tree rises to extreme heights of about one hundred and seventy-five feet, with the trunk developing to a diameter of more than five feet. The timber has been commercially important for centuries, being employed for many purposes allotted to oak in the West. For this reason, and in part from the appearance of the wood, teak has been referred to as the oak of the East.

Rather widespread misunderstandings have permitted East Indian rosewood to be accepted as teakwood, despite the fact that the former timber is considerably darker in color and heavier than teak. These misconceptions are associated principally with furniture and smaller articles made in the Orient during the last hundred years, particularly in China, where both timbers were imported.

In color, teak varies from a straw yellow to a medium shade of tobacco brown, often with lighter or darker streaks or irregular markings. It is a hard and strong wood with a great resistance to decay. The texture varies from medium coarse and uniform, to coarse and uneven. The grain is generally straight, and growth-ring figures appear prominently in the usual tangential cuttings. Other surfaces may display some mottling, giving an effect that is reminiscent of a coarse mahogany. Frequently the appearance is midway between oak and walnut in color and grain. A soapy feeling is characteristic of the wood, and a scent that may be agreeable, like that of old leather, or rather unpleasant.

An air-dried weight of 40-45 pounds per cubic foot represents a considerable reduction from that existing in the live tree. The natural moisture, with a large quantity of fluid resinous matter that clogs the vessels, renders the undried timber so heavy that it will not float. Therefore the trees are girdled[25] or ringed several years before they are felled, permitting the wood in the trunk to dry out as it stands.

After felling, the timbers may lie for various periods of time before they are moved to a water course. As stands of teak no longer exist near the seaports, water transit often entails journeys lasting for hundreds of miles along riverways. Before such removal can be initiated the heaviest work is carried out by elephants. These animals have served for many years in hauling timbers out of the hot teak forests, particularly after the wood came into great demand for shipbuilding. Hundreds of elephants were acquired by single owners after this time, and great numbers of water buffaloes.

Elephants are said to be proud of their great strength, enabling a single pachyderm to lift a half-ton log on its tusks or drag a tree trunk of six times its weight. They are also used to pile cut timbers, which they stack as methodically as similarly trained humans. In the teak forests they are worked for only a few hours a day, over an equally short period of working months. It is said that when a bell sounds at the end of a working period they are even more prompt than other workers in leaving a job, no matter what point they have reached in their allotted tasks.

Fires have repeatedly spread through large areas of the teak forests and it was thought during the nineteenth century that controls would result in improvement of the standing timbers. It was found, however, that the trees actually benefited in vigor by the normally disastrous effects of these conflagrations.

Teakwood has been employed to a considerable extent in the manufacture of Oriental furniture and smaller articles, but not so largely as might be indicated by a wide acceptance under this romantic name of other darkly stained or normally darker

62. A Dutch carved teakwood and ebony cupboard Courtesy of the Rijksmuseum, Amsterdam.

Eastern timbers. Occasionally the wood is found in pieces executed by native craftsmen for colonial residents, supercargoes or other ship's officers. Such examples generally appear in designs that follow European styles, with Oriental origins indicated by ornamental details or constructional methods. In still rarer instances timbers received in Europe were incorporated in furniture of local manufacture.

THE ILLUSTRATED EXAMPLES

Fig. 62

All of the flat and molded surfaces of the architectural cupboard are of teak, as are the carved details of the arches and spandrels. While sculptured effects of European furniture produced during this period, *circa* 1650, were often executed in boxwood or other native timbers, the pilaster masks and demifigures of the present piece are carved in ebony.

Fig. 63

The source of the cylinder-front desk is evidenced by its tectonic features and the characters used in designating the positions of the drawers. As an example of Chinese work it is almost unique in so closely approximating a British design, in this instance one popular from about 1780. The irrationalism of the Chinese copyist is indicated, however, in the molding work. The frieze drawers are edged with a cock bead, a customary feature of the time, while in the pedestal sections the drawer fronts have been left unmolded, and the same type of beading has been applied to the framing members, following an earlier method practiced to some extent in the British Isles after its introduction from the Continent during the early years of the eighteenth century. Double sets of carrying handles add to the inference that this piece was specially made for a ship's officer concerned with trading activities carried on in the vicinity of Canton.

63. A Chinese teakwood cylinder desk in the Georgian taste Courtesy of Arthur S. Vernay, Inc.,
New York City.

53. SAL

Sal or sal tree, *Shorea robusta,* is a wood yielded by one of India's largest and most important timbers, growing to a height of one hundred and fifty feet, and a circumference of twenty-five feet in the trunk. For centuries this wood has been used by Indian craftsmen in the production of furniture and decorative woodwork. Sal varies in color from medium tan to deeper brown tones, and to reddish hues. It is harder and stronger than teak, but not quite so durable. The texture is moderately coarse, a close, interlocked grain producing striped figures in quartered surfaces. An aromatic resinous substance contained in the vessels is used as a base for producing incense. The weight ranges from 50 to 60 pounds per cubic foot.

54. AMBOINAWOOD

The amboinawood tree, *Lingoum indicum,* is native to the East Indies, and in particular to the island of Ceram whence its richly figured burls were formerly shipped to Europe by way of Singapore, a concentration point for rare East Indian timbers during the nineteenth century. The normal trunkwood of this tree has never received a commercial interest, hence the more valuable burl-

wood is recognized simply as amboinawood, without any qualification. Webster gives the same spelling for this name as that given for the island of Amboina, rather than Amboyna, as more commonly used.

An ample coverage of the delicately figured wood is given by *The Cabinet-Maker's Assistant:*

Amboyna wood is imported in oblong, irregularly shaped slabs, ranging from 2 to 4 feet long, from 4 to 24 inches wide, and from 2 to 8 inches thick. In its general expression it resembles the burr of the yew tree, [but] it is much softer in the wood, and is more minutely and uniformly figured, being full of small curls and knots. It is also more yellow in colour than the yew, and ranges between an orange and chestnut brown, and frequently red brown.

It is an exceedingly beautiful and highly-ornamental wood. Its available size, figure, and colour recommend its use in the manufacture of small cabinets. It is, besides, frequently used in veneering more extensive surfaces, such as loo table and tea table tops. In such cases, from the irregularity of form in the wood, and from the abrupt and transitory character of the fibre, the joinings require to be waved and indented.

Considerable skill and care are requisite in the surface finish of this wood. It is generally, but not uniformly, soft; and, in consequence, does not pre-

64. A Queen Anne or early Georgian inlaid amboinawood dressing and writing table Courtesy of the Victoria and Albert Museum, London. 65. A George III inlaid amboinawood and East Indian satinwood card table Courtesy of Biggs of Maidenhead.

66. A Regency brass-inlaid amboinawood and Brazilian rosewood sofa table at Buckingham Palace Reproduced by gracious permission of Her Majesty the queen. Copyright *Country Life.*

67. A Louis XVI amboinawood *secrétaire à abattant* Courtesy of Morton Lee, London.

sent a firm or equable resistance to the action of tools. In working it, a keen edge, little bite, a quick and steady hand, are important points to be attended to. A chief difficulty in bringing this wood to a perfectly smooth or flat surface when polished, arises from irregularities in its expansion, caused by its general softness, and unequal absorption of moisture.

This is usually remedied by reducing these asperities and inequalities by the action of pumice and oil. This process darkens and deteriorates the appearance of the wood in some degree. Amboyna wood is now of less frequent use than formerly. It is sold at 1s. 6p. per foot of veneer.

Howard records the weight as 39 pounds per cubic foot.

The twisted grain and burl eyes of amboinawood are displayed in patterns that are quite similar to, but more pronounced than those of burl poplar, and more delicate than those occurring in thuja, which may appear in a similar light tan color.

Although amboinawood was imported into England during the early part of the eighteenth century it is seldom found in furniture of designs associated with the walnut period. At the turn of the century veneers of this type became fairly popular in British cabinetwork of Sheraton and Regency designs. In France, Parisian *ébénistes* showed some partiality toward the use of *bois d'amboine* during the Louis XVI period, an interest which may in part account for later selections of burl ash and burl elm in productions of Empire or Restoration designs.

THE ILLUSTRATED EXAMPLES

Fig. 64 From the designs of several related types of wall and dressing mirrors, and that of another tall dressing table in which the straight legs are joined by an elaborate cruciform stretcher, it is apparent that the first piece here was made at the close of the Queen Anne period or early in the succeeding Georgian decades. Thus this particular example documents an initial European use of Amboinawood, and a reappearance of straight legs in the finer cabinetwork of the time.

Fig. 65 In the card table of *circa* 1790 veneers of East Indian satinwood, on the four planes of the legs and the edge of the folding top, harmonize with a golden-toned amboinawood employed for the upper surface, the frieze and die panels. The sofa Fig. 66 table is one of a pair said to have been made for Princess Charlotte at the time of her marriage with Prince Leopold, in 1816. Here rosewood panels serve as foils for the typical brass inlays of the period, and an ormolu collar at the base of the pedestal gives balance to the matching paw feet.

Fig. 67 The choice *secrétaire* is by Adam Weisweiler, one of the most brilliant *ébénistes* of the Louis XVI period, apparently with the collaboration of Gouthière, the famous Parisian *ciseleur*. A *bureau de dame* completed through this same collaboration, and supplied to Marie Antoinette in 1784, features exactly matching terms with demifigures in the form of canephoroe. The decorative plaque repeating the theme of the pilasters is of Sèvres porcelain, a material favored by Weisweiler in several of his most important projects.

55. WILD SERVICE TREE and ROWAN TREE

The wild service tree, *Sorbus torminalis*, native to Continental Europe and England, usually appears as a small tree although a few specimens have attained record heights of eighty feet. While it is not a common timber, Sophie von Roche saw "numerous articles of straw-coloured service wood charmingly finished with all the cabinetmaker's skill" on her visit to the establishment of George Seddon in 1786. English craftsmen of rural communities also utilized this timber for furniture and smaller household articles. In the solid and as veneers it also appears as the *bois de sorbier*, or *cormier* of French *ébénistes* and *marqueteurs*.

The heartwood ranges in color from the lighter pinkish-tan shades found in other fruitwoods to the reddish cast of cherrywood, and it may be marked by darker veinings. It presents a fairly hard surface with a fine and uniform texture. Varying from the more common fruitwoods in one particular respect, rays are not discernable in ordinary visual examination, or through a lens of ten diameters' magnification. The weight is about 40 pounds per cubic foot.

A closely related species, the rowan tree, *S. acuparia*, produces a wood that is very similar to that of the wild service tree, and also to that of the whitebeam. This species is frequently referred to as the mountain ash, from the resemblance of its leaves to those of the true ash. Its heartwood possesses a reddish-brown color, and is distinguished by a compact arrangement of very minute vessels resulting in an exceptionally fine texture. It is a strong and elastic timber, restricted in use only because of its limited dimensions. During the past it was found to be serviceable in turnery, in supplying handles for table implements, furnishing parts of musical instruments, and for other small purposes.

56. APPLE

The apple has been propagated to such an extent that species originally native to temperate zones of Europe and North America now appear in more than two thousand varieties. Formerly associated with the genus *Pyrus*, this category of trees is now separately classified as of the genus *Malus*. The wild apple, or crab apple, *M. pumila*, is the progenitor of the common apple, *M. sylvestris*, which the Romans introduced into Britain.

Apple trees generally attain heights of from twenty to fifty feet with average commensurate diameters. The wood is of a light to medium pinkish-tan color, sometimes marked by streaks or fairly wide bands of a darker pigmentation. It is a hard and close-grained material with imperceptible pores and rays. Growth-ring figures may be either very mild or rendered more prominent by thin dark lines appearing in tangential surfaces. Cuttings marked by the darker streakings mentioned above are obtained most commonly from very old trees. The weight averages around 48 pounds per cubic foot.

In the production of old furniture and smaller objects it is apparent that a use of applewood was confined to localities in which sizable growths developed, and felled limbs or entire trees became available from time to time. Contrasting with its more customary use as a solid material, the wood was at times employed as a veneer, generally in central areas of the Continent where this timber was fairly popular during the early nineteenth century, and in France where it is known as *bois de pommier*. A number of English and American pieces casually identified as made of applewood have been found to display prominent rays. These, and additional structural features, have indicated that such pieces were actually made from unusually pale cuttings of cherrywood.

57. BEECH

The European, or common beech, *Fagus sylvatica* Linn., is widely distributed throughout Europe, from Scandinavia and the British Isles to Spain and Hungary. During Romanesque times Scandinavian and German scribes cut their records in blocks of beechwood, and, as a building material, the timber is known to have been used in England by the thirteenth century. The tree attains a height of one hundred feet and a butt diameter of four feet, thriving satisfactorily in poor soil or under other unfavorable growing conditions.

Beechwood is generally of a light pinkish-tan color, though it may appear in whiter or browner tones, the latter colorings formerly considered as representative of the best quality timber. It is a moderately hard wood, with a fine, uniform texture, and a straight grain developing mild growth-ring figures. Rays furnish a characteristic feature of identification, occurring in two sizes, the smaller of which cannot be seen without a lens. The larger rays appear distinctly as reddish-brown flecks which are displayed most prominently in radial sections. Although other timbers were usually preferred for bending purposes, beech may be easily treated in this manner after it has been steamed. The weight varies between 43 and 55 pounds per cubic foot.

The principal fault of beech as a furniture wood has been well known since the seventeenth century when its use was decried as "subject to the worm." An attraction which it holds for the furniture beetle has resulted in considerable harm to many examples in which it appears. Damage of this nature may be apparent within a few years of manufacture, gradually spreading to more resistant woods combined with beech as surfacing veneers.

As one of the most readily available and serviceable timbers, beech was widely utilized by Euro-

68. *(Left)*. A Régence-Louis XVI inlaid beechwood commode. 69. A Queen Anne beechwood child's armchair Courtesy of Arthur S. Vernay, Inc., New York City.

70. A George III carved beechwood armchair Courtesy of Arthur S. Vernay, Inc., New York City.

ably from the earlier flat or carved trelliswork designs.

THE ILLUSTRATED EXAMPLES

A very large proportion of the seat furniture produced in Paris and in other leading cities of France, prior to the Directory, was made of beech or *bois de hêtre*, including many examples now in private and public collections that are believed to be of walnut. It was but seldom that beech was employed as a principal surface material of the cabinetmaker, even in rural productions such as the plainly shaped commode. This late eighteenth-century example, patterned after a Louis XIV design, is furnished with ribbanded, pearl-molded handles and escutcheons in the Louis XVI taste. In many so-called reproductions of French furniture it is difficult to determine whether a Louis XIV or a Louis XVI composition has been attempted. Indeed original designs are in certain instances quite similar, and those of earlier derivation were drawn upon by some of the foremost artists of the later period. The mixture of styles is certainly amusing, and not inharmonious, in the present piece which, from the inlays simulating *cannelures*, or wide flutings, was obviously not intended to receive the usual painted finish.

Fig. 68

The Queen Anne and Late Georgian chairs represent a limited number of frames produced in the British Isles after the close of the seventeenth century in which beech was utilized as an unconcealed primary material. Lengthy rays, characteristic of quartered surfaces, are prominently displayed in the splat of the child's chair, *circa* 1710-1720, an interesting model and one in which the use of a common timber is quite understandable.

Fig. 69

A more typical use of beech, as this wood was customarily employed in metropolitan work of the eighteenth century, is represented in the design and execution of the shield-back armchair, *circa* 1775. Hepplewhite's later adaptations of this upholstered form were presented as "Cabriole Chairs." If this appellation was meant to coincide with the French term *chaise en cabriolet* it should have been applied only to models in which he represented the backs as concave in plan. As usual the frame of this chair was originally painted or gilded.

Fig. 70

58. PEAR

Numerous varieties of pear trees are derived from the wild pear, *Pyrus communis* Linn., which originated in Asia and southern Europe. These

pean craftsmen after the close of the seventeenth century, either as a principal framing material of seat furniture, or for various concealed structural purposes. In the former use the exposed wood was generally finished by painting, japanning or gilding. Beech might also be substituted for walnut or other woods in the rear uprights of seat furniture and as the foundation of veneered back splats, when it was usually stained and finished to match the color of the finer timber. During the nineteenth century it was frequently treated to imitate mahogany and rosewood, and following an earlier practice it was also ebonized.

Chippendale and his contemporaries offered many "Designs of Chairs after the Chinese Manner" to be used in conjunction with lacquer furniture and in rooms hung with "India papers." The continuing popularity of Chinese wallpapers, which did not become dutiable until 1794, extended through the reign of George IV, who is known to have acquired a particularly fine set. Imitation bamboo chairs produced to answer the requirements of this decor are at times assigned to the Chippendale period, although varying consider-

trees have been grown principally in Italy, Switzerland, France, Germany and the Tyrol. In southern regions the wild pear attains a height of from twenty to sixty feet, yielding a wood that is highly suitable for the manufacture of furniture and for other fine purposes. The tree has been cultivated in England, though it has seldom been available there as a timber. A similar scarcity has also existed in America, but nevertheless "Pear Tree" does appear in the stock records of our earliest cabinet-makers.

Pearwood is frequently distinguished by a flesh-like color, at other times appearing in soft apricot tones, or in deeper and redder hues. Very minute pores and vessel lines account for an unusual uniformity and smoothness in texture. Rays, too, are indistinct, though they may be faintly visible in radial sections as small flecks of a deeper tone than the ground tissue. Growth rings have very little effect on the surface appearance, but the irregular character of the grain may result in some mottle figures. Certain timbers grown in the vicinity of northern Italy develop fiddle-back figures of great

delicacy. The weight averages between 45 and 50 pounds per cubic foot.

Wherever pearwood was available during the sixteenth and seventeenth centuries it was selected for special uses in the production of furniture, for smooth or carved members or details executed in the solid, or as an inlay material—when it might be stained to simulate ebony. The following century saw these utilities extended in marquetry work, as *bois de poirier* became more popular in French *ébénisterie*, and in the more delicate carved embellishments of cabinet pieces, a use favored by certain British craftsmen.

THE ILLUSTRATED EXAMPLE

This is a frame made by Joseph Bonzanigo, 1740-1820, an Italian carver who is believed to have executed some commissions in Paris. Bonzanigo also worked in ivory, a material rivaled here by the fine texture of the pearwood employed for cameo-like appliques that are set in ebony. The moldings display equally smooth, figureless surfaces, and the pearl-chain fillet again exemplifies the fine nature of this wood.

Fig. 71

59. PLANE TREE
or LONDON PLANE

The Oriental plane, *Platanus orientalis* Linn., was introduced in Europe during the sixteenth century, and in England where the American plane tree or buttonwood, *P. occidentalis* Linn., was transplanted from Virginia in 1640. Later the London plane, *P. acerifolia*, appeared, apparently as a result of hybridization, and as a cultivated British tree for this species *is never found growing wild.*

In 1842 the English botanist, Selby, drew attention to the then recognized differences between the Oriental and the Occidental or American plane—without any mention whatsoever of the hybrid species. Of the Oriental plane he wrote:

In the south of England and around London, where specimens are most numerous, the largest trees mentioned by Loudon seem to have attained a height of from seventy to ninety feet, and a diameter of trunk of from three to upwards of four feet. The oldest recorded British specimen is that at Lee Court in Kent, which was seen by Evelyn in 1683, and was then a fine tree.... In Scotland it grows as far north as Ross-shire...and in Ireland it seems to grow vigorously.

As a timber, the wood of the Oriental Plane is almost unknown throughout the greater part of the

71. A Louis XVI carved pearwood and ebony *cadre*

72. A George II inlaid plane tree chest of drawers

73. A George III plane tree parquetry "commode" Courtesy of Norman R. Adams Ltd., London.

south and west of Europe, but in Greece, Persia, and other native habitats it is extensively used, not only in cabinet work, but in common carpentry and joinery. Olivier tells us that its wood is equal to that of any European tree for cabinet-making, and that it is almost exclusively employed by the Persians for their furniture, doors, windows, &c. When young, the wood is of a yellowish white colour, but as it acquires age becomes brown, streaked with reddish veins, and when polished is not unlike the wood of the best walnut.

According to the same authority "it would appear" that the species introduced from America "had, in Evelyn's time, become much more common than the Oriental Plane, which it had then nearly supplanted." Nevertheless his account indicates little use of the tree as a timber, though he recorded it at more than one hundred feet in height, and with a trunk circumference of twelve feet. "The timber of the Occidental Plane may be said to be scarcely known in England, as it has hitherto only been planted for its ornamental properties, and never with a view to profit; from Michaux we learn that, though of a close grain and susceptible of a high polish, it cannot, from its liability to warp, be used for delicate cabinet purposes, but is made into bedsteads and other bulky articles; its colour when old is dull reddish brown, and the medullary rays, extending from the centre to the circumference, and which divide the concentric rings into numerous sections, are very distinct and visible."

Current descriptions of the London plane, and its wood, coincide in many points with Selby's notes on the Occidental or American plane, rather than the Oriental species. This might well indicate that the London plane developed in Britain as a result of a more widespread propagation of the former, rather than the latter species. It might also indicate that his notes were based in part on observations of the unrecognized hybrid species. In any case it will be recognized in this country that the following remarks on the London plane are generally descriptive of our American buttonwood.

Botanists now recognize the London plane as a separate and distinct species, growing more plentifully in the British Isles than other members of its genus. This tree is also considered the only plane worthy of notice as a British timber, the dimensions duplicating those given by Selby for the Occidental plane. The wood varies in color from medium shades of tan to reddish-brown tones. It is fine and uniform in texture, with obscure vessels but fairly distinct growth rings. The grain is normally irregular, but decorative figures which may result from

this circumstance are largely or entirely absent. The most characteristic feature of the wood results from an unusual development of broad and numerous rays, an eighth of an inch or more in breadth, and appearing as pronounced flakes which are profusely, and often evenly, distributed through quartered surfaces. As lacy effects frequently result from these crowded markings of London plane, cuttings of this nature are also referred to as lacewood. The weight varies from 30 to 45 pounds per cubic foot.

Sheraton noticed that plane tree was "in many places in the country used by Cabinet makers instead of beech for painted chairs, or the fly joint rails of card and pembroke tables." These substitutions for beech (and for sycamore) have been verified, but in addition, the lacy cuttings of plane tree were also employed for finer purposes during Sheraton's time. They appear from time to time in the smaller articles of cabinetwork, up to the size of a portable table, that were produced around the close of the eighteenth century. Still less frequently plane tree may be seen in larger pieces, in rare instances indicating a use of the wood several decades prior to Sheraton's appearance in London.

THE ILLUSTRATED EXAMPLES

The chest of drawers with brushing slide is a production of *circa* 1745. Except for a use of walnut in the panel bandings and for facing the bracket feet, all of the exposed surfaces are of plane tree. Whether the wood for these veneers was obtained from a London plane, an Oriental plane, or another tree of the genus *Platanus* is, according to confirmation by Mr. J. L. Stearns, quite impossible to determine from an examination of the wood itself. — Fig. 72

An interesting synthesis of structural forms and decorative materials is exhibited in the parquetry "commode," *circa* 1770. The floreted trelliswork inlays of the doors and sides are set off by quarries of plane tree, and the front panels are bordered with rosewood. It is difficult to determine the striped veneers solely through examination of the photograph, but these appear to be of rosewood, in which the sapwood may be as light in color as that of laburnum, or of laburnum itself. — Fig. 73

60. CHERRY

The European wild cherry, *Prunus avium* Linn., known in France as *l'merisier*, grows abundantly throughout Europe to about the fifty-fifth parallel, and to a lesser extent in the British Isles. An extreme height of about one hundred and ten feet is recorded, and a butt diameter of two feet—which may certainly be exceeded.

When freshly cut the timber is usually of a reddish-tan color, with exposure turning to the average light tones of Honduras mahogany. However, in some instances the color may be as dark as the deepest hue ever to appear in West Indian mahogany. Finished surfaces display a moderately fine and even texture, accompanied by a good luster and a certain amount of oiliness. The grain is generally straight, often producing moderate growthring figures in the usual tangential cuttings. Rays may appear in such material but they are more pronounced in radial sections. The wood is also noted for its toughness, and it has little tendency toward shrinking or warping. Weights vary from 35 to 50 pounds per cubic foot.

St. Lucie, mahaleb or Austrian cherry, *P. mahaleb*, is closely similar to European wild cherry except for a somewhat grayer color. This wood was utilized principally in Austrian and South German furniture. A violet dye and a cordial are prepared from the fruit of the tree, and its flowers and young leaves are used in perfumery.

Cherrywood was widely favored on the Continent, in both branches of the furniture crafts, with a range of interest extending from Austria to Scandinavia during the eighteenth and nineteenth centuries. A lesser attention was granted this material in the British Isles, despite Evelyn's report at so early a date as 1664 that "The Black Cherry wood grows sometimes to that bulke, as is fit to make

74. A Dutch cherrywood child's kettle-base armoire

75. A Connecticut River valley carved and inlaid cherrywood secretary Courtesy of Ginsburg & Levy, Inc., New York City.

stools with, Cabinets, Tables, especially the redder sort which will polish well."

Cherrywood was especially popular with French craftsmen, a popularity which was not confined to furniture produced in provinces other than *Île de France*. The timber was also employed in Parisian ateliers, generally in the production of *meubles usuels*—which American collectors delight in calling "French provincial." The most darkly colored cherrywood appears in pieces emanating from the large cities or smaller towns of southern provinces. *Cerisier* is the term applied to wood obtained from cultivated trees, which is often distinguished by a milder grain than that occurring in timbers produced by *l'merisier* or wild cherry.

The American black, or wild cherry, *P. serotina*, grows throughout the eastern half of this country except in southern Florida, with its range extending into southern Canada. Supplies of this timber formerly rivaled those of our light-brown walnut, but the species is no longer abundant. The tree attains a height of one hundred feet, with the trunk free of branches for seventy feet and measuring four feet in diameter.

Of a light or medium reddish-tan color, the wood is moderately hard, straight in the grain, and usually rather plain in appearance. A mild type of growth-ring figure is displayed in some cuttings, and in rare instances swirl, feather-crotch, or wavy figures distinguish the choicest selections. The texture is fine and uniform, with pores so small as to be indiscernible without the aid of a lens, though they may be indicated as fine vessel lines in longitudinal surfaces. Rays are visible as small flecks appearing in radial sections. Although burls are not uncommon, veneers of this nature were not featured until comparatively recent times. The weight averages around 35-36 pounds per cubic foot.

During colonial and Early Federal times black cherry was an important cabinet wood, particularly in the states situated above Pennsylvania and New Jersey. In New England and New York it was used in producing seat furniture, general cabinetwork, clock cases and various other household requirements. Local timbers were particularly favored in Connecticut, not only in fashioning the simpler pieces for which the average workman might choose a relatively inexpensive material, but in many, if not the majority of the finest examples executed within that state. These include elaborately pedimented highboys and secretaries, and chests of drawers in single or double stages, their façades frequently enhanced with yoke-shaped contours, or with blockings similar to those of Rhode Island designs.

THE ILLUSTRATED EXAMPLES

Restrained lines in the cupboard section and kettle base of the small armoire, *circa* 1750, offer a pleasant contrast to the more usual elaborated productions of Dutch "cabinet-workers." The cherrywood is of an excellent quality, with a warm yellowish-red surface tone. Apparently the knots appearing in the balanced door panels were intended to add interest to the otherwise plain character of the wood. According to usual practice the carcase work has been carried out in oak, and in this instance the drawer linings are nailed into position without any use of dovetails. Fig. 74

The pedimented secretary bears certain resemblances to cabinet pieces produced and labeled by Daniel Clay, a cabinet- and chair-maker of Greenfield, Massachusetts, where he was born in 1770, and worked from 1784 to 1806. After this time Clay moved to Mansfield, Connecticut, and continued his activities in this town until 1821. Awaiting more positive documentation as a production of this maker, or possibly of a still undiscovered compeer, the present example is conservatively ascribed to an origin within the confines of the Connecticut River Valley. Fig. 75

61. RED CEDAR
(A softwood)

The red cedar, *Juniperus virginiana* Linn., also known as the pencil cedar, is indigenous to the eastern half of this country and to the West Indies; attaining a height of about ninety feet and a butt diameter of more than three feet. The heartwood is generally of a deep reddish-tan color, rather similar to that of yew, but this may vary toward much darker red or even purple tones. The sapwood has a pale yellowish tint when freshly cut, deepening to a light tan hue with long exposure. Red cedar is a medium-soft but durable wood, with a fine texture and a fairly straight grain—except when it is diverted by knots. It is rather brittle but not difficult to work with, and it takes a smooth, silky finish.

This wood is distinguished by a structure resembling that of yew, for the uneven growth rings are also formed with narrow, dense, summer-wood bands. As a result, these bands appear in longitudinal surfaces as fine, deep-toned, linear markings, which are particularly characteristic of the two woods, although somewhat similar features of growth are noticeable in other softwood timbers. Like all cedarwoods, in which the true cedars are of the genus *Cedrus*, this juniper species possesses a pleasant aromatic scent. The weight is 30 pounds per cubic foot.

Supplies of red cedar were received in England during the seventeenth century. The wood imported from Virginia was noted by Evelyn as "nearest to the Bermuda juniper, both yet exceeded by that from Carolina." Howard mentions the use of pencil cedar in the reception hall of the Skinners' Company, in Howgate Hill, executed shortly after the Great Fire of London; noting that its fragrant scent was still clearly perceptible. In its use as a furniture wood, red cedar was utilized principally in the British Isles and favored as a superior material for the drawer linings of fine cabinet pieces. In this capacity it was employed rather sparingly at first, usually in the smaller drawers of such pieces, and later also for the larger drawers in chests of drawers, bureaus, secretaries and other pieces where the clean appearance and fragrant scent of the wood might prove more advantageous than a use of pine or oak. After the turn of the eighteenth century red cedar was occasionally utilized as a principal surface wood of furniture produced in the British Isles.

In its modern use as a mothproof lining for storage chests and closets, Malcolm H. Sherwood has pointed out that veneers of red cedar are purposeless: "The best manufacturers use lumber at least three-fourths of an inch thick, since experimentation has shown that the aroma from thinner stock is not sufficient to prevent moth damage. Here knots, far from being defects, are actually specified; for the more knots, the more pungent the odor. . . . A moth may live and lay her eggs in cedar-lined chests and closets, yet the aroma from the cedar oil will kill the larvae as soon as they hatch, and it is the larvae, not the moth, that make colanders of clothes." Moths are frequently found in cedar-lined closets usually soon after their construction.

62. THORN

Among the larger and more important thorn trees of Europe are the hawthorn and blackthorn. The former species, *Crataegus oxyacantha* Linn., is sometimes referred to as the whitethorn. In England, Scotland and Ireland it grows to extreme heights of around forty-five feet, with circumferences of more than ten feet at the widest portion of the bole.

As a tree, the hawthorn retains a shrublike form, with a short, typically irregular main stem that is twisted and deeply furrowed. In addition, the wood has a strong tendency to split and warp in drying, so that this species is of little value as a timber. In color, it is generally of a pinkish-tan hue, with more of the pink toning than appears in applewood or pearwood, both of which resemble hawthorn in structure.

Selby's description disagrees with British governmental authority regarding the color of this wood, mentioning "a pale yellowish white colour." This author also notes "a firm, hard texture, and close grain, susceptible of a fine polish"; and a weight of fifty-seven pounds, three ounces.

Blackthorn, *Prunus spinosa* Linn., is best known in relation to Ireland, where two of the products yielded by these shrubs and trees have frequently gone hand in hand—shillelaghs, and the flavoring extracted from their sloe plums to be used in making gin. Howard stresses the desirability of another product: "If sound wood of even, narrow widths could be secured, it would make an attractive decorative wood for inlay, comparable with the best of other woods imported for that purpose."

In common with plumwood of the same genus, Irish blackthorn develops a rich reddish-tan heartwood, and when freshly cut it is commonly marked by purplish streaks. The wood is close and firm in texture, with finer pores and less distinct growth-ring figures than appear in cherry. Rays are visible as minute flecks appearing in quartered surfaces.

Veneer pieces of Tunbridge wares have been labeled simply as "thorn." At times these veneers

76. A George III tea caddy inlaid with oyster pieces of blackthorn Courtesy of Arthur S. Vernay, Inc., New York City.

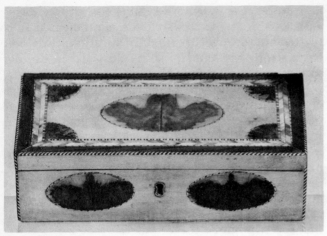

77. A George III inlaid holly and blackthorn caddy

ness was generally kept under lock and key in tea caddies fitted with one or more canisters, or in larger, equally decorative chests, tea poys, etc.).

63. PLUM

The plum, *Prunus domestica* Linn., in numerous wild or cultivated varieties of trees and shrubs, thrives in the south of France, in Spain and in Italy. This species develops a reddish-tan heartwood, and a fairly wide sapwood of a straw-yellow hue. The wood is hard, very fine and uniform in texture, with rays appearing as small but distinct flecks in the radial section. Weights range from 35 to 50 pounds per cubic foot.

Plumwood, or *bois de prunier*, in veneers displaying both heartwood and sapwood areas, was employed by some of the finest cabinetmakers working in France, Germany and Scandinavia during the eighteenth century. Veneers of this type are found principally in tables of various types that became popular during or after the middle decades of the eighteenth century. The designs of these pieces, and the choice of material, often suggest a southern provenance, but plumwood was by no means restricted in use as, according to the best Swedish authority, natively grown trees supplied the wood that was selected by leading artisans of that country. On occasion these veneers were also employed in the inlaid wares of Tunbridge Wells.

display deeper shades of color than the pinkish-tan associated with hawthorn, or than Selby's "pale yellowish white color." Therefore it would appear quite likely that the thorn employed in these, and in other veneered productions of the British Isles was at least in part cut from blackthorn shrubs or trees. A diagonal section of a blackthorn branch, displaying irregularly formed heartwood in the central portion, was obtained by John Hingston from an old craftsman of Tunbridge Wells. This cutting is very similar to others that were inlaid in Late Georgian tea caddies, and in other Irish pieces of even larger dimensions. It was labeled "English Blackthorn," a legend which Mr. J. L. Stearns has corrected to "Irish Blackthorn." Whether this thorn was used in Continental work has not been determined, though the blackthorn, *prunillier*, and the hawthorn, *aubepine*, are indigenous to France, and to other European countries.

THE ILLUSTRATED EXAMPLES

Fig. 76

Fig. 77

Transverse sections of Irish blackthorn stems or branches are featured in the octagonal tea caddy, *circa* 1785, and in the plainer oblong box. The shallow box bears a close resemblance to a rising compartment contained in a harlequin pembroke table (illustrated in *The Dictionary of English Furniture* and other English publications, but now owned by a New York collector), which is inlaid with additional ornamentation more definitely indicating a date of *circa* 1790-1800. (*Caddy*, spelled *catty* during the late seventeenth and eighteenth centuries, is derived from the Malay *kati*, a weight of one and one-third pounds. This standard, as also the Malay *picul* and *tael*, was employed throughout eastern Asia in the buying and shipping of tea [*ch'a, tsia* and later *tā*], which, because of its costli-

THE ILLUSTRATED EXAMPLES

A skilled Parisian use of plumwood is patent in the design and execution of the small writing table, which bears the pontil mark of "Migeon," apparently denoting Pierre Migeon II (b. 1701, d. 1758) in this notable family of French *ébénistes*. The dark inlays, contrasting with the heartwood-and-sapwood veneers, appear as ebony in the reproduction but they are of a varying, dark reddish-brown wood that can not be determined without marring a principal surface.

Fig. 78

In comparison with much of the furniture produced in Paris during the greater part of the eighteenth century, structural techniques appearing in the *bureau plat*, *circa* 1760, are of a high order, but the secondary woods noticed in examining this piece were suggestive of an origin outside of the capital city. If this is possible the *bronze doré* work, particularly the elaborate *chutes* or capital mounts of the legs, must surely have been obtained in Paris or cast from Parisian originals. However, an equal simplicity in the chevron- and diamond-matched

Fig. 79

78. A Louis XV plumwood marquetry *table à écrire* Courtesy of M. Gaston Bensimon, New York City.

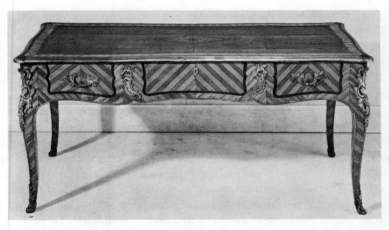

79. *(Above)*. A Louis XV inlaid plumwood *bureau plat*. 80. A Louis XV inlaid plumwood *bibliothèque*

veneers of the bookcase, regarded by native experts as a Parisian example, tends to suggest the preceding piece as possibly a production of the same city. Cases of this type and quality were more generally executed in violetwood, tulipwood, or other exotic timbers, the doors being fitted with grilles or wire network—in the present instance replaced by glass panels.

64. YEW
(A softwood)

The yew, *Taxus baccata* Linn., is a widely distributed species of shrubs and trees growing throughout most of Europe and the British Isles, with a range extending eastward to the Caspian Sea. It is one of the most enduring trees, living for well over two thousand years, while many centuries of growth are known to have elapsed before certain specimens have shown any signs of decay. In bygone times there was a common saying that a post of yew would outlast one of iron.

The word *yew* was also used to designate a long bow made of this material, and prior to the Elizabethan period in England the wood was restricted to the manufacture of these weapons. Its demand was so great at this time that additional supplies were imported from the Continent. As the yew was often grown in churchyards its twigs or branches have become emblematic of grief.

The tree seldom reaches a height of more than sixty feet, but the irregularly formed bole develops to a great size, attaining an extreme circumference of fifty feet or more. English trees are recorded at more than three feet in diameter, though in that country today such sizes are rarely found equal to those recently obtained in Caucasian logs measuring from fourteen to twenty-eight inches in width. A particularly fine quality of yew was formerly obtained from the neighborhood of Loch Lomond in Scotland, where, near the close of the eighteenth century three hundred trees were felled on one small island. The tree also grows wild through most of the Lake District, in Surrey, Sussex, other sections of England, and in Ireland.

In its heartwood, yew is generally distinguished by an orange-tinted, medium-brown color, though in rare instances this may approach a deeper, purplish brown. The sapwood, which was frequently utilized in combination with the heartwood, possesses a creamy-yellow hue. Since the tree is an evergreen of the *Coniferae* group, it may be fitting to liken the general coloring and appearance of the wood to cedar. In these respects there is a superficial resemblance to American red cedar—in the

81. A George I inlaid yewwood side table Courtesy of Biggs of Maidenhead.

color tones of the heartwood and sapwood, in the clearly marked growth lines, and in the small eyes or knots that are often distributed throughout both of these areas.

This wood is hard, tough and resilient, with a high resistance to indentation. It is characterized by a fine texture, a compact grain which may be either straight or shallowly interlocked, and it takes a smooth, lustrous finish. Finished surfaces soon acquire a slightly deeper shading, and with adequate polishing they may take on an appearance of greater age than they actually possess. Rays are not distinct in this timber, which is one of the heaviest of the softwoods—weighing 38-48 pounds per cubic foot.

A particularly identifying feature results from the character of the growth rings, which are clearly

82. *(Left).* A George II inlaid yewwood secretary Courtesy of Phillips of Hitchen Ltd. 83. A George III carved yewwood architectural bookcase Collection of A. Randolph Brett, Esq., High Close, Baldock, Hertfordshire.

84. A George III inlaid yewwood card table

marked by a narrow zone of dense summer-wood occurring in each annual layer. These markings appear in tangential surfaces as thin, clearly defined lines of a darker tone than the ground color. They may run through some areas with a certain degree of parallelism, or they may develop with a more graphic fluidity. It is these lines in particular that serve as a principal means of differentiating burlwood cuttings of yew from amboina and thuja.

The irregular and shrublike growth of the yew, in which lower parts of the bole frequently give off new rising branches, accounts for the tiny knots that appear in the wood. At the ramifications of the branches and near the roots the wood "is marbled and veined in a way surpassed by few of the finest foreign cabinet woods." Occasionally burls add to these more highly figured sections of timber, developing in irregular hemispherical formations that may extend for seven feet or more along the trunk. Imperfections in wood of either type are filled in with patches of a sounder nature, which are often seen in examples of old furniture.

It has been generally recognized that yew possesses a high degree of resistance to attack by larvae of the furniture beetle, a fact born out by the healthy state of many pieces of antique furniture executed in this wood. Nevertheless British governmental authority points out that yew is "Liable to attack by the Common Furniture beetle, particularly in the sapwood."

This timber has been employed in the production of British furniture ever since the Elizabethan period, either as a solid material or, with the advent of the cabinetmaker, as a veneer. With the advance of the furniture crafts in Ireland the wood became quite popular there,* and it was used to a much lesser extent in Scotland. Toward the close of the eighteenth century yew was also added to the inlay materials then used for oval paterae, bandings and other linear decorations of conventional types. Later "Yew-tree" appeared among the finest woods recommended for moldings and veneer work in *The London Cabinet-Makers' Union Book of Prices.*

Austria also produced a considerable amount of furniture in yew, particularly at the turn of the eighteenth century, and the Germans extended some favor to this material. It was employed principally for inlaid work in France, where the plain wood is known as *bois d'if,* and the burlwood as *racine d'if.*

THE ILLUSTRATED EXAMPLES

As a principal medium of fine furniture yewwood will generally be found in pieces of highly individual designs, such as those in which each of the following specimens have been fashioned. Richly figured burl veneers employed for the upper portion of the kneehole table, *circa* 1730, are in

Fig. 81

---

* Concentration on the present study of cabinet woods has been of great help toward confirming my findings in regard to Irish furniture of the highest quality, as this appears in the more sophisticated or cosmopolitan designs which have been, and continue to be so highly prized by collectors of "Old English" furniture. The finest of such examples executed entirely or largely of yew are for the greater part of Irish, rather than English origins; a fact that has been totally unnoticed or speculated upon by English writers on the subject. Indeed, adding to these pieces their companions in walnut, mahogany, padauk, the satinwoods, rosewoods, etc., the appearance of such fine woods combined with excellent woodworking skills has resulted in the assignment of numerous Irish examples to *London* origins, even to individual shops such as those operated by Giles Grendy, Vile and Cobb, Chippendale, etc.

harmony with those of the walnut dressing mirror. The cabriole supports of this table are of walnut, painted to simulate the rarer wood, and they are ornamented with knee lappets of a type favored in Holland, and to a lesser extent in America.

Another interesting use of yew veneers is seen in the secretary with mirrored door, *circa* 1725-1745. Here they are combined with herringbone bandings and cross-grained borders of walnut. Various other pieces appear from time to time displaying this same combination of woods with yew as the featured material. These will indicate the high esteem in which the rarer wood has always been

Fig. 82

85. A George III inlaid yewwood commode Courtesy of Arthur S. Vernay, Inc., New York City.

held, without detracting from the importance of walnut, for bandings and other inlays were customarily selected from among the finer, though in such instances not the rarer supplies of exotic and native timbers.

The architectural bookcase of a later, Adam, period, is a most exceptional example of work performed in highly figured yewwood. With great lavishness in this instance, timbers that might have yielded an abundant supply of fine veneers have instead been employed in solid cuttings. Veneer work is incorporated in the designs of this case, however, appearing in the cornice. There what seems to be a fret meander is actually an inlaid band of reciprocal candle or gutta motifs. The brass network grilles and drawer handles are original, and retain traces of their former water gilding.

A pair of card tables is represented by the single

Fig. 83

specimen of half-round shaping, *circa* 1790. All surfaces of the top, including the edges, and the legs are veneered in swirl-figured yewwood marked by scattered eyes. The folding flap is faced with fan sectors converging on a mahogany center. In the commode with reverse diamond-matched drawer panels, *circa* 1780, the stiles are inlaid with anthemion and husk pendants. The featured heartwood-and-sapwood veneers may be compared with those of the preceding and following examples in plumwood and laburnum. On the Continent similar contrasting effects were at times achieved by combining veneer strips obtained from the heartwood portions of two entirely different, light- and dark-colored timbers.

A Parisian use of *racine d'if*, with unusually contorted sapwood markings, is shown among the illustrations of furniture produced in ebony.

65. MULBERRY

The mulberry was brought to Europe from the Far East and India. By the tenth century it was propagated on the Continent, particularly in Italy and Southern France where *Morus alba*, the white mulberry, thrives best. This variety is grown especially for its leaves, on which the silkworm feeds. The black mulberry, *M. nigra*, which is planted chiefly as a shade tree and for its fruit, was the first of the two species to be introduced in England. St. James's Park and Greenwich Park were chosen by James I in 1609 as sites for mulberry gardens, though few of these trees remain in London or elsewhere in England today. Seven years later the Bermuda Company sent out mulberry seeds to the islands under its authority, and in 1627 an act was passed requiring fifty plants to be set in every share of land for three successive years. These island growths eventually attained heights of from twenty to twenty-five feet.

From one to about fourteen stems are developed in the growth of a mulberry tree. English specimens of *M. nigra* are recorded as reaching heights of thirty-five to forty feet, the greatest butt diameter given at eighteen inches. The largest recorded specimen of *M. alba* measured forty-five feet in height and twenty-two inches in the diameter of the trunk.

Toward the close of the seventeenth century the mulberry received a considerable degree of attention from English landowners and appeared in many private gardens. Celia Fiennes, who visited many great homes at that time, mentions in her diary that timber obtained from these trees was used at Lord Orford's in Newmarket: "The Hall is wanscoated with wall nut tree—the pannels and Rims round with mulberry tree, yt is a Lemon Coullour."

British governmental authorities make no distinction between timbers obtained from the two *Morus* species. They describe mulberrywood as possessing a reddish-yellow or medium brown heartwood when freshly cut, with prolonged exposure darkening to dull reddish-brown tones, not unlike those of tawny mahoganies, or even to bronzelike hues. Blackish streakings may occur in this portion of the wood. The sapwood is light yellow when freshly cut, taking on duller tones over a period of years. The wood is coarse and irregular in texture and grain, its general appearance resembling locustwood rather closely. Moderately broad to broad rays appear distinctly in radial surfaces of mulberrywood, contrasting to the finer rays of locust. Evelyn declared that the mulberry "suffers no kind of vermin to breed on it, whether standing or fell'd." The weight is recorded at 37-45 pounds per cubic foot.

Regular trunkwood of the mulberry tree is suitable for the production of seat furniture and cabinetwork, and until recent times this type of timber was available for such purposes in temperate regions of the Continent. All of the aged wood that I have seen, which has been positively identified as mulberry, has displayed a rich reddish-brown heartwood, very similar to, or slightly darker than that of yew. The deep yellowish-tan sapwood has been quite similar to that of yew in color, and darker than any average "lemon" tone, or the shades developed in the heartwood portions of citronwood, satinwood or a medium-colored applewood. The extent to which highly figured veneers of mulberrywood appear in English cabinetwork is still undecided.

A number of English bureaus and secretaries have appeared in elaborately marked veneers which have been designated by some authorities as mulberrywood, and by others as maplewood. These examples are usually characteristic of work performed by the London firm of "G. Coxed and T. Woster," and in several instances have retained original trade labels bearing the names of these two cabinetmakers. The firm is believed to have flourished from about 1690 to 1736, the year in which Woster is known to have died.

It may be considered quite singular that Evelyn thought so little of such a fine and richly figured material—if the veneers employed by Coxed and

87. A Regency inlaid mulberry knurl-wood and West Indian satinwood work-box Courtesy of Ginsburg & Levy, Inc., New York City.

86. A mulberrywood teapot, cup and saucer Collection of Mr. and Mrs. Edward H. Pinto, Oxhey Drive, Middlesex.

Woster were actually obtained from large mulberry trees in which these rare configurations had developed. In the 1706 edition of *Sylva* the diarist prefaced his remarks on the mulberry by saying: "It may possibly be wonder'd by some why we should insert this tree amongst our forest inhabitants; but we shall soon reconcile our industrious planter, when he comes to understand the incomparable benefit of it, and that for its timber, durableness, and use for the joyner and carpenter, and to make hoops, bows, wheels, and even ribs for small vessels, instead of oak, &c. though the fruit and the leaves had not the due value with us, which they deservedly enjoy in other places of the world."

Evelyn was inclined to enlarge upon the merits of elaborately figured timbers, and to associate their use with the "cabinet-maker" rather than the "joyner and carpenter." It would seem that such a diligent observer, well acquainted with the "knurs and nodosities . . . rarely diapered" that distinguished the finer cuttings of maple, would be as well informed about another equally handsome timber if it was currently available in London. Still, he offered no such information in regard to the mulberry tree, though he devoted more than ten pages to its fruit and leaves.

Selections of maple buttwood or gnarlwood employed in varied pieces of American furniture are often closely similar to the veneers appearing in Coxed and Woster examples. They are generally characterized by dark brown flamelike, crisped (rippled), or otherwise undulated markings, set off against light yellowish grounds, or grounds that take on this coloring with the application of a plain yellow or orange varnish. Somewhat darker markings emerge or are strongly emphasized by this same treatment. Such veneers are also notable for a more compact arrangement of the wood tissues than occurs in most burlwoods. That veneers of this type may have been introduced in England from the Continent is indicated by the fact that in a number of such cabinets they are inlaid with brass or other metal stringing lines—just as those of early Coxed and Woster pieces were inlaid with narrow pewter bandings.

It is evident that a pale yellow color, such as that providing the basic tone of all maple timbers, could only appear in long-matured heartwood veneers of mulberry as an extremely rare phenomenon. From all authoritative descriptions of the English wood it seems that Celia Fiennes' "Lemon Coullour" can indicate only very new and untoned material from young trees. Therefore, considering the number of bureaus and secretaries that were produced in the controversial veneers, it is difficult to believe that the material represented is in fact mulberrywood, rather than maple.

On the other hand, veneers displaying orange-toned backgrounds have been noticed in a few English pieces remembered as possibly executed in mulberrywood. Still, even this surmise cannot be sustained unless British authorities finally determine that mulberry stumps, or gnarled portions of the trunks, were formerly available in light ground colorings and in dimensions suitable for these large cabinet purposes. The only aid offered in this direction by Continental experts is concerned with color. M. Clouzot associates a "white and yellow" coloring with ordinary mulberrywood. This he mentions, along with spindle tree, wild stock and other rarities discovered in his researches as appearing among the inlaid decorations of French eighteenth century cabinetwork.

THE ILLUSTRATED EXAMPLES

A long search for specimens of antique furniture that might be definitely considered as executed in mulberrywood has not been too successful. The tone and normal graining of this wood is shown in the teapot, cup and saucer made of material **Fig. 86** obtained from a mulberry tree planted, prior to 1616, in William Shakespeare's garden at New Place, Stratford-on-Avon, and felled in 1756. It is fairly safe to assume that the sides and top surface of the workbox, *circa* 1815, are of mulberry knurl- **Fig. 87** wood. Although the dark brown markings are quite similar to those of either brownish or blackish effects appearing in maple knurlwood, the ground color is several shades deeper than the darkest yellowish-tan hue occurring in this other wood.

66. LABURNUM

The common laburnum, *Laburnum anagyroides* or *Cytisus laburnum* Linn., is indigenous to northern Italy, Germany, Switzerland, and to France where the wood is known as *bois d'aubour*, or *faux-ébénier*. It is a small tree growing to heights of about twenty feet, a size attained in the British Isles where the plant was introduced during the sixteenth century. The alpine laburnum, *L. alpinum*, is also native to Central Europe and France, with a variety of this species appearing in Scotland.

In its heartwood laburnum varies from a golden-brown to deeper brown colorings. These tones are

88. A George II inlaid laburnumwood card table Courtesy of the Victoria and Albert Museum, London.

89. A George III inlaid laburnumwood pembroke table Courtesy of Mallett & Son (Antiques) Ltd., London.

During the late seventeenth and eighteenth centuries, oyster pieces, obtained by cutting thin cross sections from stems or branches of laburnum trees, were utilized as parquetry veneers of British cabinetwork. Larger veneers and solid cuttings were employed in the British Isles throughout the eighteenth century, frequently in examples of the finest metropolitan character. At the beginning of the nineteenth century laburnumwood was employed in the manufacture of chairs and musical instruments, as well as for the more usual cabinet purposes, and it was then recorded as the most valuable timber growing in Scotland.

91. A George II laburnumwood center table Courtesy of Biggs of Maidenhead.

THE ILLUSTRATED EXAMPLES

Forms such as those displayed in the card table, *circa* 1725-1740, and the small center table of about the same date, came into vogue at the time when mahogany was introduced in the construction of British furniture. In the top sections of both these pieces strips of laburnum veneers are so adroitly matched and butted together that the joins are practically imperceptible. A minimum of solid material, well within the limits of this timber, was required in fashioning the round tapered legs. The center table is additionally remarkable as in this particular instance the veneers are entirely of laburnum heartwood.

The height of metropolitan elegance is reflected in the coffret on stand, *circa* 1760-1770. In the

Fig. 88
Fig. 91

Fig. 90

90. A George III inlaid laburnumwood coffret on stand Courtesy of Hotspur Ltd., London.

sometimes tinged with red or green, and they darken with long exposure. The narrow sapwood is of a whitish- or yellowish-tan hue. Laburnum is a hard and durable wood, with a medium-fine texture, and generally possesses a straight grain. Fine rays appear distinctly in radial sections. Plainsawed material displays growth-ring figures with deep-toned veins resulting from contrast between the bands of soft tissues and fibers. Weights vary from 50 to 57 pounds per cubic foot.

quality of the veneers employed for all showing surfaces, including those of the elaborately compartmented interior, and of the mounts, which are of silver, this piece rivals the dainty *tables de dame* that Parisian *ébénistes* occasionally produced in plumwood. During the Chippendale period it was customary to bevel chair and table legs according to the manner in which those of the pembroke table have been treated, whether or not they were braced by a cross stretcher. The chamfer thus formed was tapered out just beneath the seat frame or table frieze. While this procedure was at times retained in transitional designs, it gives some aid, in conjunction with the other features exhibited by the present table, in denoting a manufacture prior to about 1775, or within the period *circa* 1760-1775.

Fig. 89

67. ZEBRAWOOD

Zebrawood was formerly designated as a product of the species *Omphalobium lamberti* (of the family Connaraceae), which is now classified as *Connarius guianensis* in this large genus of tropical American shrubs and trees. The wood was first received in England during Sheraton's time, and was described in his *Cabinet Dictionary*, 1803, as "streaked with brown and white as the animal is, whence it has its name." Supplies were never plentiful, and by 1820 it was said that they were no longer obtainable in any quantity. A continued scarcity is no doubt responsible for some confusion in current descriptions of the wood, and in its botanical designation.

Later in the nineteenth century Laslett noted zebrawood as a product of *C. guianensis*, "an elegantly marked furniture and cabinet wood of British Honduras." Of present-day authorities, Titmus takes the most definite stand in regard to this particular timber among the many others which have come to be known by the same name: "Zebrawood is a little known cabinet wood of the Connaraceae family, being the product of a small tree, the *Connarus guianensis*. It is a lightweight hardwood that has good working and finishing qualities, though only moderately durable. It is chiefly noteworthy for its beautiful and distinctive figuring, consisting of a striping of dark reddish-brown on a creamy background."

The Cabinet-Maker's Assistant alludes to this tropical American timber in its description of calamander, where it is mentioned that "the figure is between that of rosewood and zebra-wood," i.e., zebrawood is more boldly and unevenly marked

92. A Regency inlaid zebrawood secretary Courtesy of the Victoria and Albert Museum, London.

than calamander. The same publication also stresses a darker coloring than mentioned by Sheraton, or by Titmus:

Zebra-wood, as its name implies, is striped in a manner resembling the skin of the zebra. On a ground of a pale buff colour are imposed, in straight lines [*sic!*], veins of a dark brown hue, clouded with black. This wood has a lively and rather gaudy appearance, but is destitute of lustre or transparency, and presents none of that agreeable variety of configuration which distinguishes rosewood. It has long been extensively used in the manufacture of drawing-room furniture, for which, in apartments that are imperfectly lighted, its smart and gairish colouring renders it peculiarly suitable....

Zebra-wood has become much less popular than it was a few years ago; the variableness of public taste will account for this to a considerable extent, but another cause is to be found in the fact, that many of the articles veneered with it have given way.... In cutting up zebra-wood, care should be taken to select the planks which have the finest figure for veneers. The plainer planks must be used in the solid for chair-wood, couch-scrolls, table-pillars and claws, and mouldings of fret panels for cabinets....

Zebra-wood, like rosewood, is indigenous to Brazil.... It is the produce of *Omphalobium lamberti*, and apparently also of a second species, for one of the trees yielding this wood is, in Portuguese, named *Burapinima*, and another, *Goncalo de para*; both of which are of considerable size, and frequently furnish planks, or hald logs, twenty-four inches in breadth. Of the amount imported into Britain during five years, we find, on an average, nearly 145 tons per annum entered for home consumption. The price current at present, in London, for wood of this kind, of fair sizes, sound, and of good figure, is about £10 per ton. Of course inferior pieces are to be had at a lower price, and selected planks are charged higher.

THE ILLUSTRATED EXAMPLE

English contributors to the classic revival, including Thomas Sheraton and Thomas Hope, repeated the chimerical projects of the late eighteenth century and introduced their own interpretations of the Egyptian style. This latter development is represented in the secretary-cabinet featuring pilasters in the form of terms with Egyptian-head capitals, a piece executed *circa* 1805, the year in which Thomas Chippendale III, grandson of the lesser known original member of this furniture-making family, submitted a bill for a library table with structural units of the same description. The two water-color paintings framed by the glazed doors of this cabinet are signed *J. Baynes*,* and dated *1808*.

Fig. 92

68. DAMSON

The damson, *Prunus institia*, is a cultivated form of the bullace which shares the same botanical designation today, though Linnaeus included this species in his classification of the plum, *P. domes-*

---

* J. Baynes, (b. 1766, d. 1837), of Kirkby Lonsdale, Westmorland, is recorded as a water-color painter who exhibited countryside views of England, North Wales, and Scotland—where he apparently carried out the Clyde scenes used to decorate the interior of this zebrawood cabinet.

tica. While damsonwood is similar to plumwood in structure, it varies in color and weight, being distinguished by a bright yellowish-red heartwood streaked with veins of lighter and darker red tones; and therefore approaching a faded tulipwood in effect more closely than it resembles plumwood. The weight is 32-33 pounds per cubic foot.

In France the plum and damson are both known as *l'prune*, though the latter may be distinguished as *l'prune de damas*. While damsonwood has not been positively identified in antique furniture of that country, it is quite possible that in their wide selections of inlay materials French *marqueteurs* would employ this wood as a substitute for the imported tulipwood.

69. ALMOND

The European almond, *Prunus amygdalus*, (*Amygdalus communis* Linn.), is one of the species of smaller trees and shrubs that supplied French marquetry workers with the materials of their trade. Almondwood, or *bois de amandier*, is not quite as fine in texture as plumwood, or damsonwood, but it is distinguished by a dull reddish-tan color, and veinings of a deeper tone, enabling it to serve in the same purposes as those more generally reserved for tulipwood in the finest metropolitan work. The weight is 43 pounds per cubic foot.

70. EUROPEAN CYPRESS
(A softwood)

The cypress, *Cupressus sempervirens* Linn., is said to have derived its name from the island of Cyprus, where it was found growing in great abundance. This tree grows to a height of about ninety feet in Mediterranean regions, and though presently known as the Italian or common cyprus it is also native to Asia Minor, and, since the seventeenth century, it has been successfully planted in England.

Varying in color from light yellowish-tan to reddish-tan hues, the wood is marked by the usual deep-toned veinings. It is harder than the better known American cypress, *Taxodium distichum*, close in the grain, easy to work, and noted for durability. The weight is given at 20 pounds per cubic foot, a surprising figure in comparison to that of 35 pounds per cubic foot associated with the softer American timber.

Cypress has been used for many centuries in producing the more sturdily built furniture of Italy,

Austria, South Germany and France. M. Ernest Dumonthier, Director of the French Garde Meuble, ascribed its use to some of the finest Parisian *ébénistes* of the eighteenth century, including Leleu, Schlichtig and Riesener. His ascriptions apply to the principal veneers of commodes and cabinets, which in general are nevertheless clearly indicative of tulipwood.

Various European and exotic woods were identified by this authority in his work *The Louis XVI Furniture*, 1922, including holly, lemonwood, satinwood, box, sycamore, maple, walnut, mahogany, rosewood, amaranth, violetwood and ebony. No reference was made to tulipwood in his work, although M. Guillaume Janneau, Administrator of the National Furniture Collection, and other French authorities have since identified *bois de rose* where M. Dumonthier claimed cypruswood.

At least M. Dumonthier has deviated from a rather general French custom of labeling all cabinet pieces as executed in *marqueterie, bois de placage, bois de couleur,* etc.—even where principal woods are amply displayed and inlaid only with simple panel bandings. Therefore his attributions of cypruswood indicate a more serious approach to the subject, and some attention may be given to his indicated belief that cypress was employed to a considerable extent in French cabinetwork of the eighteenth century.

In the genus *Cupressus* there is also the weeping cypress of China, *C. funebris*, a species yielding a light yellow wood with red veinings, which appears in old Chinese furniture. In addition, the Himalayan cypress, *C. torulosa*, produces an orange-tinted and darkly-veined brown wood that was used in Indian furniture, temple fittings and sculptures.

71. TULIPWOOD

Scientists offer different opinions in regard to the botanical designation of the Brazilian tulipwood tree, and indeed variations in timbers delivered to Europe during the eighteenth and early nineteenth centuries indicate that at least two different species, or subspecies of the genus *Dalbergia* are responsible for these supplies. It is generally conceded that tulipwood is obtained from an undetermined species of this genus, which includes the Brazilian violetwood, rosewood and palisander. Webster gives the species as possibly *Physocalymma scabberimum*, of the family Lythraceae. Record considers this to be incorrect, stating that tulipwood "is intermediate between specimens of *Dal-*

bergia and *Tipuana.*" In addition, a further variety of tulipwood was introduced from the East Indies at some unspecified time before the publication of *The Cabinet-Maker's Assistant*, wherein it is mentioned as "held in high esteem by French cabinetmakers."

The Brazilian timber, obtained from Bahia and Pernambuco, in the northeast coastal section of that country, has been shipped in billets of from two to seven inches in diameter—sizes that were standard during the early nineteenth century. It is usually of a creamy-tan or flesh-pink color, marked by more or less fine and parallel streaks of strawberry-pink or fuller rose tones—so that in effect the colorings of a yellow and red tulip blossom are reproduced in the usual tulipwood veneers. These colors are subject to considerable fading with long exposure, frequently bleaching out until the ground becomes almost white, and the linear markings are displayed in lighter, pinkish hues. The wood is very hard and dense, often splitting badly when sawed into veneers. Like rosewood obtained in this same region, Brazilian tulipwood possesses a roselike scent. The weight varies from 50 pounds to as much as 65 pounds per cubic foot.

While all of these properties are characteristic of the tulipwood (*bois de rose*) commonly used in

93. A Louis XV tulipwood and amaranth marquetry occasional table

94. A Louis XVI tulipwood parquetry
table de milieu

French furniture of the Louis XV and later style periods, and to a lesser extent in other Continental work, some examples produced in Europe, and particularly those executed in the British Isles around the close of the eighteenth century appear in veneers that are considerably darker in coloring and coarser in texture. Vessel lines are frequently displayed in "furry" effects that are less pronounced in the light-toned wood, but are quite distinct in other *Dalbergia* timbers, and are also characteristic of padauk and sabicu. As a result of these variations in color and texture it has been

thought that a number of Early Georgian examples were executed in tulipwood, whereas the material actually present was identifiable either as padauk or as sabicu.

The East Indian timber mentioned as "French Tulipwood" in *The Cabinet-Maker's Assistant* was obtained chiefly from Madras. It is described as "much straighter in the grain, and softer, than the Brazilian wood . . . the darker streaks present a more decided contrast to the ground color, which is orange-red. This wood is resinous, but has no odour." Although a very scant description, it seems possible that this timber is related to, or is of the same *Dalbergia* species as that found in Madagascar. *Vide* MADAGASCAR ROSEWOOD.

THE ILLUSTRATED EXAMPLES

Fully developed rococo designs did not appear in Parisian furniture until the middle of the eighteenth century. Projects of 1745, and in some instances those of 1750, still retained much of the baroque spirit. In fact a large proportion of so-called Régence furniture was actually produced between 1723 and 1750, while various compositions displaying Régence effects were evolved during the later decades of the century.

Transitional stages in the development of structural forms and ornament are portrayed by the tables selected to indicate three successive phases in the progression of Parisian designs. Representa-

95. A Louis XV tulipwood marquetry *table de milieu*

96. A Louis XVI tulipwood and amaranth parquetry *secrétaire à abattant*

97. A Regency inlaid tulipwood writing table Courtesy of Arthur S. Vernay, Inc., New York City.

tive of the period 1755-1765, the example with pierced three-quarter gallery features mother-of-pearl in its marquetry work, and bears the stamp *BVRB*, attributed to the Flemish *ébéniste* Boucher, a master in Paris from about 1736 to some undetermined time after 1765. Exhibiting later features in its fretted bandings and gilded bronze *chutes*, the small occasional table serves to illustrate a close approach to the Louis XVI mode in work executed *circa* 1765-1770. The table with straight legs and fitted writing drawer, dating from the early years of the Louis XVI period, *circa* 1775-1780, is stamped with the pontil mark of Etienne Levasseur, received as a Paris master in 1767.

A stamp of *Joseph* impressed on the carcase work of the *secrétaire à abattant* apparently refers to Gaspard-Joseph Baumhauer, son of the more illustrious Joseph, a master of the rococo school who died in 1772. In its severe form and ornamentation this piece recalls the drawings published by Jean-François Neuforge in 1768, which, obviously derived in part from prototypes of the Louis XIV period, nevertheless foreshadowed the more austere developments of 1775-1785. The darker framing veneers in the Louis XVI secretary are of amaranth. The treatment in general, including the use of *bronze doré* bosses and matching pilaster fillets, is remarkably similar to the work of Jean-François Leleu (M.E. 1764, d. 1807).

The writing table of *circa* 1800-1810 is modeled after a Sheraton design of 1792. In each lateral stepped plateau is a compartment which swings out when a catch is released by pushing a button centered in the ormolu patera immediately above it. A number of these tables have appeared in satinwood and mahogany, but the over-all use of tulipwood veneers in this instance is exceptional.

72. MADAGASCAR ROSEWOOD

During the late eighteenth and early nineteenth centuries supplies of two different timbers from the island of Madagascar were received in England and America. Records of the time may refer to "Madagascar" or "Madagascar Wood," which is more apt to be Madagascar ebony, a true black ebony of the genus *Diospyros*. The other timber from this island in the Indian Ocean is Madagascar rosewood, produced by an undetermined species of *Dalbergia*.

Madagascar rosewood is the product of a tall, slender tree yielding logs of about eight feet in length, and up to twelve or fourteen inches in diameter. It is lighter in coloring than the related East Indian rosewood, and considerably lighter than Brazilian rosewood, in fact the general appearance is such that Madagascar rosewood is often used as a substitute for tulipwood in the present market, and apparently it served the same purpose when first received in the West. The basic color varies from light to medium rose-pink hues, while the prominent veinings appear in much deeper and redder tones. It is a hard and strong wood of a character quite similar to that of tulipwood, and like this other timber it frequently splits when sawed into veneers. Sherwood records the weight as 55 pounds per cubic foot.

73. ACACIA

The Acacias are better known for their valuable gums and tanning extracts than as sources of commercial timbers. Of the many plants comprising the genus *Acacia*, a majority are native to Australia where they grow as shrubs, or as trees attaining extreme heights of over seventy-five feet, and butt diameters in excess of four feet. There they are also known as "wattles," a name adopted during early colonial times when their long pliable branches or split stems were used in making wattles or hurdles.

Varying in color from yellowish-red to deeper and browner tones, acaciawood is frequently marked by dark brown or blackish veins or streaks. The general appearance may be quite similar to that of rosewood, a resemblance noted by Laslett in connection with certain unspecified Australian timbers of the genus. The wood is commonly hard, tough, and difficult to work, except in turning, but capable of offering fairly smooth and lustrous surfaces. In texture it may vary from fine to coarse, while the grain may be straight, wavy, or interlocked. Weights range from 40 pounds to as much as 65 pounds per cubic foot.

THE ILLUSTRATED EXAMPLE

In its principal veneers the piece shown displayed a number of features varying from those of the more popularly used rosewoods. Therefore comparison was made with specimens of true acacia —a darker wood than the false acacia of Europe. Variations in color, texture and grain were then more perceptible and the identification was thus established. Rosewood veneers were employed for the corbelled stiles of this piece, offering a quiet contrast in relation to the rarer wood. At the top

98. A Regency inlaid acacia and rose-wood cabinet

of the stiles appears a standard *fleur-de-lis* pattern which was employed during the early decades of the nineteenth century.

74. STINKWOOD

Stinkwood or *stinkhout, Ocotea bullata,* is a South African timber that is seldom given the less inelegant name of Cape laurel. Laslett recorded the tree at twenty feet in height and eight inches in diameter, also noting the timber as not unlike walnut. In color, this wood varies from light yellow tones through medium shades of brown to much darker hues. It is moderately fine and uniform in texture, displaying either subdued or pronounced growth-ring figures. An interlocked grain produces handsome stripe figures in quartered surfaces. When the timber is worked an unpleasant odor is noticeable, but this is not perceptible in fully seasoned material. Weights range from 45 to 55 pounds per cubic foot.

East Indian craftsmen, and apparently specially trained natives, employed this wood in producing furniture used by Dutch residents of the Cape Colony. It appears in chairs, tables, commodes, secretaries, wardrobes and other pieces which often approximate Dutch designs of the late seventeenth, eighteenth and nineteenth centuries. The finer of these cabinet pieces were frequently enhanced with silver handles and escutcheons elaborately *repoussé* with baroque or rococo ornamentation.

75. WALNUT

The European walnut, *Juglans regia* Linn., is comprised of several varieties which may be designated as Persian, Turkish, Circassian, Italian, Spanish, French, Rhenish, and English walnut. As a scattered forest tree the walnut thrives in isolation, or in small groves intermixed with other growths, rather than in large stands. For many centuries this tree has been specially planted in selected positions, in fields connected with farmlands, in dooryards and along roadways.

During the sixteenth and seventeenth centuries the walnut was propagated in Italy, Germany, Switzerland, France and in the southern part of England. In mentioning the Continental trees, Evelyn wrote that "Burgundy abounds with them, where they stand in the midst of goodly wheatlands, at sixty, and an hundred foot distance; and it is so far from hurting the crop, that they look on them as a great preserver, by keeping the grounds warm; nor do the roots hinder the plow. Whenever they fell a tree (which is only the old and decayed) they always plant a young one near him; and in several places twixt Hanaw and Frankfort in Germany, no young farmer whatsoever is permitted to marry a wife, till he bring proof that he hath planted, and is a father of such a stated number of walnut-trees, as the law is inviolably observed to this day, for the extraordinary benefit which this tree affords the inhabitants.

"The Bergstras (which extends from Heidelberg to Darmstadt) is all planted with walnuts; for so by another ancient law, the borderers were obliged to nurse up, and take care of them; and that chiefly, for their ornament and shade; so as a man may ride for many miles about that countrey under a continued arbour, or close-walk; the traveller both refreshed with the fruit and the shade."

The European walnut attains a height of about one hundred feet, when the diameter of the trunk may be around four feet. Although the tree is especially common to the warmer southern portion of the Continent it grows well in more northerly situations. The Romans probably introduced this species in England, where it is not particularly abundant today, though formerly existing in large plantations. It does not follow that geographic locations alone will effect variances in walnut timbers, for those of distantly separated areas are frequently quite similar in appearance, while markedly contrasting properties may be developed in different trees growing within a single locality.

The wood varies in color from light, to very dark grayish-brown tones. It is generally medium-coarse but uniform in texture, and straight in the grain, with growth rings affecting its appearance according to their distinctness or imperceptibility. Stripe, roe, wavy and mottle figures are brought out by radial sawing. Particularly rich markings may occur in wood obtained from the centermost portion of certain logs, while the outer portion of the same heartwood will be of a much plainer description. The blackish pigment figure of this species may appear in varying degrees of prominence, or these depositions may be entirely absent. In the finest cuttings obtained from walnut butts, crotches and burls these pigmentations occur as irregular dark brown or black "smoky" patterns. Imperfections in veneers of this nature often entail replacements, which are noticeable as the patches found in many examples of old furniture. Rays are imperceptible, or faintly visible in the radial section of some timbers. Weights vary from 38 to 48 pounds per cubic foot.

The essential character of this medium-hard wood renders it highly satisfactory for chair- and cabinet-making, and also for fine carving. After thorough seasoning it is less affected than most other cabinet woods by variations in climatic conditions. The principal disadvantage as a structural material is a susceptibility to attack by larvae of the common furniture beetle. Seat furniture dating from the early or middle decades of the eighteenth century is often found with portions of

99. A Louis XV walnut marquetry commode

the members so entirely reticulated that only the outer polished surfaces remain, literally as shell sections.

Italian walnut may be light in color, rich in graining, and marked by elaborate pigmentations; or it may be exceptionally dark and quite plain. The darker wood appears in many examples of furniture produced during the Renaissance period and later. It is still common today, and preferred by Italian, French and American *truqueurs*, or fakers, who do not wish their handiwork to be revealed by the appearance of new, light-colored surfaces when their applied finishes are removed.

Until quite recently large quantities of Italian walnut were shipped from the east-coast port of Ancona. These supplies have become famous for their light brown color, wavy grain figuring and a high degree of blackish pigmentation. They have also contained a certain proportion of burlwood. The name of Ancona walnut, long associated with these and similar timbers, has been continued in use to the present time although it now has very little meaning, for the same name has been applied to various darkly streaked walnut timbers originating in the Mediterranean countries and in eastern Europe.

Perhaps the height of folly in the use of this name was reached in the dispersal of the Leverhulme collection, wherein one lot was described as a set of Queen Anne side chairs in Ancona walnut. The fact that very little old wood existed in the entire set, and that this material or the great amount of new wood could not possibly be assigned to an Italian origin, did not deter an expert brought here from England to catalogue the collection. This forced attribution included an early eighteenth-century date, lavished upon new and old wood without recognition of the extensive replacements.

Spanish, French and Rhenish walnut timbers are often closely similar in appearance and general character. This is true of plain material, and of that displaying the richer grain and pigment figures. The more elaborately marked of these timbers attained wide fame during the seventeenth and eighteenth centuries, particularly those obtained from the region of Grenoble, which were considered equal in all respects to the best Bolognese walnut.

Circassian walnut is also equal to the finest Italian wood, and may display more elaborate pigment figures than any timbers grown elsewhere in Europe. Markings of this description are developed in uncultivated trees of the province, but they are particularly characteristic of those planted in open farmlands. The best Circassian supplies are considered superior to those formerly shipped through Ancona, while various districts in the adjoining Caucasus region also produce timbers of superior quality. Circassian trees are generally felled by cutting the trunk very close to the ground, to obtain the greatest amount of richly figured

101. A George III carved walnut "commode"

100. A Danish inlaid and parcel-gilded yoke-front secretary
Courtesy of the Schleswig-Holsteinisches Landesmuseum, Kiel.

wood without uprooting the stump.

According to prevailing conditions of growth, English walnut displays the usual variations in color, texture, figure and weight. The wood is generally distinguished by gray or fawn tones, but in some instances it may be dark brown or even blackish, and marked by still darker streaks. It is fine to medium-coarse in texture, with vessel lines noticeable as dark hatchings. The grain is usually straight but at times somewhat wavy. Pronounced pigment markings and wavy grain figures occur in a relatively small proportion of timbers. Fine rays appear distinctly, or with moderate clarity in radial sections. The average weight is 41 pounds per cubic foot.

The American walnut, *Juglans nigra* Linn., is widely distributed in the eastern portion of this country, where, "for want of yew" it supplied the first English colonists with needed material for their bows. Forest timbers have been largely planted by squirrels burying walnuts at some distance from the spot where they have fallen. Dimensions of the American trees exceed those of European growths, reaching one hundred and fifty feet in height, and six to eight feet in the diameter of the trunk. Although the botanical name cannot be disassociated with an implication that the wood itself is black, it is the bark of the tree that commonly presents the blackest coloring found in this timber, aside from the darkest markings of stumpwood and burls.

In the sapwood American walnut is almost white. The color of the heartwood ranges from a light tan or grayish tan to a very dark brown. Occasionally dark, irregular pigment streaks are present, running more or less in the direction of the grain. The lightest tones and most attractive grain figures are developed in trees that have grown in open land. A certain proportion of forest trees yield the darkest wood, and these growths usually produce a straight-grained timber with no finer markings than those resulting from the distinct character of the growth rings.

American walnut is moderately hard, but more difficult to work than European walnut. The pores are irregular in size, gradually decreasing in each growing season, a fairly regular disposition resulting in a moderately coarse but smooth texture. They are visible as fine, dark vessel lines appearing in all longitudinal surfaces, in radial sections accompanied by equally fine rays displayed as light-toned flecks. Trees that have grown in open ground may produce timber marked by striped, waved or

102. An Early Georgian inlaid walnut chest-on-chest

mottled figures. Irregular growths, crooks, forks, stumps and burls yield other highly prized veneers. The weight is 38-39 pounds per cubic foot.

Virginia walnut is a darkly colored timber produced by a southern variety of *J. nigra*, the variety introduced in English arboriculture during the seventeenth century. During Evelyn's time it was recognized that this particular walnut came "from Virginia . . . where they have three or four sorts." The lavender-tinted, or darker purplish-brown color of the wood is generally recognized in England when it appears in old Irish or English furniture, and it is designated there by its correct name although "Virginia Walnut" is seldom if ever mentioned when the same wood appears in our own antique furniture.

According to Sheraton, the "Black Virginia Walnut" had been laid aside some forty or fifty years prior to his time. Some fifty years later the timber was returned to favor in England, though it was maintained that "In quality, it is decidedly inferior to that of European growth." This opinion does not, however, apply to American walnut as a whole—which is recognized as the finest and most valuable wood of American forests, and considered superior to European walnut in many respects. A decided advantage of Virginia walnut in foreign use is afforded by its ability to withstand the damaging effect of the furniture beetle, a characteristic that for many years has been considered a principal asset in the British Isles.

Following an Italian use of walnut as a principal cabinet wood, during the fifteenth century, a general popularity spread northward. Early in the sixteenth century the wood was adopted by craftsmen working in France, where it is known as *bois de noyer*, in Spain, in the Germanic states and the Netherlands. Later it was specified in regard to occasional examples of furniture executed for wealthy English landowners. The seven-

104. An Elizabethan carved and inlaid walnut buffet Courtesy of the Victoria and Albert Museum, London.

103. A Danish carved, parcel-gilded and inlaid walnut block-front secretary Courtesy of the National Historiske Museum, Frederiksberg.

During recent dissertations on the walnut used in Early American furniture of the southern states, it was concluded that the name *Virginia walnut,* which appears prominently in old inventories of the South, was formerly employed "to differentiate it from its close relatives, the hickories" (!). This is indeed a sorry conclusion. Apparently the basic properties of our native woods mean very little to those engaged in research of this type.

teenth century witnessed a more extensive use throughout all of Europe, fostered by the employment of veneers and the development of parquetry and marquetry techniques in lieu of intarsia work.

Continental timbers were requisitioned in England during the seventeenth century, and in the following decades it was still customary to send to France and Italy for the choicest wood. The scarcity of English walnut is indicated by Evelyn's statement, in 1706, that "were this timber in greater plenty amongst us, we should have far better utensils of all sorts for our houses, as chairs, stools, bedsteads, tables, wainscot, cabinets, &c. . . . What universal use the French make of the timber of this sole tree, for domestic affairs, may be seen in every room both of poor and rich."

A common use of walnut was never entirely abandoned on the Continent, although it was largely forsaken in metropolitan cabinetwork when mahogany came into vogue. This continuous popularity was interrupted at times when shortages occurred as a result of severe weather and storms. Major events of this nature took place during the winter of 1709, when many of the trees in central Europe were killed, and in the summer of 1788, when a wind and hailstorm "tore up by the roots, and destroyed all the trees from Valence to Lisle."

After Mahogany became the favorite material of English craftsmen, *circa* 1735-1745, they soon discontinued the production of walnut furniture.

105. A George II carved walnut card table Courtesy of Biggs of Maidenhead.

However, during the second half of the eighteenth century the latter still continued to be imported in Ireland, from the Continent and America, and to be used there either as a surface wood or for concealed structural purposes. *The Cabinet-Maker's Assistant* recorded a return vogue in English furniture of the Early Victorian period: "The introduction of mahogany and other exotic woods, it is true, effected a great change in the general taste, and caused walnut for a long period to be regarded only as a material for gunstocks. . . . Within the last few years another change has taken place, and walnut furniture has again become popular."

This publication draws attention to the high value set on walnut timbers then obtained from Italy and France, "particularly those of Auvergne," noting also that inferior parcels of walnut were delivered from Smyrna. It is of interest that no reference is made to Circassia as a source of timber at the time, and unlikely that "inferior" wood from

this province was shipped through Smyrna. Circassian walnut was apparently introduced a short time later, for this wood was especially favored in Early Victorian furniture retaining certain features of late Regency designs.

While America was colonized during the period in which walnut furniture was to be found in many European cities, few of the earlier colonists were acquainted with such developments, and circum-

106. A Philadelphia carved walnut highboy Courtesy of Ginsburg & Levy, Inc., New York City.

stances did not permit the expression of metropolitan tastes until after the turn of the seventeenth century. Therefore the "walnut period" in this country was comparatively brief, though the wood remained in use long after mahogany had became the preferred medium of colonial furniture.

The walnut that appears predominantly in Early American furniture is characterized by a light brown, or grayish-brown color, not too unlike the

107. A Philadelphia carved walnut highboy Courtesy of
Joe Kindig, Jr. & Son, York, Pennsylvania.

basic tones of English, French and certain other
Continental timbers. This variety of American walnut was employed in colonial and Early Federal
examples produced in New England, New York,
New Jersey and in many of the finest pieces executed in Pennsylvania.

Shop practices and the techniques of many individual craftsmen working in this country were by
no means restricted to the precepts observed in
England. Hence walnut was never entirely abandoned in this country and it may be found to a
limited extent in seat furniture and cabinetwork

executed during our extended Chippendale and
Hepplewhite periods. As a result of this continued
use of walnut here, certain Irish, Welsh, Scottish
and even Continental productions, partially or
entirely made of walnut, are sometimes accepted
as of American provenance—since it is at least recognized that the appearance of this wood precludes
a late eighteenth-century origin in England. The
fact that European walnut is thus accepted as
American walnut (except where American walnut
may have been returned here in manufactured
form), even where unfinished surfaces have been
examined, is indicative of the close similarity existing between European walnut and American
(light brown) walnut.

Virginia walnut was not highly valued by American craftsmen. According to this single study it
would appear that a limited use of the timber was
confined principally to craftsmen working in the
smaller towns situated below Philadelphia. The
lavender- or purple-tinted wood appears in seat
furniture and cabinetwork indicating these southerly origins. At times designs of such pieces are
clearly indicative of Irish influence, with only
minor details attesting an American provenance
in certain chair frames. Of the pieces observed, few
have possessed any particularly outstanding claims
to quality.

THE ILLUSTRATED EXAMPLES

Collecting interest now focused on fine examples suited to current decors is of course largely
concerned with French furniture of the quality
possessed by the small commode, *circa* 1765. **Fig. 99**

Numerous types of yoke-front and block-front
shapings were evolved in Danish and German furniture produced between 1730 and 1770, and in
rural areas these contours were continued until **Fig. 100**
1800 or later. Examples such as the yoke-front secretary with cock-beaded drawers are generally
ascribed to the first half of the century, at which
time the pediment with reversed scrolls was a
characteristic feature of such northern designs.
However, in this piece the inset quarter-round
colonettes of both sections, and the quadrantal
shaping of the writing lid indicate a production
of 1750 or thereabout. The block-front secretary **Fig. 103**
with lip-molded drawers, *circa* 1770, exhibits veneering skills commensurate with the carved and
gilded details. Apparently through intention, the
markings of each halved door panel form a remarkably accurate depiction of a steer's head.

Both of these secretaries are furnished with writing-lid supports, or lopers, of scant vertical depths —following a customary Continental technique. In British and American cabinetwork these supporting bars are generally of a vertical depth coinciding with that of the topmost long drawer or mock drawer. However, the Continental loper is found in some British writing pieces of the early eighteenth century, and the English loper was adopted by some craftsmen of the Continental districts in which English designs and working methods were followed.

Fig. 104 The design of the buffet or sideboard is indicative of work accomplished in England at the close of the sixteenth century, a time when walnut was highly prized but seldom available to British joiners. There is very little oak in the construction of this piece, but fortunately bog oak is displayed as the dark triangulate inlays of the cornice, and as the rhyming inlays of the intarsia border beneath the lowest shelf.

Fig. 111 Some years ago the editor of a New York magazine published the armchair from the Victoria and Albert Museum as a "Holland Armchair (c. 1720)." This is but one of numerous abortive attempts, based on assumed but unqualified authority in another field, to claim Dutch influence as a strong motivating force in the development of American furniture designs. In the majority of such speculations the examples singled out, to illustrate an unrecognized influence, have been of Irish origins, and they have been compared with American pieces strongly influenced by Irish designs.

Neither of Dutch provenance nor of Dutch design, the Victoria and Albert Museum chair was most definitely produced in the British Isles *circa* 1730-1750 or even slightly later, after mahogany was generally employed by the finest London craftsmen qualified to produce equally sophisticated designs.

The more knowledgeable English dealers in antique furniture generally label pieces such as those represented in the foregoing illustration as "Early Georgian," without any direct reference to the city or country of origin. Often with complete awareness of the provenance of these pieces they do not choose to contradict nonprofessional but prolific writers on the subject who unquestioningly accept them as English, and describe them as such to their readers, and to clients advised in purchases of antiques. This appears to be the logical course for dealers to follow until a more healthy situation arises from a thorough clarification of the subject, which is now in preparation. In the meantime, and without further laboring of the subject elsewhere

in the present work, it should at least be pointed out that these handsome and finely executed chairs are actually quite typical of the skills perfected by Irish chairmakers.

108. An Early American Virginia walnut chest-on-chest

Of approximately the same period as the preceding chair, the two card tables exhibit pronounced serpentine shapings that were followed by various modifications in the folding and stationary portions of the top. With the immediately ensuing developments the frieze might follow rounded or crosset- Fig. 10⁵ Fig. 11⁶

109. A New England inlaid walnut highboy

110. A George II carved and inlaid walnut card table Courtesy of Arthur S. Vernay, Inc., New York City.

ted oblong forms, or the front and sides of the supporting frame might be perfectly straight. In regard to the table with needlepoint playing surface, the wood surround and counter wells set within this applied panel are inlaid with a narrow billet-chair banding, and the frieze contains a pair of swing-out candle disks. The table with claw-and-ball feet may in all likelihood have been produced *en suite* with a number of chairs, for several of the latter frames have appeared, in walnut and burl walnut, with exactly matching front rails and legs, the veneered backs centering a type of splat in which median spurs are joined to the curved uprights.

Fig. 102 The chest-on-chest with brushing slide, *circa* 1735-1750, is similar to a number of examples found in Ireland, Wales, Scotland, and the western counties of England. The niched stellate inlay is a feature repeated in an interesting secretary with gilded eagle finial, owned by the Victoria and Al-

bert Museum, and also in other tallboys with cock-beaded, rather than lip-molded drawers.

A prolonged use of Walnut in the British Isles, long after mahogany had become firmly established as the principal medium of London furniture, is evidenced by the "commode" with double doors beneath a range of frieze drawers. The design and **Fig. 101** execution of this piece, and the condition in regard to aging, attest a date of *circa* 1765-1785. The handling of the stiles and bracket feet is markedly weak, and the top has been framed up in a manner which has resulted in damage to the initial surfacing and to a replacement veneering in mahogany. Simulated drawers surround the central swirl-figured panel of the doors, which open with fret-pierced stays, revealing interior drawers and sliding trays. That this commode was formerly contained in a famous Warwickshire collection is no indication that it was originally produced within that county or in England. All indications point to

Irish workmanship, certainly not of the highest order, and an Irish choice of material.

In America the cabinets and wardrobes favored by European householders were largely replaced by our highboys, which, with their companion lowboys continued to follow Queen Anne and Early Georgian lines well into the nineteenth century. The smooth cabriole leg, as featured in seat furniture dating from about 1730, soon replaced the turned supports of the earliest examples. A refined version of this leg is presented in the example with scrolled pediment and niched drawers, a production of *circa* 1740-1760. It will be seen that a similar recess with stellate inlay appears in the illustration of a British chest-on-chest with canted and fluted pilasters (102).

Of the two Philadelphia highboys, the example with ribbed Irish feet is according to all features of design the earlier by some ten or fifteen years. The one with greater enrichment is representative of work performed in that city between 1765 and 1780. Both pieces display an extravagant use of

Fig. 109

Fig. 107

Fig. 106

solid swirl-figured and mottled walnut. In the earlier example material with a number of sound knots (which are as solid and hard as the surrounding wood, and firmly fixed in position) has been utilized to gain rich feathered effects in solid crotchwood.

Determination of *Juglans nigra* as Virginia walnut will at least confirm an origin in southern Pennsylvania or New Jersey, or in a more southerly state. This particular evidence indicates a southerly origin in the instance of the chest-on-chest, *circa* 1760-1780.

Fig. 108

Since there is no other definite means of identifying Virginia walnut (even through microscopic examinations), except through its color, cutting the wood lightly at some inconspicuous point is the one resort when all surfaces of an object have toned to average walnut-brown tones. In some instances, however, it will be found that unexposed surfaces still retain some of the original lavender or purplish tones of the wood, when such verification will not be necessary.

76. SISSOO

The sissoo, *Dalbergia sissoo*, is an Indian timber that is closely related to the native blackwood or rosewood tree. An alternative name, shisham, may be applied to *D. latifolia* or its wood, which *The Cabinet-Maker's Assistant* described as a superior variety of sissoo. The tree reaches a height of eighty feet and an extreme diameter of about four feet. Its timber is lighter in color than East Indian rosewood, possessing a warm brown hue, with golden or dark brown streaks. A hard, firm and even texture permits a fine surface finish. The weight is 48 pounds per cubic foot.

This wood is especially noted for its strength, elasticity, durability, and lack of tendencies toward warping or splitting. As a result of these qualities, sissoo has been regarded for many centuries as one of the best, if not the finest cabinet wood of India. There it has been largely employed in the production of native furniture, and for other woodwork embellished with delicate and often highly intricate carved effects achieved through the particular nature of the wood.

111. A George II carved and inlaid walnut armchair
Courtesy of the Victoria and Albert Museum.

77. PRINCEWOOD or CANALETE

Princewood, better known today as canalete, is a product of the Spanish elm, *Cordia gerascanthus* Linn., a large tree endemic to the West Indies and Central America. Laslett employed the scientific name in mentioning this timber as somewhat important in Trinidad, noting also that in Dominica it was called rosewood—though the genus *Cordia* is not botanically related to the *Dalbergia* species. The first supplies of this wood to be received in England were designated as prince wood or princes wood, names appearing in records that date from the seventeenth century. Diameters of the round billets or logs obtained in modern commerce seldom exceed ten inches.

In its ground color, princewood is frequently of a medium walnut-brown tone, but deeper violet-tinted hues are also common. Rather delicate pigment lines, like light and dark charcoal markings, follow the general direction of the grain, but in a very irregular fashion, producing fairly light cloud-like patterns in tangential surfaces. Effects of this nature are far less pronounced than in the rosewoods. The timber is hard, strong, and elastic. It is dense in structure, with a very even texture, and no particular figure in the grain itself. The weight is about 53 pounds per cubic foot. In relation to the *king* of fine timbers, princewood—which in the present market is about equal to rosewood in value, —is purchased at less than half the price of kingwood (*vide* VIOLETWOOD).

At the time that princewood was first received in England it was employed in producing various articles of furniture destined for use by royalty, and by the nobility then engaged in lavish building operations. Records indicating this favor include those kept for the British royal household. "Princes wood" is the designation used in a seventeenth-century inventory of Ham House, Surrey, where some of these pieces still remain. In mentioning the wood as an inlay material of English craftsmen, Evelyn referred to it merely as a "red" wood, though further qualification might be expected from the verbose diarist had he been well acquainted with its reserved, rather than striking, particolored appearance.

78. COURBARIL

The courbaril is a tropical American locust tree, *Hymenaea courbaril*, valued for its timber and for the resin courbaril copal. Laslett noted the species as a large tree of Trinidad, "with close, hard, and very beautiful timber." The tree grows abundantly in the West Indies, but attains particularly gigantic growths in the Guianas and Brazil, where the trunk develops to a circumference of eighty-four feet at the ground and sixty feet where the butt becomes cylindrical. Alternative names are West Indian locust, South American locust, locust gum and courbaril plum.

In its heartwood courbaril varies from a light brick-red color, through richer and deeper orange-red tones to a dark brown. It is "diversified by streaks of a lighter and darker hue . . . [that] frequently expand into irregular flakes [*silver grain*], which deepen to nearly black, and by presenting a varying contrast with the lighter tints, enhance and beautify the general expression." Courbaril is a diffuse-porous wood with its larger vessels inducing a medium-coarse coarse texture. Growth rings are distinct to the unaided eye. Weights range from 55 to 70 pounds per cubic foot.

Clouzot believed that courbaril was "perhaps the same wood" as the ébène rouge of French eighteenth-century marquetry work, but these two woods are products of different species and the imported locust is noted for a flake figure which does not appear in the latter timber. *The Cabinet-Maker's Assistant*, quoted above, asserted that courbaril "has hitherto been comparatively little known to British cabinet-makers, but from the elegant and ornamental character of the articles of furniture, manufactured of this wood and shown by the Austrians in the Great Exhibition, it is probable that it will soon be introduced into general use in this country."

79. SAPANWOOD

Sapanwood, *Caesalpinia sappan* Linn., is more important as a soluble red dyewood than as a timber. Tropical American varieties of this genus yield logs that have been used for both purposes, but sapanwood was the first of the so-called Brazilwoods to be received in Europe—from the East Indies. The heartwood is characterized by a brilliant orange-red color, a very fine and uniform texture, and an exceptionally high luster. Rays are too fine to be seen except through magnification.

There was a limited use of sapanwood, as a veneer, in European furniture of the seventeenth and eighteenth centuries, while an extended use occurred in the Dutch colonial possessions of the East Indies. As the name *sapan* has been employed synonymously with *Brésil*, some French records are not clear, but it is likely that *C. echinata*, rather than *C. sappan*, is indicated in most instances; *vide* BRAZILWOOD.

80. LOGWOOD or CAMPECHE

Among the first Central American timbers to

arrive in Spanish, Portuguese and British ports during the sixteenth century, one was simply designated as logwood. Later this particular timber, of the many received in log form, was given the botanical name of *Haemotoxylon campechianum* Linn., referring to a dark coloring principal, haematoxylin, obtained from the heartwood for use in dyeing fabrics and leather, and to the port of Campeche whence the wood was shipped. Today logwood is alternatively known as campeche, campeachy, campeacheawood, and, in France where it was employed as a medium of eighteenth century marquetry work, as *bois de Campêche.*

At a candle auction[26] held in Salters Hall, London, in 1702, the prize cargoes of two ships contained logwood, Nicaraguawood, *brazilletto, mohogony* and *ebbone.* The first three are dyewoods, with *brazilletto* possibly indicating brazilette, another species of *Haemotoxylon* which yields the compound brazilin. "Nicaraguawood" and "Brazilette" are names that were often used synonymously, while either of these woods or logwood might be referred to as "Hypernic" (*vide* BRAZILWOOD).

Logwood is obtained from a medium-sized tree producing logs of small diameters. The bright-red heartwood is strong, brittle and rather difficult to work, but it takes a very smooth surface and a high polish. More precisely, the diffuse-porous character of the wood results in a coarse but even texture, an interlocked grain is present, growth rings are fairly distinct, and fine rays appear in the radial section. Titmus remarks a sweet, distinctive taste, and a violetlike scent. The weight ranges from 50 to 65 pounds per cubic foot.

81. BRAZILWOOD

In Gothic times *braise* referred to live or glowing coals. From the stem of this word *brazil* was derived and used in application to the fiery red brazilwood. A legendary island of the North Atlantic, appearing on a map of 1325, was believed to abound with this wood which had formerly been obtained from the East. The island was searched for by mariners hoping to locate an additional source of supply. Finally identified with the discoveries of the Portuguese in South America, the brilliantly colored wood gave its name to the country of Brazil. It was also taken as a type of hardness, whence the common dialectal English expression "as hard as brazil," and use by writers such as the English poet, Francis Quarles, 1592-1644, "Are my bones brazil, or my flesh of oak?"

Brazilwood is the product of various trees in the genus *Caesalpinia*, which appears in both hemispheres. Of those growing in tropical America, the most important is *C. echinata*, found in the region of Bahia, in Brazil. Laslett noted *C. brasiliensis* and *C. crista* as appearing in the Bahamas. These brazilwoods are known also as brasilete, *brésillet*, hypernic, Pernambuco wood, *bois du Brésil* and *bois de Pernambouc*. The wood of the two last named botanical species, and of one other, *C. vesicaria*, has been additionally classed as brasiletto, or, in both English and French spellings, *braziletto*.

Despite their importance in the past, little information is available concerning these different species and the properties of their woods. Casual descriptions of brazilwood mention a rich, bright red color, and a bright, metallic luster.

Laslett's use of braziletto, to indicate *C. crista* and *C. brasiliensis* of the Bahamas, gives some credence that brazaletto, appearing on a specimen wood block of about his time, may indicate a similar timber, rather than brazilette of the differing genus *Haemotoxylon* (*vide* LOGWOOD). The specimen, obtained with others representing a nineteenth-century collection of tropical American woods, may therefore bear describing here.

This brazaletto is of a rich orange-red color, lighter in hue than any mahogany of exceptional hardness and weight. It is of a diffuse-porous nature, with compact tissues forming a very fine and smooth surface texture. A walnutlike growth-ring figure is apparent in all four verticle faces, one showing a delicate band of cross mottles along a grain stripe, and all containing one or two small eyes. The wood is so hard that at each end of the block a band saw has "jumped," leaving evidences which were not satisfactorily removed when it was recently planed and varnished. In comparison with the other specimen blocks, representing woods of recorded weights, that of the particular wood, brazaletto, must be in the neighborhood of 55-65 pounds per cubic foot.

During the time that Portugal and Spain were powerful as trading nations, brazilwoods from tropical America were important items in shipments made to the Iberian Peninsula, eventually appearing elsewhere in Europe through direct trade and seizures of these nations' ships. However, despite the rich color and figure found in some material, brazilwood never became popular with furniture craftsmen, apparently because of its hardness, knottiness, and the difficulty in working it generally. Also, though sizes are not recorded, it is possible that these were of limited dimensions, restricting use of the wood to skills exercised by the turner and inlayer. Evelyn records the latter use, which was continued when *bois du brésil* was employed in France during the eighteenth century. In the production of turned, or partially turned work, brazilwood was fashioned into cups, bowls, and other table articles, and into handles for various utensils, all of which were more often made of European woods or of lignum vitae.

82. SNAKEWOOD

Snakewood, *Piratinera guianensis*, of the family Moraceae, is found in Central America and northern areas of South America. Among its alternative names, speckledwood and leopardwood are quite descriptive. Others include tortoiseshellwood, letterwood, *bois de lettres*, *bois de lettres de Chine*, *bois d'amourette moucheté*, and *bois lézard*. The tree is recorded at heights of over one hundred feet, but the commercially valuable heartwood portion of the trunk is generally obtained in diameters of only one to five and a half inches. A wide sapwood is removed before the small logs are shipped.

The coloring of the heartwood varies through deep reddish-tan shades to brighter, copper-tinted reddish hues, with much darker or blackish pigment spots appearing prominently in tangential surfaces. These markings may consist of fairly circular and closely spaced spottings, resembling the smaller patterns of leopard skins, or they may be more irregular and separated by larger areas of unfigured wood. They may also run together in banded formations, such as those associated with the markings on a mackerel's back. The wood is fine and uniform in texture, and straight in the grain, with minute rays appearing in radial sections. Weights range from 77 to 83 pounds per cubic foot.

It has been said that during the seventeenth, eighteenth, and early nineteenth centuries snakewood was employed as an inlay material of English furniture, that during part of this time it appeared in French marquetry work, and that it was used as a border veneer of Early American furniture. It is believed here that the wood may be considered a great rarity even in nineteenth-century use. *The Cabinet-Maker's Assistant*, 1853, mentions only a current utilization: "Its adaptation to cabinet-work being much restricted by the smallness of its size, it is principally used in veneering picture-frames and in turnery, and in the more expensive kinds of walking sticks."

83. RED ELS

Red els, *Cunonia capensis* Linn., is a South African species that takes the form of a small tree or shrub in which the bark has some importance as a source of tannin. Known to the Dutch as *rood els*, the wood was employed in producing furniture used by early settlers of their Cape Colony. It is distinguished by a cedarlike color, and indeed has been erroneously designated as red cedar though the plant is a hardwood species. Red els is hard, strong and close in the grain, but noted as light in weight. Further details are not available because of a restricted use during the past and a present lack of commercial interest in this wood.

84. SPANISH CEDAR

The Spanish Cedar, *Cedrela ororata* Linn., is native to tropical America and in particular to the West Indies, producing an important hardwood timber that is alternatively known as Havana cedar, West Indian cedar, bastard Barbados cedar, swamp cedar and cedrelas. This tree is not a cedar in the botanical sense, as it belongs to the mahogany family (Meliaceae), but the wood does possess a fragrant scent which is quite similar to that of the true cedars.

Supplies of Spanish cedar are available in dimensions up to forty feet in length and forty inches in width. The appearance and scent of the wood is well known to everyone who has handled a cigar box, from which the additional names of cigar-box cedar, and more properly cigar-box mahogany, have been derived. Its reddish mahogany color and moderately coarse, rather uneven texture are well known. The grain is generally straight, but occasionally irregular, though never so interlocked as in the more valuable mahoganies. Despite a rather brittle nature the wood is easily worked and quite satisfactory for drawer linings, trays and similar casing work. While these were the usual purposes in which the wood served British cabinetmakers of the Late Georgian period, Howard draws attention to mottle, curl, and crotch veneers of old cabinets and grandfather clocks, identified by him as Spanish Cedar. The weight is 27-34 pounds per cubic foot.

Prior to the middle of the eighteenth century "Spanish Cedar" was also received in the American colonies, and stocked by our leading cabinet shops. However, where "Cedar" or "Red Ceddar" are mentioned in old inventories of raw materials or home furnishings, or "Red-Sedar"—appearing as early as 1711, it is problematical whether these names apply to Spanish cedar or to the native red cedar, *Juniperus virginiana*, for both of these woods have been referred to as red cedars in the past.

Some of the earlier records identify cabinet pieces as made of *cedar or mahogany*. As these identifications were often made by local cabinetmakers, and since the cedar used for mothproofing storage spaces is hardly mistakable for a mahogany, it would appear that this form of identification was employed only where differences could not be established between Spanish cedar and the more valuable mahoganies.

Further confusion may result from former references to "Havanna or "Havannah," names which might apply to Cuban mahogany, but also to "Havannah Cedar," as Spanish Cedar was called. Thomas Sheraton's brief mention of "Havanna" or "Cuba Wood," which he believed to be so named solely "because Havanna is the chief town in the island of Cuba," is no more descriptive of an inferior Cuban mahogany than of Havana cedar: "A kind of mahogany somewhat harder than Honduras wood, but of no figure in the grain. It is inferior to Spanish wood . . . [and] . . . is pale, straight grained, and some of it only a bastard mahogany. It is generally used for chair wood, for which it does very well."

85. AFRICAN CHERRY

The first use of African cherry, *Mimusops heckelii*, as a furniture wood occurred in the colony founded by the Dutch at the Cape of Good Hope. There this native timber was formerly known as hard pear, another misnomer since the species is not related to either genera of these other fruitwoods. In modern commerce the wood is also called makore, or cherry mahogany—from a resemblance to true 'mahogany, and the appearance of dark growth lines in some material, recalling these markings of cherry.

Dimensions of the tree may reach one hundred and fifty feet in height and nine feet in diameter. The wood is frequently redder than mahogany, but it varies from a pinkish tan, through dull browns, to deep reddish- or purplish-brown tones, and at times it is marked by irregular veins of still darker hues. Usually it is harder, heavier and finer in texture than mahogany, and it takes a good, smooth surface. Straight-grained material has a rather plain appearance, but when the grain is interlocked, stripe and mottle figures occur, sometimes rivaling those of Cuban mahogany. The small

pores are generally filled with a bright gum, while equally fine rays may appear with some clarity in radial surfaces. The weight is 40-50 pounds per cubic foot.

86. BERMUDA CEDAR

Bermuda cedar, *Juniperus bermudiana* Linn., provided the colonists of this small island group with a principal material for the construction of their furniture. Accounts of the earliest visits to Bermuda mention a great abundance of cedar trees rising above the other endemic growths of evergreens and palms. The oldest specimens are recorded as attaining trunk diameters of about three feet, a measurement contrasting to the *very small size* of timbers later observed by Laslett.

This cedar has a reddish-brown mahoganylike color, a fine and uniform texture, and a grain that is normally straight, developing no pronounced figures. It is not a particularly ornamental wood, the plainness of longitudinal surfaces being relieved to only a moderate extent by vessel lines such as those seen in light-weight mahoganies, and occasionally by mild types of growth-ring figures. An aromatic scent is scarcely noticeable after very long exposure. In his brief mention of this species, Laslett indicated that the timber was "much lighter than that of Cuba," which he charted as an average weight of 27½ pounds. It would appear that this opinion is open to some contention, particularly in regard to former supplies which apparently were somewhat heavier, possibly weighing about 35 pounds per cubic foot.

Bermudian craftsmen employed the island cedar in constructing chairs, tables of various descriptions, chests, cabinets and other household necessities. More common uses extended to the production of numerous woodenwares that were exported during the seventeenth and eighteenth centuries, along with hats, baskets and cordage made from the leaves of the native palmetto.

Prohibition against the exportation of Bermudian timbers, mentioned here under SATINWOOD, was circumvented to some extent by embodying cedar planks in packing cases, to contain other products of lesser value. These planks were frequently used in widths up to thirty inches or more. The "chests" became so large that in 1679 a ruling was introduced which forbade total weights in excess of fifteen hundred pounds.

Contemporary notices indicate a strong approval of the Bermuda timber in England. In the proceedings of the Privy Council, dated 1658, a recommendation was made for "an order to purchase a parcel of cedar lately brought from the Bermudas, for the ceiling of Hampton Court." At a general court of the Somers (Bermuda) Islands Company, held in 1667, a member applied for permission to import three tons of Bermuda cedar "to pleasure friends for kindnesses received," a request which was granted. Despite the ban issued in 1632 to restrict the exportation of this timber, later in the century a Lady Clayton was also able to obtain Bermuda cedar to use as a wainscoting material in her London house.

87. NARRA

The Narra is the national tree of the Philippine Islands. Governmental authority there distinguishes two separate species, *Pterocarpus indicus* and *P. vidalianus*, each yielding both yellow and red wood. In some instances the inner core of the trunk is yellow, with the balance of the heartwood portion appearing in a reddish color. Timber that displays pronounced yellowish tones is designated as narra amarilla or narra blanca, and that which is definitely reddish in hue is classed as narra encarnada. The tree grows to an extreme height of only forty feet, but the trunk attains a diameter of more than six feet.

In their full range of color tones the narra woods vary from a pale yellowish cast, through salmon hues to a deep blood red. As a result of a very close relationship existing between these *Pterocarpus* species and *P. dalbergioides,* narra encarnada frequently approaches the general appearance of a faded padauk. The Philippine timber is hard and strong, with a medium-fine, uniform texture, and a fair luster. The grain is often straight, but at times it is crossed, wavy or interlocked, producing stripe figures and cross mottles. A faint cedarlike scent is characteristic. Weights range from comparatively light to comparatively heavy, averaging around 44 pounds per cubic foot.

Philippine furniture of the eighteenth and early nineteenth centuries indicates a native preference for the narra encarnada resembling a medium grade of mahogany. These productions might indicate Chinese, or even Japanese influence, but greater controls are noticeable in examples following Late Georgian and Victorian styles, frequently with Spanish modifications. This singular mixture of influences may be seen in the Philippine sideboard illustrated in the previous publication of this series, *A Directory of Antique Furniture.* For some unaccountable reason the intermixture of foreign ele-

ments, and no doubt a fairly close approximation of mahogany, resulted in the assignment of that piece to a Baltimore origin.

88. CORAL WOOD or BOIS DE CORAIL

Coral wood is a product of *Adenanthera pavonina* Linn., one of the two red sandalwood trees. This species is indigenous to Indian, Burma and the Andaman Islands, but has been naturalized in the West Indies where it is known as Barbados pride. The seeds of the tree, known as "Circassian seeds," are used in the Orient for making necklaces, armlets, etc.

Howard believes that supplies of *bois de corail* were probably received in France from Indo-China, or from French possessions in the West Indies. He describes the timber as maturing "to a bright golden red, or to a coral shade, so that it might easily be mistaken for a Spanish Mahogany. It possesses a very rich mahogany figure. . . . The pores are fairly large, and often surrounded by a ring of loose tissue. The medullary rays are straight, exceedingly fine, and very numerous. . . . Weight 56 pounds."

The same authority repeats a quotation which Holtzapffel (1852) took from Bergeron, an earlier botanist: "Coral Wood was named for its colour. When first cut it is yellow, but soon changes to a fine red or superb coral. It is hard and receives a fine polish . . . the *Bois de Corail* of the French is the wood of *Adenanthera pavonina*, which is . . . sometimes confounded with Red Sanders Wood." This confusion has continued into the present century. M. Clouzot connects the two different woods with the species yielding red sanderswood: "Santal rouge ou caliatous, bois de corail (*pterocarpus indicus*), rouge mêlé de jaune et de brun."

89. MAHOGANY

Mahogany was given the botanical name of *Swietenia* by Nicholas Joseph Jacquin, of Leyden, who in 1760 chose this means of honoring a fellow townsman and botanist, Baron Geraard Von Swieten. The name was subsequently changed to *Swietenia mahogani*, a designation which included all of the mahoganies, although differences in quality were recognized and understood to result from "the soil on which they have grown." Not until 1886 was mahogany from the American mainland distinguished as *Swietenia macrophylla*, thus distinguish-

112. A Queen Anne or Early Georgian inlaid mahogany center table Courtesy of Biggs of Maidenhead.

ing between Honduran timbers and those of the West Indian Islands, which continued to be designated as *S. mahogani*.

The mahogany tree attains an immense size, often one hundred and fifty feet in height and ten to twelve feet in the diameter of the bole, with the trunk bare of branches for about half the total height. These tropical American trees appear in scattered positions with two to an acre comprising a very good stand. Cutting operations of more than a century ago, in Honduras, entailed work by a gang of twenty to fifty men, working under a *captain*, and accompanied by a *huntsman* who would ascend one of the tallest trees to locate the positions of others. Selected timbers were cut by an *ax-man* working on a stage elevated from ten to fifteen feet above the ground, as the base of the trunk consisted of undesirable wood with immense buttressing roots.

Paths and any necessary bridges leading to a river were cleared and built by these gangs. After the trees had been felled and cut into logs, these sections were squared to lessen their weight, to facili-

tate their removal to a watercourse, and to insure the least possible amount of final shipping space. The dressed logs might weigh as much as fifteen tons in exceptional instances. They were first moved on trucks, with two drivers managing about seven pairs of oxen, and because of the intense heat this moving was done at night with the aid of torchlight.

At the riverside logs identified by the initials of the owner were thrown into its course to await the rise of a flood that could float them to the sea. When this occurred the logging gangs followed in flat-bottomed canoes, or *pitpans*, to facilitate their progress toward a boom formed at the mouth of the river. Here they were assembled, joined into rafts, floated to the wharf of the owner, and then dressed further for shipment. The greater part of a year would have elapsed before all of these operations were completed, with major phases of the undertaking dependent upon conditions set by seasonal changes.

The great favor extended to mahogany ever since

the middle of the eighteenth century is certainly well merited. Aside from its rich color tones and handsome figures, other important virtures have established it as an ideal cabinet wood. It is uniform in structure, with not too much tendency toward shrinking or swelling after proper seasoning. There is little likelihood of warping or splitting after manufacture, unless this wood is employed in conjunction with another of uncongenial nature. In addition, the heartwood (but not the sapwood) possesses a capacity for repelling attack by the larvae that have damaged or ruined so much furniture made of other woods.

The latter virtue was stressed by *The Cabinet-Maker's Assistant* a century after mahogany came into general use: "Mahogany, of all kinds, possesses another valuable property, namely durability; and in this respect it is equal, if not superior to, any other wood with which we are acquainted. Although, while in the tree, it is subject to the ravages of various insects, we have never seen nor heard of any instance, in which, after being manufactured, it has suffered from this cause. It cannot be reckoned an exception to this statement, that when planted in thin clamps or veneers on any of our home-grown hardwoods which fall speedily to decay, it should be perforated by the insects which destroy them; for we never find it attacked when detached from other woods."

Mahogany timbers of different geographic areas develop variations and *similarities* in their properties according to existing conditions regarding soil and climatic conditions. Thus, supplies formerly obtained in Trinidad have been noted as closely approximating those of Santo Domingo, while Nassau timbers of the past, and those recently cut in hilly sections of Central America, have also approached the Santo Domingan wood very closely.

113. A George III carved mahogany side chair Courtesy of Maple & Company Ltd., London.

These conditions are additionally responsible for the range of color tones appearing in mahogany timbers, the lightest of which possess yellowish or pinkish hues when freshly cut, while the darkest are distinguished by deep reddish- or purplish-brown shades. The erect axis of the tree tends toward the formation of a straight grain, but other factors influencing the structure of the wood produce a greater variety of grainings and figures than are found in any other genus.

Hardness and weight, affected by rapidity of growth, form a principal difference between Cuban and Honduran timbers. The harder and heavier Cuban wood is produced by trees that reach a diameter of twenty-four inches after a full century of growth, while Honduran trees that attain an equal diameter in seventy-five years yield wood that is softer and lighter in weight. Variations in weight now range from 28 to 48 pounds per cubic foot,

while timbers formerly obtained from giant slow-growing island trees might weigh considerably more than this higher figure.

In view of the variances and parallels that are found in mahogany timbers it is often difficult, if not impossible, to differentiate island and mainland species. According to American governmental authority, "if the place of origin is not known, it can not be determined from an examination of the wood."

West Indian mahogany, the first to be received in Europe, was obtained in Jamaica, Puerto Rico, Santo Domingo, Cuba, and in the smaller islands of this group extending from the Bahamas to Trinidad. Spain controlled the greatest amount of territory in which supplies were available. Aside from the great forest lands in Central America, South America and Mexico, this country owned part of

114. A George III parcel-gilded mahogany dressing mirror with label of John Elliott Courtesy of Ginsburg & Levy, Inc., New York City.

115. A George III inlaid mahogany sideboard

116. *(Right).* A George III mahogany basin stand Courtesy of M.
Comer of London Inc.

117. A George III inlaid mahogany
dwarf cabinet Courtesy of Arthur S.
Vernay, Inc., New York City.

118. A New England mahogany block-front secretary

119. A Philadelphia carved mahogany highboy Courtesy of Ginsburg & Levy, Inc., New York City.

120. A Goddard-Townsend carved mahogany lowboy Courtesy of Ginsburg & Levy, Inc., New York City.

Santo Domingo, exercising complete control over Cuba and Puerto Rico, some of the Bahamas, Trinidad, and other islands of the Lesser Antilles. In contrast, the English controlled Jamaica and a number of small islands, including Barbados, some of the Bahamas, and Bermuda. Jamaica was the center of British trade, and here supplies of mahogany from the Spanish islands were collected to be forwarded to England as "Jamaica Wood."

It is said that timbers originating in the Spanish possessions were designated as "Spanish Mahogany" to indicate their reception from non-British territories. Nevertheless, this name was applied more specifically to Santo Domingan mahogany, a significance held by *The Cabinet-Maker's Assistant*: "Spanish or St. Domingo mahogany is grown in the island of St. Domingo or Hayti"; while other West Indian timbers were frequently distinguished according to the different islands on which they were found.

As a class, West Indian mahoganies are darker in color, silkier in texture, closer in grain, harder and heavier than any others of their genus. They are often distinguished by whitish chalklike deposits in the pores, contrasting to the black specks or lines that may appear in the grain of Honduran timbers. Still, as Howard points out, these lighter-colored desposits also appear in some of the latter wood. It may be well to mention here that West Indian and all other true mahoganies display vessel lines that are visible as dots, short grooves or hatchings, or longer linear markings, according to whether the wood has been cut across the grain, at an angle, or with the grain. These minute openings and channels, and also the appearance of rays in quartered sections, help to distinguish true mahogany from various other woods used in substitutions.

Jamaican mahogany was apparently well known in England prior to large-scale importations from Puerto Rico and Santo Domingo. According to *The Cabinet-Maker's Assistant*: "Of the earliest importations, those from the island of Jamaica furnished a great proportion of the largest and most beautiful wood, of which we have seen several specimens in old furniture, marked by a wild irregular figuring and deep colouring, more resembling tortoise-shell than the mahogany in use at present. The trees nearest the sea were cut first, those near streams capable of floating them to the sea followed, until all the mahogany which would repay the cost of its transmission had been removed. We learn from missionary intelligence and books of travel, that many noble trees are yet standing in different parts of the island, which the difficulty of removal alone has preserved."

This mahogany was also the first to be noted in official British import records. It is listed, within the period covering Christmas, 1699, to Christmas, 1700, as "Jamaica, wood, mogogany, 36 pc £5." Although such timbers were received in the American states until long after the middle of the eighteenth century, a notice of 1748 declared that "The true Mahogany, which grows in Jamaica, is at present almost all cut down."

Jamaican trees were later selected, in conjunc-tion with others obtained in Honduras, for trans-planting in India—an event which took place in 1795. More than a century later two trees that had been growing in the Botanical Gardens of Calcutta were cut down and shipped to England, arriving there in the winter of 1922-3. Howard saw the trees and ascribed them to the species *S. mahogani*, describing their wood as equal in quality to that grown in Santo Domingo. While he had no certain information regarding the history of these trees, it would seem quite possible that the age of the larger, *about 129 years*, could link it with the transplant-ing mentioned above. If this is so the comparison would indicate the close resemblance between Jamaican timber, though grown on Indian soil, and that of Santo Domingo.

Santo Domingan, or Spanish mahogany, in the best timbers of the past was distinguished by a fine texture, a close grain, and a weight frequently in excess of 50 pounds per cubic foot. The poorer

121. A Dutch inlaid mahogany *grande secrétaire*

123. A Late Louis XVI acajou *Moucheté secré-taire à abattant*

122. A George III carved mahogany kettle-base secretary

selections were grayish and smutty in appearance, with an open grain accounting for a much lighter weight. Citywood, obtained from St. Domingo City, according to *The Cabinet-Maker's Assistant* was chiefly of "a rich generous hue, varying from gold colour to ruby; but its superiority over other importations consists principally in the transparency and beauty of figure by which it is distinguished. . . . From the celebrity attained by the exports from St. Domingo city it has become customary to carry the growths of other localities coastwise thither, and ship them for foreign markets under the common name. The cargoes thus collected are ordinarily of less value than those which consist of wood grown in districts more adjacent to the city; the latter is therefore usually distinguished by the name of the city."

The Santo Domingan timber was not, as sometimes believed, shipped to England principally during the earlier decades of the eighteenth century. Exportations amounted to 5,217 board feet in 1801, increasing to 55,005 feet in 1821, and to 7,525,461 in 1841. About one-sixth of these supplies were received in Great Britain, with almost half arriving in Liverpool where timber buyers from the United Kingdom, France, Germany and Russia made purchases. At this period logs of small sizes were shipped in increasing numbers, making the Santo Domingan wood available to cabinetmakers at moderate prices, not exceeding those paid for Honduras mahogany.

Laslett described the Santo Domingan timber of his time as very similar in quality to that of Cuba, "but of much smaller dimensions." Of their rich markings he especially mentioned that "near to the top of the stem, where it branches off, there is generally a rich and pretty feather or curl in it, which is much prized by cabinetmakers, especially when it is of sufficient length for table tops, or the fronts of drawers." These crotch or *curl* blocks had been particularly favored in England around the close of the eighteenth century, when many Santo Domingan trees were felled to obtain them. The balance of the tree trunks had then been left to decay, but they were retrieved more than a half century later. Despite some damage to their perimeters, many were found to retain a large proportion of sound wood of magnificent colour, texture and figure.

Cuban mahogany was known to former cabinetmakers as nearly equal to Spanish or Santo Do-

mingan mahogany in hardness, texture and general appearance. Still, this timber is usually paler in color, and lacks the "force of expression which distinguishes good Spanish wood," nor does it acquire "the same rich mellow appearance from lengthened exposure after being manufactured." Blemishes that occurred in some of the Cuban supplies, appearing in dark brown spots or streaks, forbade use of this affected wood as a surface material. Such timber was recommended, in 1853, for the sliding rails of telescopic tables, and "beds for veneering [as] Cuba wood will be found to offer a greater resistance, and to stand better than even Bay Mahogany."

In general, Cuban mahogany is of a light reddish color when freshly cut, rapidly turning to a richer and deeper tone, and it presents a lucent surface that is rather cold to the touch. It ranks next to Santo Domingan mahogany in heaviness, averaging around 40 pounds per cubic foot. Much of the Cuban timber displays handsome markings, including crotch, swirl, plum pudding, blister, stripe or roe figures, and various types of cross or splash mottles.

The Cabinet-Maker's Assistant also drew attention to the fact that "Wormholes [existing in the

124. An Early Federal inlaid mahogany sideboard

logs] are common to all kinds of mahogany, but they occur less frequently in Cuba wood than in the others . . . wood partially affected with this blemish, may be wrought up as a bed for veneering on, when only the veneered side is exposed, as in the tops of loo-tables; probably, also, in the veneered gables and ground-framing and panelling of the doors in rosewood cabinets, the inside of which are imitation grained."

Honduras mahogany, *S. macrophylla,* generally varies in color from pale reddish-tan to medium red-brown shades, although darker tones may occur. In contrast to the majority of West Indian mahoganies, which darken with exposure, the color of this Central American wood fades to golden, or even decidedly grayish tones. It is also characterized by a more open texture, a straighter grain, and a greater softness. Either black or white deposits may occur in the vessels, but the former phenomenon is a more constant feature of the

125. A George III carved mahogany secretary-cabinet Courtesy of Smith & Watson, Inc., New York City.

wood. The finest Honduran timbers of the past were at times more showy in their markings than those obtained in the West Indies, appearing with stripe, roe, mottle, fiddle-back, crotch and swirl figures. While the weight usually ranges between 29 and 38 pounds, some wood may weigh as much as 48 pounds per cubic foot.

Bay mahogany (as mentioned above) or *baywood* are terms used in reference to the softer and lighter timbers obtained on the tropical American mainland. It is said that when these timbers were first received in the British Isles they were not recognized as true mahogany, and therefore they were designated by the latter name. Sheraton declared that

the principal kind of mahogany in use amongst cabinet-makers . . . generally bears the name of Honduras mahogany, and sometimes Bay-wood, from the bay or arm of the sea which runs up to it.

The difference between Honduras and Spanish wood is easily perceived by judges, but not by others unskilled in wood. The marks of the former are, as to size, its length and width, which generally run much more than in the latter wood. We seldom import any much more than 2 feet 2 inches broad and 10 feet long, and generally not more than 21 or 22 inches broad. Honduras wood will frequently run 12 to 14 feet in length, and from 2 to 4 feet wide. In rare instances, there have been some 6 or 7 feet over.

The grain of Honduras wood is of a different quality from that of Cuba, which is close and hard, without black speckles, and of a rosy hue, and sometimes strongly figured; but Honduras wood is of an open nature, with black or grey spots, and frequently of a more flashy figure than Spanish. The best quality of Honduras wood is known by its being free from chalky and black speckles, and when the colour is inclined to a dark gold hue. The common sort of it looks brisk at a distance and of a lively pale red; but, on close inspection, is of an open and close grain, and of a spongy appearance.

An earlier recording raises a question regarding the origin of the name *bay*wood. English lumber operations on the American mainland were first concentrated in the Gulf of Mexico, at the point then known as Campechy *Bay.* Writing in 1757 Edward Burke declared that the Spanish had recently driven the English out of the *Bay,* and that their operations were then transferred to the *Gulf* of Honduras.

In his section devoted to Honduras mahogany, Laslett wrote that "This tree, which was formerly found in great abundance in the forests of Central

America, near to Belize, was first imported into England about 1724 or 1725. . . . The quality of the wood varies very much, according to the situation in which it is grown; that which is produced on a firm soil and in exposed places, and notably that grown in the northern district, being by far the best, while the timber produced on the low moist grounds is generally soft, spongy, and inferior."

Until about 1820 veneers cut from Honduran timbers "were nearly as much used as those cut from Spanish wood." After this time a poor quality of timber was exported, suitable for use by cabinetmakers "chiefly for veneering upon, for inferior parts, or for articles of solid furniture."

African mahogany was not received in Europe until about 1830, at which time "a considerable quantity of it was bought up and manufactured into furniture." This date also marks Jussieu's broad designation of the African timber as *Khaya senegalensis*, in which he substituted the native name for the mahogany tree, *Khaya*, for *Swietenia* in a previous designation made by Desrousseaux in 1789. Different species were eventually recognized, of which the most important is *Khaya ivorensis*, obtained principally from the Ivory and Gold Coasts, and from Nigeria.

The African tree, including its foliage, flowers and fruit, is closely similar to the western species. Timbers are distributed through native districts on an average of only a single tree to six or eight acres of land. Heights of one hundred and fifty feet are reached, and diameters of eight to ten feet in the trunk, which is often bare of branches for a hundred feet. Average dimensions of present-day logs extend to thirty-six feet in length and five feet in diameter.

When freshly cut the African wood is a bright pinkish or salmon color, soon changing to a light or medium reddish-tan hue, sometimes with a slight purplish cast. It is further distinguished by slightly larger pores, and a milder texture than other mahoganies. Stripe and roe figures appear with some frequency, often more pronouncedly than in Honduran timbers. More extravagant markings may also occur, including mottle, raindrop, blister, crotch and swirl figures. Single logs, which are often more than ten tons in weight, have marketed for as much as twelve thousand dollars when the choicest figures have been anticipated. Weights range from 25 to 48 pounds, averaging around 35 pounds per cubic foot.

Spain was the first nation to export mahogany

from the West Indies, and the first to employ the timber in fine woodwork. The earliest known use of this wood in Europe is recorded as taking place between 1563 and 1584, when the Escorial was built by Philip of Spain and its great library furnished with choir stalls, desks, cases and other stationary woodwork of mahogany. (A similar use in England occurred in 1680, with the building of Nottingham Castle.) Spanish exportations to other European countries are said to date from around 1720, a time also set as marking Holland's entry into this trade. The new material did not come into general favor on the Continent, however, until the middle of the century, although it does appear to a limited extent in Dutch furniture of a decade or so earlier.

Suggested dates for the first appearance of mahogany in English furniture range from the Elizabethan period to 1724—the latest year associated with the famous candle box of Dr. Gibbons.[27] Accounts of purchases made in this year for the

126. A George III carved and inlaid peacock-feather mahogany secretary Courtesy of Needham's Antiques, Inc., New York City.

127. A George III carved mahogany "French" armchair

128. A George III carved mahogany side chair

129. A Philadelphia carved mahogany side chair

British royal household provide a more substantial documentation, proving that the wood was then employed in the making of "2 Mohogony Desart tables, 2 Mohogony Clothes Chests, and A Mohogony Supping Table."

While some few pieces of English furniture were produced in mahogany around 1725, a moderate acceptance of the new wood, even by London craftsmen, did not occur until about 1730-1735. Examples displaying features of design that are associated with the Queen Anne and George I periods have frequently been assigned to dates of *circa* 1710 to 1720, despite the fact that unstudied details point to later origins. Such pieces are usually typical of work performed where London designs were tardily received and sometimes retained for lengthy periods of time, particularly in Ireland where basic forms were modified or enlarged upon in catering to local tastes.

It is also believed that when relatively heavy, and dark or darkly stained mahogany appears as a principal medium of construction, such material indicates the very earliest of English importations. This type of wood, or treated wood, was by no means confined to English use, but appears in Irish and Welsh furniture made during the middle decades of the century. Quite a number of examples that have been published to illustrate the earliest use of mahogany in England actually indicate so-called "provincial" work carried out in other cities

long after the wood had become a permanent feature of London designs.

At first relatively plain grades of mahogany were received in the British Isles. In fact a great amount of furniture continued to be executed in the plainer timbers as long as Chippendale designs remained in vogue. Still, some imports provided rich swirl-grained wood that was employed either in solidly constructed pieces or those partially surfaced with veneers. As greater attention was given to the more elaborately marked timbers these were selected and cut to display various stripe and mottle effects, blister and plum-pudding figures. Full crotch figures were not featured until the so-called Hepplewhite designs were evolved.

The first supplies of African mahogany to be received in England (*circa* 1830) proved unsatisfactory after their manufacture into furniture. According to *The Cabinet-Maker's Assistant* the freshly cut wood had a "fleshy colour, which, on continued exposure, deepened into a dirty purple, of a most disagreeable appearance. Nor was it only in colour inferior to genuine mahogany; it altered more in drying, did not hold glue so well, and, consequently [these qualities] served to drive it out of the market; and it has now fallen into entire disuse."

American traditions indicate some use of mahogany in this country during the turn of the seventeenth century. Nevertheless contemporary records provide the only satisfactory documentation, a form of evidence best presented by William Macpherson Horner, Jr. Through the researches of this author we now know that just prior to 1708 the stock of Charles Plumley, cabinetmaker of Philadelphia, contained "2 Mohogany Plank . . . 36½ foot @ 16d.," and "3 Inch Board Ditto . . . 48 foot @ 6d."; also that two or three years later William Till, a joiner of the same city, owned "Mahogany Board . . . 209 foot @ £5 4s.," and "Mahogany Scantling . . . 42 foot @ 17s. 6p."

In regard to privately owned mahogany furniture Horner cites "A Mohogany Chest of drawers & Table," and "A Mohogany Bedstead," purchased by an Elizabeth Coates in 1721 for "£9 16s.," and "11s.," respectively. He also points out that in the large Philadelphia house occupied by Johnathan Dickinson, a trader in West Indian mahogany, prior to 1722 the principal rooms were "furnished predominantly with mahogany pieces."

These reports might tend to indicate that mahogany came into wide public favor in this country before, or at least at the same time that it attained a considerable degree of popularity in England. Yet this is not the case. Walnut remained in fashion here to compete with mahogany during the middle

of the eighteenth century. While many craftsmen then owned good stocks of both mahogany and walnut, others still concentrated on walnut. Horner shows that in 1748 another Philadelphia joiner, Thomas Gant, owned hundreds of feet of walnut but only "2 Boards of Provedence Wood," which might be interpreted as Bahama mahogany, and "64 feet of Spanish Cedar."

During the middle of the century some colonial craftsmen evinced a partiality for the best mahogany displaying rich swirl figures. Such timbers were often utilized in the solid for cabinetwork and, in rare instances, for spooned vasiform splats of chair backs—a particularly lavish expenditure of valuable wood.

Plainly figured and swirl-grained mahogany continued in use here as long as yoke-front and block-front furniture was made, which is to say until the close of the century. The richest of these timbers were at times additionally enhanced by lively mottle figures. With the introduction of designs inspired by Thomas Shearer and George Hepplewhite more elaborate "flashy" figures, in veneers, came into vogue. Panel surfaces then exhibited the characteristic stripe, mottle and brilliant swirl effects, but the repertory of mahogany figures was never

130. A Louis XV acajou marquetry *table à écrire*

131. An Early Federal inlaid mahogany card table

132. A George III mahogany spider-leg table

133. A Philadelphia carved mahogany side chair Courtesy of Ginsburg & Levy, Inc., New York City.

134. A George III inlaid mahogany chest of drawers Courtesy of Needham's Antiques, Inc., New York City.

so extensive in this country as in the British Isles. Though full crotch figures are occasionally found in earlier examples of American furniture they were not featured here until the time of Duncan Phyfe, the most notable exponent of fine quality mahogany in the history of furniture making.

When mahogany was introduced in French *ébénesterie*, during the middle of the eighteenth century, it was given the name of *acajou*. Yet this application of the word had been used in England long before that time, when, in 1622, John Evelyn referred to the then little-known wood as "Acajou." This name is derived from the Portuguese *acaju* or *caju*, and is of Tupian origin, apparently through the northern culture of these tribes; it is also applied to the Spanish cedar, to the cashew tree (yielding *noix d'acajou*), and the marinheiro.

At the time of its earliest use in French cabinet-ware *acajou* was utilized principally in veneers that were laid so as to achieve striped effects through color variances in the normal graining. Later the wood was cut to display the stripe and roe figures produced when the grain is interlocked; veneers of this type being designated as *acajou satiné*. In contrast to other preferences the plainer mahogany came into fashion during the late eighteenth century, employed either in the solid or as veneers, and generally finished to display a deep but rich, even coloring. During this time the later Louis XVI, and Directoire designs were often executed in plum-pudding mahogany, *acajou moucheté*. Then, also, French joiners first turned their skills to the fashioning of seat furniture in mahogany, a use of the wood which was withheld as long as cabriole forms were featured in their work.

Pierced splats were generally featured in British chairmaking at the time that the paw foot came into vogue, *circa* 1735. After this time mahogany frames were also carved with foliage motifs. As a conventional London practice, laterally projecting knee brackets of cabriole legs were outlined with leaf scrolls which curved upward, rather than in the reverse direction.

THE ILLUSTRATED EXAMPLES

Fig. 112 According to standards set by the majority of English experts the small center table representing a very early design in mahogany might be dated *circa* 1700-1710, while other opinions might extend this date to *circa* 1715 or somewhat later. In any case the grace of line expressed in the continuous frieze and angular cabriole legs is typical of the Queen Anne period. Mr. F. R. Stamp, a specialist in such rare examples, states that when this piece was acquired from a very old collection it was carefully cleaned and put in good condition, and not until this work had been carried out was it discovered that the top was veneered in mahogany, rather than walnut, and the solid frame found to be of the same wood.

Fig. 113 Typical of work performed in western areas of these islands where Dublin, rather than London, was the principal center of the arts, this paw-foot chair features an interlaced splat of a type which was varied to conform with models incorporating plain cabriole legs, those terminating in claw-and-ball feet, and "French" legs with whorl terminals. After the introduction of straight legs the same splat was combined with either plain or elaborately fretted underframes. The shoe (at the base of the splat) is carved with a classic molding, and the angle bracing bars of the seat frame are of beech. These bars are secured by cut plug nails, a technique observed in other work of this general area. This chair and five others remaining with it are stamped with set numbers, the highest of which is *XIV*—proving that they were originally included in a much larger suite which must have contained the usual pair of armchairs.

A number of matching chairs, also with beech rails and open bar braces, and quite possibly in part at least from the same set, have found their way into collections of American furniture. (An exactly matching armchair in the Winterthur Collection has been claimed as one of the finest examples ever made in New England, its typically Irish whorled arm terminals being considered as probably unique!) The rear legs of the illustrated chair are finished with the type of squared club foot that was long favored in Ireland, and which appears on a number of imported wing chairs that have been described as of Philadelphia origins.

Recent tests have indicated that the physical and mechanical properties of mahogany do not quite equal those of walnut in strength, rigidity and shock resisting ability. Possibly through a greater

135. A Massachusetts inlaid mahogany and West Indian satinwood writing cabinet Courtesy of Ginsburg & Levy, Inc., New York City.

reliance on the structural merits of earlier supplies, but also due to contemporary developments in design, British furniture of 1755-1770 was produced with thinner and more tortuous elements than had been attempted in the usual productions of the walnut period and those executed in mahogany prior to this time.

Slender turnings such as those employed as clustered colonettes in mahogany tea tables and urn stands, and as individual members of simpler tables and stands, have proved entirely satisfactory in these uses. The latter form of support was adopted in spider leg tables of the Chippendale period, which in various stationary and folding structures became widely popular at that time. A rather unusual version of a spider-leg drop-leaf table, *circa* 1760-1770, the example with book ledge and swing-out candle disks is intended to fold and stand against a wall when not in use. The basin stand with spindle supports, of about the same date, is illustrative of many similar pieces constructed without the convenience of a mirror, which in this instance can be adjusted at various angles and heights.

An advertising label used from 1762 to 1767 by the Philadelphia tradesman, John Elliott, is affixed to the mahogany dressing mirror, thus estab-

Fig. 132

Fig. 116

Fig. 114

136. A George III carved mahogany
side chair

lishing the approximate date of manufacture. Although this label clearly states in English and German that Elliott "imports and sells all Sorts of English Looking-glasses," it is nevertheless generally looked upon here as a "maker's label." With such evidence nonprofessional experts on American furniture have attributed all sorts of disparate frames and their glasses to the hand of this busy storekeeper. While the pine appearing in Elliott's imported wall mirrors has been permitted to serve as equal evidence, it is unlikely that the hardiest of Elliott enthusiasts would fail to recognize the difference between American oak and the European variety employed for the drawer linings of the present piece.

In regard to the secretary with kettle-form base, this type of *bombé* shaping was embodied in some of the finest walnut and lacquer cabinets executed between 1730 and 1750 in Saxony, where other examples, such as *torchères*, tables and wall mirrors produced during the earlier years of the century, were frequently contrived in designs that were paralleled in English compositions of slightly later dates. From 1740 to 1770 the kettle-form base became popular elsewhere in Germany and in Holland, more often than not interrupted by horizontal breaks and vertical chamfers, and during the same period these contours were introduced in Denmark and Sweden.

Fig. 122

London projects of 1700-1750 not only followed structural forms that had previously appeared in Saxony, but in some instances they also repeated ornamental details that had been evolved in that state, especially in the capital city of Dresden. It is therefore apparent that designs and probably working skills were transmitted from the one furniture center to the other, skills which in many instances were based in part on Parisian trainings. It is also likely that similarly trained artisans were employed by William Vile, *fl.* 1750-1767, known to have supplied Queen Charlotte with an "exceedingly ffine" kettle-base secretary in 1762, and possibly by his partner, John Cobb, *fl.* 1750-1778, equally famous for a number of elaborate marquetry commodes in the French taste.

In Queen Charlotte's secretary the sides of the long drawers follow the shaping of the base, as in the piece illustrated here, a method of construction superior to that more generally followed in European examples of this description wherein these lower drawers are arranged with the sides in vertical alignments. In an important slant-front secretary ascribed to Vile, the customary English use of lopers to support the writing lid has been forsaken in favor of two narrow metal quadrant stays of a type more characteristic of Saxon workmanship than that of any other Continental area.

Although kettle-base designs were adopted in England after mahogany furniture had become fashionable there, a good many British productions have appeared with walnut surfacing veneers. These important projects, and some of those executed in mahogany, are frequently ascribed to Dutch origins. However, no expert responsible for such attributions has ever seen a comparable Dutch example. Furthermore, while many of these pieces are finely constructed with a plentiful use of oak as a carcasing material, it will generally be found that pine has been employed for the drawer partitions or elsewhere in the framing work—further proof that such pieces were not produced in Holland.

Fig. 122 The present example was apparently made several years later than the William Vile secretary of 1762, and in Ireland rather than England. In general design it displays a strong relationship to the kettle-base secretaries and chests of drawers produced in Massachusetts after 1770, at which time similar rococo finial cartouches became regular features of Philadelphia highboys. While decided contrasts to English techniques are not too noticeably present in the overall design, the writing interior has been treated in a characteristically Irish manner.

Numerous designs of furniture in the Chinese taste were included in the drawings of Thomas Chippendale, Thomas Johnson, William Ince, Thomas Mayhew, and Robert Manwaring, as published in London from 1754 to 1765. In addition to these conceptions of the popular mode, Sir William Chambers' *Designs of Chinese Buildings* was available to craftsmen intrigued by the decorative possibilities of the pagoda roof and open-fretwork patterns. The ease in which this style was assimilated, and these proffered schemes were adapted to suit individual tastes, resulted in some highly original work—such as that represented in the small **Fig. 125** break-front cabinet with pagoda crest and open-fretted doors, *circa* 1760-1780.

In Chippendale's designs of 1755-1762 his plates devoted to various types of cabinetwork are plainly hatched with horizontal lines, indicating that he was then better acquainted with the plainer grades of mahogany than with the more highly figured material employed in his own shops from about 1765 to the time of his death in 1779. On the other hand, Hepplewhite's (and Sheraton's) drawings are shaded to give the effects of rich mottled, striped, swirl- and crotch-figured veneers.

Bedsteads were always important, and usually expensive items in the furnishing of fine British

137. A George III inlaid mahogany tilting-top table Courtesy of Needham's Antiques, Inc., New York City.

homes. Up until about 1745 it was still fashionable to cover the turned posts, testers and other parts of these structures with the newest types of silks, embroideries, damasks and other fabrics that were currently available. If, as it has been thought, common articles of household use had been largely produced in mahogany from 1710 to 1735, why then had the rich appearance and other merits of this new wood been overlooked in the making of tall-post bedsteads, even in the homes of the nobility?

Once the decorative and structural merits of mahogany were widely known, including its natural resistance to attack by the furniture beetle, it was adopted as a standard material in production of the tester bedstead. In this capacity the wood was first used only for the showing front posts—apparently at a date not earlier than 1735. During the middle of the century the tester might also be fashioned in mahogany, while the rear posts and backboard generally continued to be made in a local wood covered with, or concealed by a fabric or curtains. These exposed parts were made from

138. A George III inlaid mahogany secretary-bookcase Courtesy
of Arthur S. Vernay, Inc., New York City.

the plainer cuttings of West Indian timbers, which are of course impossible to determine specifically.

From about 1770 to 1780 the techniques of British furniture makers, including those of Chippendale himself, were affected to some extent by the work of Robert Adam and his entourage of foreign artisans. However, the various pattern books issued in London from 1788 to well after the close of the century had more far-reaching effects in the British Isles, in various areas of the Continent, and in the American states. Of these publications *The Cabi-*

net-Makers' Book of Prices received the most continuous interest as its issues appeared intermittently from 1788 to the middle of the nineteenth century, illustrating models of earlier inspiration along with those indicating the latest developments.

Hepplewhite's designs produced the same varying degrees of interest as those of Chippendale. Certain of his offerings were highly acceptable in London, while others had greater appeal to craftsmen, especially chairmakers, working in such towns as Copenhagen, Hamburg, Berlin, Dublin, Salem, Baltimore, etc. His renditions of the French cabriole leg are entirely lacking in sophistication and grace, suggesting a current lack of acquaintance, at least on his part, with the elegant designs of "French" chairs previously executed under the supervision of Robert Adam.

All of the chairs shown here are representative of designs evolved between 1775 and 1790. While Hepplewhite showed several chairs in which the front legs match those of the example with oval back, this type of leg is merely a refinement of a slightly earlier and heavier form. The open shield back, as featured by Sheraton as well as Hepplewhite, is considered to have been popular in London a decade or so prior to 1788. In fact Hepplewhite's much copied shield-back design of 1787, in which an oval splat centers a pointed urn and triple-leaf cluster, is, according to a recent museum publication, now attributed to a date of *circa* 1775.

In the more highly figured wood of the swell-front sideboard, *circa* 1790, the facings of the two deep drawers are known as *blind-crotch* veneers. This term is applied to swirl-figured veneers cut from a log in which the full crotch figure with central feathering has not materialized. Full crotch figures are presented in the oblong and oval veneer panels of the open-shelf serving piece, *circa* 1795. Here the unusually light color of these veneers gives an effect almost like that of West Indian satinwood. The surrounding veneers are in plain-cut mahogany of an average coloring.

The tilting top of the small pillar, or breakfast table, *circa* 1795, is veneered in flat-cut mahogany of unusually fine and lustrous markings. A single join, even though off center, would be of little consequence to the maker of such a piece as long as he was able to obtain such a satisfactory result with the swirl-figured and brilliantly mottled wood. An extraordinary use of swirl-figured veneers—laid in the reverse direction to that followed almost without exception during and after the eighteenth century—is exhibited in the bow-front chest of drawers, *circa* 1800-1810. Here the flush top with shallow inlaid frieze is typical of a treatment followed in Scotland.

Selections of mahogany employed from 1775 to 1800 are represented by taller case pieces. Plum pudding mahogany of an exceptional quality, with markings resembling those of a peacock's tail coverts, is shown in the lower section and door frames of the secretary-cabinet with flat-arched pediment, *circa* 1790-1800; wherein the festooned urn-shaped astragals approximate a design shown by Hepplewhite.

The secretary-bookcase with urn finials, also *circa* 1790-1800, is inlaid with oval panels of crotch mahogany, and the balance of the front surfaces display stripe and roe figures with fine mottlings. The last of these pieces, a small break-front bookcase of *circa* 1800-1810, also presents a choice selection of finely marked wood, in this instance with the lower cupboard doors featuring feather-crotch panels.

The Philadelphia side chair with solid splat surmounted by a rococo foliated cabochon cartouche is a production of *circa* 1760-1775, the same general period as that of the Philadelphia chair with pierced splat centering a tassel pendant. In both examples the cabriole legs are fashioned with deep knee brackets, those of the former piece outlined with down-curved leaf scrolls—a typical Irish treatment.

Refined craftsmanship is reflected in the lowboy with the deeply molded top, apparently produced by John Goddard or Job Townsend of Newport, *circa* 1760-1770. These pieces and their companion highboys should also be studied according to other details, as well as on a basis of overall design and carving. In the majority of instances the drawer fronts are of flat-sawed wood, either of plain quality or with swirl or crotch figuring, and they are finished with a thumb molding. The Philadelphia highboy, *circa* 1760-1775, presents an interesting variation from these usual treatments. Here the drawer fronts are faced with quarter-sawed veneers, and edged with a cock beading—in the more up-to-date method of British-trained cabinetmakers.

Another of our highly appreciated block-front examples, the secretary with scrolled pediment, *circa* 1765-1780, commanded an auction price that ran well into five figures. The door panels with brilliant sunbreak effect are contained within scrolled surrounds and flanking pilasters, a favorite Irish treatment.

The card table in swirl-figured veneers, *circa* 1810, is of Baltimore origin. Inlays similar to those of the legs, and the same type of fan segments are also found in tables believed to have been produced either in New York or New Jersey. A sideboard with comparable decorations, exhibited in the Boston Museum of Fine Arts, has been published both as an example of New York origin, and also as probably made by Mathew Egerton of New Brunswick, New Jersey.

Another of these still problematical pieces is the sideboard shown here, also made at about the same time in this general vicinity. The front shaping is more graceful than in the majority of related

(margin figure references: Fig. 138, Fig. 139, Fig. 133, Fig. 129, Fig. 120, Fig. 119, Fig. 118, Fig. 131, Fig. 124; left margin: 127, 128, 136, 115, 117, 137, 134, 126*)*

139. A George III mahogany break-front bookcase Courtesy of Arthur S. Vernay, Inc., New York City.

the city as well as the lesser craftsmen. These *meubles usuels* might be simplified versions of the latest *meubles de luxe,* or of those previously made for a wealthier clientele. A late version of the Louis XVI style, the present example was produced shortly after the turn of the eighteenth century.

Another piece that has been suggested as representative of French craftsmanship, on the basis of design and extraordinary technical skills, is the important secretary with finial eagle and trophies surmounting a pipe-organ clock. This *chef-d'ouvre* was executed in Amsterdam during the early years of the nineteenth century for Louis Napoleon, King of Holland. When not in use the writing chair is moved forward into the kneehole space, and the hinged sections of small drawers are closed against the similarly lettered interior files.

Fig.

90. THUJA
(A softwood)

Thuja is a burlwood obtained from the sandarac tree, *Tetraclinis articulata,* which is indigenous to the Atlas Mountains of Morocco and Algeria. This is the famous thyine tree, yielding an incense used by priests in ancient times, when the wood was more greatly valued than gold. It is said that the wife of Cicero owned a thuja table that cost the equivalent of some fifty thousand dollars.

This timber has been known in Europe since it was first introduced into Spain by the Moors, but French and British cabinetmakers did not discover the decorative possibilities of thuja (or *bois de thuya*) until the latter half of the eighteenth century.

Sherwood gives an interesting account of the causes resulting in particularly fine burls: "When the French régime began, early in the nineteenth century, rigid forest control was set up and the waste of standing timber largely ceased. For centuries the natives had started fires whenever they wished to clear small plots of ground; the cleared tracts, temporarily ample, were enlarged at frequent intervals. Such clearing, of course, caused great devastation but, paradoxically enough, also caused burls of the choicest character to form on the roots of burned thuya trees. That burls should form is a strange phenomenon, for as a rule needle-leaved trees do not propagate from root sprouts, yet a burl is just that, a moss of dormant fruit buds that never develop. . . .

"Found in the Atlas Mountains and nowhere else on earth, the greatest stands of thuya today are in a narrow belt some hundred miles inland

examples, including the few that are known to have been produced by Egerton, and the veneering work is also of an unusually fine caliber.

An interesting combination of crotch veneers has been employed for the principal surfaces of the cabinet with medianly hinged writing section, *circa* 1800-1810. The more highly figured mahogany veneers, appearing in the upper portion, are balanced by lower panels of West Indian satinwood cut in full crotch-swirl veneers.

Fig. 135

The small writing table is a Parisian production of *circa* 1770 in which mahogany has been employed as the principal surfacing material. On the strength of an impressed mark this piece has been attributed to Pierre Migeon II, an *ébéniste* who died in 1758.

Fig. 130

Plum-pudding mahogany, or *acajou moucheté,* as employed by French cabinetmakers, is presented in the façade of the *secrétaire* with mirrored doors above the *abattant.* This piece is also representative of the plainer type of furniture supplied to the Parisian *bourgeoisie* by the leading *ébénistes* of

Fig. 123

140. A George III inlaid thujawood cylinder desk Courtesy of Needham's Antiques, Inc., New York City.

from Mogador, the shipping point for most burls. To find these rare growths is no mean task; never very large they must be plowed for, since there is scarcely a stump to guide the searcher. Grubbed out, they are shipped to France, where until recent years we could buy only the veneer at a very fancy price."

In common with the amboinawood tree, only the burls of the sandarac tree are valued and utilized in the production of furniture. Veneers obtained from these burls vary in color from reddish-tan to almost blackish tones. Selections appearing in old furniture generally possess a medium reddish-brown hue, slightly darker and richer than that of an average mahogany. The grain figure is more pronounced than in amboinawood, presenting more

141. A George III inlaid West Indian satinwood and thujawood dwarf cabinet Courtesy of Biggs of Maidenhead.

heavily shaded effects. The eyes, also, are darker and more clearly defined, appearing either in diffused arrangements or in considerable numbers islanded together amid lustrous swirls of surrounding tissues. Thuja is a brittle wood, often developing wavy cracks in old veneer surfaces. Resinous deposits give the freshly cut timber a sweet aromatic scent. Sherwood states that the heavy oil content also gives the wood a "greater weight than might be expected." In his Table of Condensed Data this weight is listed at only 19 pounds per cubic foot, apparently a typographical error. Other authorities avoid considerations of weight.

THE ILLUSTRATED EXAMPLES

In Thomas Sheraton's design for "A Cylinder Desk and Bookcase," dated 1792, the shaping above the writing interior and the arrangement of that section are somewhat similar to the treatments followed in the thuja example here with two long drawers beneath the pull-out slide. The second cylinder-front desk is surfaced with veneers that are much lighter in tone. Comparison with those of the examples illustrated in the section devoted to amboinawood will serve as an important means of differentiating the figures developed in these two timbers, and of emphasizing the more delicate and compact markings of amboinawood.

Another view of the low cabinet is shown (33) in the section devoted to West Indian satinwood, as the exterior surfaces are principally veneered in that material. The interior drawers are paneled in thujawood, banded in West Indian satinwood,

Fig. 142

Fig. 140

Fig. 141

142. A George III inlaid thujawood cylinder desk
Courtesy of Arthur S. Vernay, Inc., New York
City.

and lined with mahogany, while lustrous, flat-cut mahogany veneers have been employed for the inner facings of the doors. All of the metal furnishings are in silver and of the period, *circa* 1790.

91. SATINÉ ROUGE

Satiné Rouge (Brosimum paraense or *Ferolia guianensis)* is a timber obtained in Brazil and the Guianas. Laslett noted the logs as measuring thirteen to fifteen inches square (with sapwood remaining to a depth of an inch or two at the angles), and fourteen to twenty-eight feet long.

Of the rarer timbers employed by French *ébénistes* during the eighteenth century, M. Clouzot mentions *satiné rouge* as "très en usage." The wood varies from a bright rich red color with a golden sheen, through the average tones of Cuban mahogany, to a somewhat deeper hue with a slight tinge of purple. It possesses a fine, uniform texture, and a luster that permits an excellent polish. Material displaying striped effects is referred to as *satiné rubane*. Rays are irregular in size and distribution. The weight is 55-66 pounds per cubic foot.

92. MORA

Mora (or petowood) is obtained from the mora tree, *Dimorphandra mora* or *Mora excelsa*, a species related to the mulberry, and which is indigenous to the Guianas and Trinidad. Laslett gave the dimensions of timbers as eighteen to thirty-five feet in length and twelve to twenty inches square; also indicating that the tree developed at the same rate of growth as the Cuban mahogany.

In regard to the wood, this same authority stated that it "is of a chestnut-brown color, hard, heavy, tough, strong, and generally straight in the grain, but has occasionally a twist or waviness in the fibre, which imparts to the logs possessing it a beautifully figured appearance, giving to them much additional value. As it takes a good polish, it would be useful as a substitute for Rosewood or dark Spanish Mahogany in cabinet-making, and might be employed for many purposes in the domestic arts. . . . The Mora possesses great strength, and contains an oily or glutinous substance in its pores, which is probably conducive to its durability." Titmus notes the texture as coarse and nonuniform, mentioning that the reddish-brown heartwood has a "figuring of darker lines." The weight is 50-60 pounds per cubic foot.

Although the mora is recognized as a valuable and abundant timber tree, supplies have seldom reached world markets during the past century. That the wood may appear in occasional examples of old furniture is suggested by an attribution of the Rijksmuseum, Amsterdam, in regard to a chest which, according to tradition is made of petowood. The piece is of simple slab construction with cut-out bracket feet. Ornamentation is provided by metal studs and *ajouré mounts* that are characteristic of East Indian, possibly Batavian, workmanship. A most interesting feature of this chest is a branded *V. O. C.* mark (*Verenigde Oost-Indische Compagnie: United Dutch East India Company*), and shipping date of 1728.

93. JACKWOOD

The jack tree of India, Burma and Ceylon produces a wood that is amply described in *The Cabinet-Maker's Assistant*:

Jack Wood is the timber of *Artocarpus integrifolia*, and is a variety of the bread fruit tree. This tree is a native of India, and belongs to a class of trees that are extensively distributed over East India, both continental and insular, and also over the islands of the South Seas. It is likewise extensively cultivated in the West Indies; its fruit being a favourite food with the negro population....

Jack wood, in colour and grain, resembles a rather coarse and inferior variety of mahogany. In cross section, the concentric rings are seen to be variously and alternately coloured in different shades of brown, the wood in plank presents a minutely streaked appearance, which, at near view, imparts to it considerable richness and elegance.

The general colour of the wood, when first cut, is yellowish brown, which deepens on exposure into a reddish brown. It is harder and heavier than mahogany, and abounds in white, gritty, silicious particles in its pores.

In India, jack wood is extensively employed for all purposes in house carpentry and furniture; and in England for cabinet work, marquetry, and turnery.

Howard writes that "in India the wood darkens to the colour of rosewood, and almost black. The grain is hard and close, and shows a strongly marked hard and soft contrary grain, which requires a very sharp tool to obtain a smooth surface.

... The pores, which are numerous and rather large, are grouped in wavy bands, and are generally filled with a bright sparkling gum. The medullary rays are very bright and well-defined, parallel but irregularly spaced. On the radial section they show strongly in numerous straight light lines, at right angles to the longitudinal grain." The weight of jackwood is 33-44 pounds per cubic foot.

94. IRONWOOD or *BOIS FER*

Many trees and shrubs yielding unusually hard, strong or heavy woods are designated as ironwoods, a term also applied to their usable woods. It is not requisite as a distinguishing feature of these woods that they will sink in water—as is sometimes believed. Some will do so as long as their full moisture content is retained, while a number will lack buoyancy after this content has been reduced. In regard to antique furniture, the term is sometimes employed when an extremely hard and heavy timber is not determinable in work produced by craftsmen of the Portuguese, Spanish, or Dutch colonial possessions.

The ironwoods range in color from almost white, through brown and red tones, to black; and they are frequently variegated in self-tones or contrasting colors. They are usually quite difficult to work, presenting hindrances to hand or machine tools that render them more suitable for solid structural requirements than as veneers. Nevertheless, one of these timbers was cut into veneers and thus employed, as *bois fer*, by French *ébénistes* of the eighteenth century. This particular wood appears in lightly streaked parti-colored effects of fawn and medium brown tones, intermixed with black, and displayed in smooth, lustrous surfaces.

Webster gives the most complete information:

The name "Ironwood" is generally associated with trees of the genera *Diospyros*, *Sideroxylon*, and *Millettia*—a genus yielding some of the finest streaked Ironwoods. It is applied locally to a wide variety of trees and shrubs, the most important of which are now recognized by the following vernacular and botanical designations:

In Africa and the adjacent islands: the White Ironwood, *Toddalia lanceolata*; several species of the genus *Olea*, including *O. capensis*; *Stadmannia oppositifolia*; *Northea seychellana*; *Gardenia rothmannia*; the Argan Tree; the Mopane.

In Asia: the Rose Chestnut; the Iron Tree, *Metrosideros vera*; the Persian Tree, *Parrotia persica*; the Acle, *Xylia xylocarpa*; species of the genus *Inga*.

In Australasia: the Stavewood, *Tarrietia actino-*

phylla; the Silver Tree, *Tarrietia argyrodendron*; *Nania vera* of Amboina; the Olive, *Olea paniculata*; the Botany Bay Olive; species of the genus *Notelaea*; the Akeake, *Dodonaea viscosa*; the Ironbark Acacia; the Australian tree *Acacia stenophylla*; the Puriri; species of the *Casuarina*; *Cassia siamea* of the Dutch East Indies; the Ridge Myrtle, *Melaleuca genistifolia*; *Memecylon edule*; any of several Ironbarks; the shrub *Myrtus gonoclada*.

In the West Indies and continental tropical America: the Spanish Stopper, *Eugenia buxifolia*; the Red Stopper, *Eugenia rhombea*, and the related *E. confusa*; the Black Ironwood, *Krugiodendron ferreum*; the False Logwood; the Colima; the Snakebark, *Colubrina ferruginosa*; the Breakax, *Sloanea jamaicensis*; the Quebracho; the Wamara or *Ferréol*, *Swartzia tomentosa*; the Joewood; *Dialium divaricatum* of British Honduras; the Genip, *Exothea paniculata*; the Bastard Ironwood, *Trichilia hirta*.

In North America: the Hornbeam, *Carpinus caroliniana*; the Hop Hornbeam, *Ostrya virginica*; the evergreen tree *Lyonothamnus floribundus*; the Mesquite, *Prosopis juliflora*, and the related *P. glandulosa*; *Olneya tesota*; the Leatherwood, *Cyrilla racemiflora*; the Titi, *Cliftonia monophylla*; the Chittamwood, *Bumelia languginosa*, and the related *B. tenax*; the Ocean Spray; the Bastard Lignum Vitae, *Guaicum sanctum*; in New Mexico, any shrub of the genus *Forestiera*; in Florida and the West Indies, the White Ironwood, *Hypelate trifoliata*, also known as Madeira Wood.

95. THE EUCALYPTS: BLOODWOOD

The genus *Eucalyptus* is comprised of about two hundred and fifty species of Australian trees in the family Myrtaceae, today found largely in western Australia where they are the most important timbers. Some secrete a considerable amount of resinous gum, whence they are called gum trees. Others, with inner fibrous bark, are known as stringybarks. A number yielding blood-red timbers are known as bloodwoods. Within this genus trees of gigantic growths are common, some of which develop to dimensions between those of the giant sequoia of California and the redwood. Heights of more than three hundred feet are recorded, while Sherwood gives a round figure of "five hundred feet tall."

Mahogany was widely popular at the time that Australia was discovered, and therefore native timbers yielding the more richly toned reddish woods were the first to be cut and shipped back to England. Bloodwood was included in these shipments, and possibly one or more of the ironbarks and so-called forest mahoganies.

The most important bloodwood is a product of *E. corymbosa*. In common with other eucalypts this species is also referred to as a gum tree and its timber as gumwood. The wood varies in color through medium to dark evenly distributed shades of red. It has a hard, medium-coarse texture, and displays no distinctive growth-ring figures. An interlocked grain may result in a light stripe figure appearing in radial surfaces. The weight is 60-65 pounds per cubic foot.

Laslett designated *E. corymbosa* as *blood gum*, and *E. paniculata* as *bloodwood*. The latter species is recognized today as one of the ironbarks, still another class of Australian timbers named for their hard gray bark. In this class *E. fergusoni* is the bloodwood ironbark. The ironbarks vary in color from medium to dark red tones, and to brownish reds, colorings that are subject to considerable fading over long periods of time. They are hard and heavy, with coarse to fine textures, and no pronounced figures are reported. Weights range from 65 to 75 pounds per cubic foot.

The forest "mahoganies" yield tallowwood, *E. microcorys*, red mahogany, *E. resinifera*, and red gum, *E. rostrata*. While timbers of this class are found in eastern sections, where they were available to the early settlers, western Australian mahogany, or jarrah, *E. marginata*, has become the best known and most important today. These "mahoganies" usually appear in colors similar to those of the ironbarks, but at times they incline toward yellowish hues. In general they are moderately coarse but uniform in texture, the grain either normally interlocked or variable, and no particularly distinctive figures are specified. They are often oily to the touch, as with others of the gumwoods. In weight they are usually somewhat lighter than the ironbarks.

Eucalyptus timbers, particularly bloodwood, were distributed by Dutch, as well as English ships, and they were employed by furniture craftsmen working in Holland's East Indian colonies. They appear infrequently in British furniture of the nineteenth century, ordinarily displaying faded surface tones of brownish, rather than reddish casts. Due to the similarities existing between so many of these timbers it is generally impossible to distinguish them specifically in manufactured form. Hence, determinations according to class are advisable, if this is at all possible, or simply as eucalyptuswood.

96. AUSTRALIAN BEEFWOOD

144

Various species of beefwoods[28] are included in the Australian family Casuarinaceae, of which *Casuarina equistifolia* is probably the most important. This category of trees and shrubs is alternatively known as the beefwood family, while other species belonging to the family Proteaceae[28] are also designated as Australian beefwoods. Analyses of these timbers do not agree in all respects, but at least they do regard the Australian beefwoods in the same light as the more widely known beefwood or balata of British and Dutch Guiana, *Mimusops globosa,* in that all of these woods possess beeflike colorings.

Colorings of the Australian timbers vary from strong to very dark reds, and through browner tones. They are moderately coarse but even in texture, and the grain may be straight or shallowly interlocked, producing stripe figures in quartered surfaces. Weights average between 55 and 65 pounds per cubic foot.

It is believed that prior to the second half of the eighteenth century beefwood (or "casuarina"), possibly from East Indian timbers, was employed in South African furniture displaying elaborate organ-front shapings, derived from Dutch models of about the same date. Since these designs were continued for some time in Holland, and for several generations in colonial work, it is more likely that beefwood appeared in the Cape Colony around the close of the eighteenth century, when the English arrived there.

After that time the Australian wood was introduced in England where it was never extensively employed. The description in *The Cabinet-Maker's Assistant* draws attention to the fact that "many woods have this name, but the sort which is commonly designated beef wood . . . is imported from New South Wales, in round logs about 9 feet long, and from 9 to 14 inches in diameter. In general color, it is more intensely red than mahogany, with occasionally dark veins, small, slightly curled, and minutely dispersed throughout the entire surface. Some specimens are pretty. It is used in turnery, in veneers for bordering and for small cabinets and brush backs, and in the manufacture of Tunbridge ware." Although this publication states that "Beefwood is known also as Botany Bay oak," it makes no mention of rays—which generally provide the most identifying feature of Botany Bay oak.

97. BOTANY BAY OAK

Botany Bay, situated on the southeast coast of Australia (New South Wales), was so named from the number of plants found on this shore at the time that it was first sighted by Captain Cook in 1770. From this late discovery, and the fact that the British settlement had not progressed to any considerable extent by the opening years of the nineteenth century, it might be expected that Australian timbers would not appear in British furniture until fairly late in the Regency period. Nevertheless, "Botany Bay" is one of the woods mentioned in the 1811 edition of *The London Cabinet-Makers' Union Book of Prices*:

WORK VENEER'D with hard wood, to be calculated on the price of veneering only, and charged extra on the shilling, on the price of veneering with mahogany, as follows:

Botany-bay or rosewood	0	0	3
Satin wood, Manilla, or zebra	0	0	4
King, tulip, Coromandel, purple, or Amboyna wood, and yew-tree	0	0	5
Ebony or snake wood	0	0	6

"Botany Bay" is also featured in this publication under the "Tables of Mouldings," the cost of "mitring, cutting, sweeping, glueing on, and sticking mouldings of Botany Bay" reckoned, with "rose, satin, or any similar woods," at two pence less than "ebony, purple, king, Coromandel, tulip or similar hard woods."

It is possible that the veneers and moldings referred to might be of Botany Bay oak, for I have seen this wood employed as a veneer of Regency furniture. However, it should be noted that in the past the same name was used in reference to beefwood (without mention of rays); and *Botany Bay wood* is a term that has been applied to African blackwood, *Dalbergia melanoxylon.*

Botany Bay oak is obtained from various Australian she-oaks, known also as forest oaks. These are species of the genus *Casuarina,*[28] comprised of trees and shrubs constituting a distinct family, Casuarinaceae, and order, Casuarinales. Early settlers in Australia applied the name *oak* to several species of trees found growing there, although the oak is not indigenous to this island continent. These timbers bear only a vague resemblance to true oak when broad and lengthy rays are noticeably present. According to one authority, the name of she-oak was derived from the sound of wind passing through the branches of these trees—in which case, when gusts of air disturb the branches of the native he-oak, the sound must surely be akin to an answering whistle.

As Botany Bay oak appears in late Georgian

furniture the color is usually of rich and full reddish tones, at times as dark as a plum red. In later cuttings the color has also varied toward browner hues. The wood is hard and heavy, distinguished by very small pores, and a fine, uniform texture. Growth rings are indistinct, therefore pronounced figures of this type are not displayed in finished surfaces. A particularly interesting flake figure is produced by fine to very broad rays that appear in quartered material. Generally the rays are broad and long, irregularly distributed and of a lighter tone than that of the ground tissues—giving a most unusual and unmistakable effect to the smooth, lustrous wood, for they seemingly "float" beneath the surface finish, as the bubble of air in a spirit level. Weights range from moderately heavy to 75 pounds per cubic foot.

98. SABICU

Sabicú is a Spanish name, probably derived from an origin in the language of the Taino Indians formerly inhabiting the larger West Indian islands and the Bahamas—where the sabicu tree, *Lysiloma sabicu*, appears as an endemic species. Laslett recorded this tree in both island groups, stating that timbers were plentiful in Cuba and that they were also sent there from the Bahamas for exportation. He described the tree as somewhat crooked and irregular in growth, indicating in a special chart that it required an average of one hundred and thirty-four years for the trunk to attain a diameter of twenty-four inches, a third of a century longer than the time necessary for a Cuban mahogany tree to reach a similar measurement. The trunk was cut into logs about ten to thirty-five feet long, and they were squared for handling purposes, when their sides measured from one to three feet.

The color of this wood varies from a medium shade of chestnut-brown, to a reddish-brown mahoganylike tone. It is a hard, strong and very durable timber, with little tendency toward warping or splitting, and it is easily worked. The sparse pores are small to medium in size, the rays too fine to be distinguished individually. A resulting firm and even texture is accompanied by a good luster in finished surfaces. The weight is decidedly heavier than that of mahogany, probably 55-65 pounds per cubic foot.

Technical descriptions of sabicu generally omit or fail to emphasize the importance of the one word that best names and describes the timber—*horseflesh*, a term that may be applied to both the sabicu tree and its wood. The appropriateness of

143. A Georgian curved sabicu card table Courtesy of Arthur S. Vernay, Inc., New York City.

this name is evident in the patinated surfaces of old furniture, particularly where the wood has been tangentially cut and pronounced growth-ring figures are displayed. While the ground casts of these surfaces may have faded to soft brown mahoganylike tones, they will usually feature rather wide elliptical bands of color in dark brown or deep blood-red shades, irregularly following the direction of the growth-ring figures. These bands of color present a most unusual effect, almost as though they had been painted in with a brush. In combination with the natural grain figure, the total effect is strikingly similar to that of a sinewy cut of raw horseflesh.

In the West Indies the name *sabicu* is generally replaced by *horseflesh mahogany* when reference is made to the grainy wood as it appears in natively made furniture of the eighteenth century or later. Also, timbers sent from the Bahamas to the American states during the later part of the eighteenth century were described as horseflesh,[29] rather than sabicu. Under the former name they were received as one of the rarer woods employed by craftsmen of the Early Federal years. Among the Philadelphia joiners and cabinetmakers to stock this material was John Gillingham, who in 1794 owned "One pair high drawers & one dressing table, horse flesh." Horner also records a costly "pr. mahogany: or horse flesh Chests of Drawers" owned by Samuel

144. A George III sabicu chest of drawers Courtesy of Arthur S. Vernay, Inc., New York City.

Bettle in 1782; and a "large dining table, horse flesh" that was in the James Bringhurst house just after the turn of the century.

From about the middle of the eighteenth century sabicu was imported into the British Isles. There it was employed in the solid or as a veneer of cabinetwork executed in the Early Georgian, Chippendale, and later classic styles. Some of the wood appearing in the finest pieces was obviously obtained from a variety of timber in which there is no decided resemblance to the appearance of horseflesh. Wood of this nature is browner than the usual horseflesh mahogany, displaying less pronounced but more irregular growth-ring figures, and it is unmarked by heavy, deep-toned pigmentations. The origin of this timber, suggested only by Laslett and Webster's authority, may be the West Indian species *Peltophorum adnatum*[29] or a related variety of the family Caesalpiniaceae, in which species of *Caesalpinia* yield brazilwood, brasiletto, and other hard, showy, and occasionally darker woods.

THE ILLUSTRATED EXAMPLES

In the partially open view of the sabicu card table it is obvious at a glance that *horseflesh mahogany* is a term well suited to describe this distinctively grained timber. While the wood itself is easily distinguished from other tropical American species, the origin of this particular table is not so readily determined. In the opinions of two experts on English furniture it is a Continental production. The choice of material suggests a European, rather than East Indian origin and the general design certainly indicates a European, but non-English provenance. Some vaguely related tables

Fig. 143

Fig. 144

were produced in Holland and Denmark, but the shape of the folding top, the straight frieze, inner knee scrolls and claw-and-ball feet are more characteristic of indifferent Irish workmanship. Individually, all of these forms were duplicated in Irish card tables produced during the third quarter of the eighteenth century. The manner in which the leaflike knee scrolls are stopped short immediately beneath the frieze is the most inexplicable feature of the entire design.

Contrasting to a solid use of this particular sabicu in the preceding example, veneers have been used in surfacing the drawer fronts, bracket feet, top and sides of the chest of drawers, *circa* 1780. In both instances the wood has been plain-sawn to bring out the characteristic growth-ring figures. According to tradition the chest of drawers was made in the village of Baldock, Hertfordshire, some thirty miles outside of London. Telescopic slides are built into the sides of the upper drawer, which contains a baize-lined writing panel, and all of the drawers retain their original brasses.

A different type of sabicu (*vide ante*) with no decided resemblance to horseflesh has been em-

145. A George III inlaid sabicu "commode" Courtesy of Mallett & Son (Antiques) Ltd., London.

Fig. 145

ployed for the oval panel and outer border of the serpentine-front commode, *circa* 1775. From the number of important cabinet pieces that were similarly treated during the last quarter of the eighteenth century it is evident that this variety of sabicu received the greater favor during that period. In some instances the wood has been confused with rosewood or laburnum, particularly where it has been combined with larger surfaces of satinwood.

99. PADAUK

Padauk is the appellation given to two closely related species of tall trees growing in the Andaman Islands and Burma. The former growths attain extreme diameters of five feet, about a foot greater than this butt measurement in Burmese trees. Traders established here in the East Indies during the early part of the eighteenth century were responsible for the first shipments of padauk to reach the British Isles. More recently the Andaman timber has come to be known also as vermilionwood or Andaman redwood.

Andaman padauk, *Pterocarpus dalbergioides*, is generally characterized by a rich crimson color,

though it may appear in reddish-brown hues, and with darker red or black streaks. It has been claimed that "this color is fast," but in surfaces of old furniture the wood has often faded to the same tones as those reached in certain pieces made of mahogany or rosewood. Lightly cutting or sanding these bleached surfaces will reveal the natural fiery tones of the Andamanese wood.

This timber is diffuse porous in structure, with the larger vessels clearly visible as fine grooves or vessel lines in longitudinal surfaces. Growth rings are quite distinct, but rays are obscure. The texture varies from medium to moderately coarse, nevertheless permitting a very smooth finish, often with an oily or soapy feeling to the touch. An interlocked grain may be present, and a small percentage of the timbers display stripe, mottle and swirl figures. The weight of Andaman padauk is 45-55 pounds, averaging around 49 pounds per cubic foot.

Burmese padauk, *P. macrocarpus*, is not considered as ornamental as the Andamanese timber, and it is harder to work for it is rather brittle. When freshly cut the color varies from a yellowish hue to a dark red, sometimes interrupted by brownish streaks. With continued exposure these tones change to a uniform but attractive golden-brown

146. An Early Georgian carved padauk low tray-top table Courtesy of Biggs of Maidenhead.

147. A George III carved and parcel-gilded padauk "lady's writing table and bookcase" Courtesy of H. Blairman & Sons, Ltd., London.

color. Other properties are almost identical with those of Andaman padauk, in fact neither wood can be positively distinguished from the other by microscopic examination of the cell patterns. A narrow stripe figure is apt to be more characteristic of the Burmese timber, and its weight is somewhat heavier, averaging around 54 pounds per cubic foot.

Former writers on the subject of English furniture have claimed a Burmese origin for padauk as found in British furniture of the Early Georgian and later decorative periods. Of all such pieces examined during the course of these studies the majority have revealed a rich vermilion or crimson color when the wood has been cut, characteristic

of Andaman, rather than Burmese padauk.

THE ILLUSTRATED EXAMPLES

The customary use of padauk as a solid material, rather than as a veneer, has been followed in the construction of the small tray-top center table of an unusually interesting design. Comparable but plainer types of supporting scrolls are found in seat furniture and side tables that English experts ascribe to the William III and Queen Anne periods; these pieces appear in walnut or lacquer, and with legs of either round or square sections, terminating in club feet. The feet of the present table are carved with the same type of uncinate, or hooked, leaf

Fig. 146

scroll that was similarly employed by James Moore of London, *fl.* 1708-1726. However, the cusped frieze panels indicate a later origin as corresponding recesses were introduced in some of the earlier examples of mahogany furniture.

Fig. 147 The design of the writing table with stepped cabinet section is similar to a drawing by Thomas Chippendale, dated 1760, in which it was intended that "The middle Feet come out with the drawer, which hath a Slider covered with green Cloth, or Spanish Leather, for writing upon." All of the carved details, fret work, and the "pagoda" molding above the drawers are gilded, presenting a pleasant contrasting effect in combination with the now softly toned surfaces of padauk, apparently of Burmese origin.

In the cabinet with cleft pediment, a piece dating from *circa* 1760-1770, the door frames have been Fig. 1 scrolled and cusped in conformity with patterns evolved some twenty years earlier. Similar treatments are found in early mahogany secretaries with slant-front desk sections, and in late walnut cabinets of various types. During the time in which the first of these patterns were evolved the writing drawer was also developed from a shallow compartment with cutaway sides to the standard English writing drawer in which a full vertical depth is given to the sides and hinged front. Although this innovation was featured in the finest London cabinetwork of *circa* 1760, it was not illustrated by Chippendale in his *Director* of 1762. After this time the slant desk received very little favor in England, although the reverse is true in regard to American furniture. On the other hand, the English writing drawer then became a customary feature of bureaus and secretaries produced within the British Isles, and it was soon adopted in America, and on rare occasions in northern areas of the Continent.

100. "ÉBÈNE ROUGE"

M. Henri Clouzot has listed "Ébène Rouge ou Grenadille" as a veneer employed in French *ébénisterie* of the eighteenth century, giving the botanical designation as *Astronium fraxinifolium*, and describing the wood as of "a reddish-brown color, striped with black, perhaps the same wood as Courbaril." This positive stand in regard to the scientific name, and ambiguity over the particular nature of the wood itself, indicates that in M. Clouzot's opinion *A. fraxinifolium* is the source of a timber similar to, or identical with West Indian locust or courbaril.

According to Titmus, *A. fraxinifolium* is the species yielding Brazilian kingswood, "a rare but important timber that is extremely popular for the making of high-class furniture and similar purposes. . . . The light-coloured sapwood is well distinguished from the heartwood which may range in colour from a lightish-brown to a red tint, with darker stripes. . . . It has an average air dry weight of 55 to 65 lbs. per cu. ft., a grain that is normally straight, and a texture that is both fine and uni-

148. A George III fret-carved padauk bookcase Courtesy of Norman R. Adams Ltd., London.

form."

Sherwood associates *A. fraxinifolium* with goncalo alves, which he considers one of the best substitutes for Brazilian rosewood. Howard believes this species to be the source of zebrawood, as used in English furniture of the past.

A veneer specimen answering M. Clouzot's general description, and bearing the label "Red Ebony," was obtained from Tunbridge Wells. As a climax to the more conflicting of the above opinions, when this specimen was submitted to Mr. J. L. Stearns it was returned with a positive identification as padauk.

Red ebony is an alternative name given to the granadilla tree, *Brya ebenus*, which is indicated by M. Clouzot's "*Grenadille*."

Granadillawood may refer to cocuswood (*vide*); to a Cocobola, *Dalbergia retusa* (*vide*); to one type of partridgewood, a chocolate-brown, hardwood of the tropical American tree *Caesalpinia granadillo*; and, in Puerto Rico, to the yellow satiny wood yielded by the tropical American species *Buchenavia capitata*. In addition, granadillawood is considered equivalent to yellow sanders, a group of yellowish woods including those produced by the mountain plum, *Ximenia americana*, of the West Indies and Florida, and the West Indian tree *Zanthoxylum elephantiasis*. Of interest to American collectors, "a Quantity of Yallowsander Wood" was listed among the losses sustained by Benjamin Frothingham, cabinetmaker of Charleston, Massachusetts, when his house and shop were burned by the British on June 17, 1777.

101. COCUSWOOD

The granadilla tree of the West Indies, *Brya ebenus*, supplies timbers of various descriptions that have come to be known by various names. One of the most important is green ebony (*vide post*), while another is cocuswood, a designation applying to the timber in which brown or reddish-brown tones are predominant.

Cocuswood varies in color from brownish-yellow hues to chocolate-brown tones, usually intermixed with darker streaks. It is very hard, brittle and oily, with a fine, uniform texture permitting a smooth, lustrous surface finish. The grain, which may be straight or wavy, has less effect on the appearance of the wood than the markings produced by the growth rings and through pigmentation. Weights vary from 69 to 75 pounds per cubic foot.

This timber holds some interest for those whose attentions are directed toward the study of turned wares, as it was employed in various forms of treen

produced in England during the seventeenth century. Later it was used principally in the making of trunchions and wood-wind musical instruments. The timber is described at some length in *The Cabinet-Maker's Assistant*:

Cocus Wood, or Cocoa Wood, is a product of the West Indies, and is imported chiefly from the island of Cuba, in logs of from 3 to 6 feet in length, and from 3 to 9 inches in diameter. The stem of the tree is irregularly figured and modulated. It is finer in the grain than rosewood, but resembles it in weight and fibre.... Cocus wood, in cross section, presents the concentric rings of growth, alternately and minutely coloured in yellow and brown. These colors, although easily distinguishable on the end view, are seen in the plank section to be so mixed and diffused as to give the wood in mass a pretty uniform yellowish brown colour, which is intermixed with streaks of a darker hue. It deepens on exposure to a dark brown, and sometimes to nearly black.

This does not possess the necessary qualities of a good cabinet wood; its small size, frequency of heart faults, general inferiority in figure, and, above all, its liability to change in colour, unfit it for extensive use. It is, however, very suitable for turnery of all kinds, and is much used in the manufacture of tubular musical instruments, such as flutes, flageolets, &c. It is sold at £5, 10s. to £6, 10s. per ton.

There is another wood bearing the name [*vide* PORCUPINEWOOD], and considered to be a variety of cocus wood... The interior wood is coarser in the grain, but presents greater variety and beauty of expression; its predominating colour is a chestnut brown, inclining to red, but veined with deeper tints. This wood is also suitable for turnery, and veneers of it are used for brush backs. It is sometimes called brown ebony. Cocoa wood is exogenous, and must not be confounded with the cocoa-nut tree, as they are widely distinct in their characters, the latter being a palm tree. Notwithstanding the long and frequent use of these woods, their botanical characters are unknown, and some uncertainty exists as to the localities of their growth.

102. PORCUPINEWOOD

Porcupinewood is produced by the coco[30] or coconut palm, *Cocus nucifera* Linn., which is believed to have originated in tropical America, but grows also in India, Ceylon and the East Indies. Only the outside portion of the stem is usable as timber. The fact that its surface markings resemble the appearance of porcupine quills accounts for the name of this wood. These markings occur as a result of orange-red or darker deposits that form in the pores and are displayed as bold hatchings or "quill marks" in longitudinal surfaces. They are set off against the color of the principal wood substance, which varies from a soft, slightly grayed medium-brown shade, to deeper and redder tones. The wood is further distinguished by a hard and compact nature, permitting a very smooth surface finish. Weights range from 50 to 70 pounds per cubic foot.

The wood of the coconut palm, or of any palm used as a commercial timber, may also be known as Palmyrawood (*vide post*). Porcupinewood has been noticed as an inlay material of nineteenth century furniture, and also in present day "restorations" carried out to refurbish a few unimportant examples produced during the Regency period.

103. COCOBOLO

Cocobolo is the product of several trees in the genus *Dalbergia*, including *D. granadillo*, *D. hypoleuca*, and *D. retusa*, native to Mexico, Panama, Costa Rica and Columbia. Timbers are exported in whole or split logs of irregular shapes and small sizes, ranging from one to three feet in length, and containing numerous defects.

The heartwood is characteristically bicolored, appearing in orange and deeper red or chestnut-brown hues, intermixed with darker or jet-black streakings. Plainer effects resemble the patterns of rosewood, while the more elaborate are comparable to the markings of tortoiseshell. Rather large but scattered pores do not have any pronounced effect on the texture of the wood, which is very hard, smooth, and marble-cold to the touch. The weight is 80-85 pounds per cubic foot.

Objects made of cocobolo, appearing from time to time in the form of turned table articles or those converted from other uses, are generally representative of material with less than a century of age. During the second half of the nineteenth century the wood was used in making bowling balls, knife and tool handles, brush backs, etc. It has also been cut into veneers, but an unusually high oil content renders it difficult to glue.

104. RUBYWOOD or SANTAL

Rubywood is a dark red dyewood produced by one of the two red sandalwood trees, *Pterocarpus santalinus* Linn., native to southern India and the East Indies. Alternative names are santal, *bois de santal rouge*, and red sanders. The timber is shipped in billets or small logs of from one and a half to about nine inches in diameter.

The heartwood is dark claret-red to almost black in color, with a figuring of darker stripings in the lighter varieties. It is very hard, medium fine and uniform in structure, and characterized by a strongly marked contrary or interlocked grain of hard and soft texture. The pores are small and generally plugged with deposits. Radial sawing may bring out a narrow stripe figure. Longitudinal surfaces can be worked to a very smooth finish displaying a glossy luster. Weights range from 60 to 75 pounds per cubic foot.

Aside from a more common utilization in dyeing, this variety of red sandalwood has been employed in Europe as an inlay material, and for small turned work. It has been claimed that the timber was also used in British cabinetwork of the Early Georgian period . . . in considerably larger dimensions than those indicated above.

105. PARTRIDGEWOOD

Partridgewood is obtained from two different species of trees in the tropical American genus *Andira*, belonging to the family Fabaceae. The name is applied more specifically to *A. americana*, yielding a heavy, mottled dark red or chocolate-brown timber that is alternatively known as Acapu. Only the scantiest of information is available concerning the structural properties of this timber, and it is apparent that findings are in part based upon studies of the second species, *A. inermis*, which produces a wood that is more properly known as angelin or cabbage bark.

Under two separate headings, of partridgewood and cabbage bark, Howard gives the same botanical designation for both of these woods, *A. inermis*, indicating that a weight of 85 pounds 15 ounces is to be associated with the former timber, and one of 46 pounds with that cut as cabbage bark. Sherwood apparently refers to *A. americana* when he mentions Brazilian partridgewood as one of the world's heaviest timbers, weighing as much as 90 pounds per cubic foot. Under the synonymous designation of *Vouacapoua americana*, the latter species is recognized by Howard as Acapu, but with a query as to whether it is to be associated with Partridgewood: "This valuable timber . . . is streaked along the grain with lighter and darker lines like partridge-wood. . . . The pores are medium-sized and irregularly disposed; they are often joined in threes and fours in short wavy lines, and are generally surrounded by a patch of loose tissue. Concentric rings are marked by an absence of pores. The

149. A Regency inlaid partridgewood dwarf cabinet with ormolu mounts Courtesy of Mallett & Son (Antiques) Ltd., London.

exceedingly fine medullary rays are very even and regular, and rather wavy in contour. . . . Weight 63 lbs."

The only recent description of cabbage bark that bears repeating is given by Howard, with alternative designations as Angelim, Partridge-wood and Pheasant-wood: "This strange-looking wood has the colour of Honduras mahogany, with a very peculiar rough grain, more suggestive of a palm growth than that of ordinary wood. A very sharp plane is required to secure even a moderately smooth surface, and even then a fine ridgy effect is produced by the very close, and yet obstinate, contrary grain. . . . Dark wavy belts of growth, crossed by very definite fine and strong medullary rays, show on the transverse section, in what is perhaps

the prettiest pattern it is possible to obtain. On this section the pores show as solid, although marked, but on the tangential section they show as open and sometimes filled."

Admitting confusion over the botanical origins of these timbers, *The Cabinet-Maker's Assistant* published their descriptions in considerable detail:

Partridge Wood, sometimes called Cabbage Wood, is brought from Guiana, the Brazils, and the West Indian islands, chiefly Cuba. There are several commercial varieties of this wood, distinguished as red, brown, black, and sweet partridge. The first three names are founded on the prevailing colours in the specimens. From the uncertainty respecting its botanical character and relations, it is highly probable that the wood of several trees is included under this name. The red sort is called *Angelim* and *Cangelim* in the Brazils, and *Yava*, in Cuba. The West Indian partridge wood is said to be furnished by the *Heisteria coccinea* of botanists, a small inelegant tree, about 20 feet high, growing by water courses. The variety imported from Guiana is the product of a tree which attains a height of 60 feet, whose name is *Boca*.

Partridge wood resembles rosewood in weight [a weight that is decidedly heavier than quoted for cabbage bark], and closeness of grain; and it has an odour like logwood. In cross section, the annual rings are distinguishable by their colour, by different degrees of hardness, and porosity. The darker they are, the harder and less porous, and *vice versa*. This circumstance is the chief cause of the peculiar figure in the wood when seen in plank, giving the general appearance of an endogen, or of one of the palm tree woods. In the most valuable examples, it has a dark and variegated appearance, resembling the plumage of the bird whose name it bears; and, according as it varies in complexional character, it is denominated Pheasant wood or Partridge wood. The predominating colour is a reddish brown, irregularly mingled, and minutely veined, and hatched in various shades of a deeper tint, approaching black. Besides these more decided colours, feathery and evanescent hues of blue and red faintly light up and beautify the general expression.

It is imported in large planks; in square, but, for the most part, in round logs, ranging from 9 to 18 and 27 inches in diameter; and is sold by weight at £5 per ton. It was formerly used by the Brazilians in ship-building, and is known in British dockyards as Cabbage wood. By the cabinet-maker it is chiefly used in small cabinets, and general turnery, in making chairs and couches; also for veneering picture frames and brush backs, and for making walking sticks, umbrella, and parasol handles, &c.

Partridgewood appears in British furniture of so-called Sheraton and Regency designs, which it may be noted here were continued, with or without obvious transitional effects, during the middle of the nineteenth century and later, and in more typical Victorian productions. At times it was employed for larger purposes than those indicated above, while it appears that Scottish cabinetmakers were inclined to a sparing use of this material, such as in the small decorative panels incorporated in their popular corner cabinets.

M. Clouzot recognized *Andira inermis* as providing a French *bois de marquetry* of the eighteenth century, designated as *epi de blé* (literally "spikes of grain") rather than *oeil-de-perdrix ou bois de perdrix* (partridge-eye or partridgewood) which he associated with a species of locust, *"Robinia prouasensis."*

150. A Regency inlaid partridgewood occasional table courtesy of H. Blairman & Sons Ltd., London.

THE ILLUSTRATED EXAMPLES

Inlays of ebony provide a quiet contrast to the partridgewood veneers of the occasional table with tapered pillar and tetrapod base, *circa* 1810. The dwarf cabinet, *circa* 1810, gives a very good idea of the varied markings that occur in this unusual wood, here combined with ebony inlays and highly decorative ormolu mounts.

Fig. 150

Fig. 149

106. VIOLET WOOD* or BOIS VIOLET

This pre-eminent cabinet wood received a great acclaim in France during the time of Louis XV, when it was designated as *bois violet* or *bois de violet*. The former term appears in contemporary accounts of furniture supplied to French royalty by such leading *ébénistes* as Antoine-Robert Gadreau (c. 1680-1751), Gilles Joubert (1689-1775), Antoine-Mathieu Criaerd (c. 1724-1787), and Jean-Henri

---

* First known as *Kingwood* in English nomenclature of the early nineteenth century.

Riesener (1734-1806); and in those enumerating the *meubles de la couronne.* Documents of this nature have been published by M. Pierre Verlet, *Conservateur au Museé de Louvre,* in his valuable contribution to the study of French furniture: *Le Mobilier Royal Français* (Paris, 1945).

In view of the extensive researches carried out by M. Verlet, an inquiry has been made to ascertain whether or not he has ever come across the term *bois du roi* in French records of the eighteenth century, or those pertaining to the reign of Louis XIV. In reply he has specified that to his knowledge "The expression *Bois du Roi* was not used in France during the period of Louis XIV, nor in the eighteenth century. The inventories use for the description of exotic woods a vague terminology which remained in use for some time under Louis XV. The name *Bois des Indes* is generally used. You know as well as I that the *ébénistes* have often varied in their designations of the same wood, especially at that period. The term *Bois des Indes* probably manifests their own incertitude.

"Regarding the name *Bois Violet*, this is found during the time of Louis XIV. . . . You will find it I think in the inventory published by Guiffrey in regard to an armoire—*Chateau de Marly*—if my memory serves. It exists in any case in the inventory by Boulle in 1720, after the fire of his atelier in the Louvre."

No further comment should be necessary in regard to the constant repetition, in England and America, of stories to the effect that this wood was

151. A Late Stuart violetwood parquetry cabinet-on-stand Courtesy of Phillips of Hitchen Ltd.

so highly esteemed by Louis XIV, or by Louis XV, that out of honor to one or the other of these rulers, and during one or the other of their reigns, the name of *bois du roi* (kingwood) was given to the newly introduced timber.

Other researches, engaged in by Amyas Phillips, Esq., director of Phillips of Hitchen, Ltd., have also indicated that the English equivalent of this name cannot be traced to a use in that country before the nineteenth century, although the terms *prince-wood* or *princeswood* appear in English records of the seventeenth century. Less concerned persons have claimed that either of these two names are pedantic, as "Princewood is now known as King-

wood." To the contrary, princewood is not even botanically related to the timber that eventually came to be known as kingwood, and rarely does it approach this other timber in appearance. If the two species cannot be differentiated, in regard to an undetermined striped *violet* wood appearing in Late Stuart furniture, it would be more appropriate to employ the name *princewood*, or *violetwood*, than to arbitrarily introduce another, particularly one that was unknown at this period.

Violetwood was never so highly esteemed by other European craftsmen as by those working in France. Nevertheless its range of use extended from Scandinavia to Italy. Palisander and *Jacaranda*,

152. A George III inlaid kingwood and yewwood sofa table Courtesy of Needham's Antiques. Inc., New York City.

obtained in the same tropical American forests, received greater recognitions in Holland and the German states. Dutch ships, and those of North German free cities were carriers of these different timbers, which, through Amsterdam and Hamburg in particular, were delivered to furniture centres of other countries. (When the *Dalbergia* timbers were received in Stockholm during the second half of the eighteenth century, one, however, is said to have been distinguished by the name of *Konïgs Holtz*. [?])

The violetwood or *bois violet* employed by cabinetmakers of the past was obtained from one or more species of *Dalbergia* native to the Guianas and Brazil. An exact determination of the species has not been discovered, due to a contemporary lack of botanic interest and, as mentioned by M. Verlet, a resulting vagueness in the terminology of the eighteenth century. Specimens of "kingwood" as now obtained from species *D. cearensis*, in timbers shipped from Ceara (Fortaleza), have far less character than the violetwood of former times; while the "Violet Kingwood," which has been introduced in modern commerce, generally displays markings similar to those of the rosewood received in Europe during the nineteenth century.

From the limited widths of violetwood veneers found in old furniture it is apparent that dimensions of the timbers never approached those of the typical rosewoods. Veneers butted together with no attempt at unusual decorative effects, or to form large quarter-matched panels, seldom measure as much as five inches in width. This limitation was overcome, additionally, by the innumerable inlay patterns that were evolved to extend and diversify the use of such a superior material.

The ground color of old veneers may appear in light or medium violet-tinted brown tones, or faded almost to the same extent as the change which takes place in tulipwood, when the lighter tones will have taken on yellowish casts. These effects lend added emphasis to the characteristic striped appearance of the wood, for its dark purplish-brown or blackish veinings are not proportionately modified.

In texture, as well as color, violetwood is somewhat similar to the finer, paler, and more delicately marked cuttings of Brazilian rosewood. However, it is much harder, heavier, and closer in the grain. It is also less oily, possessing a fainter aromatic scent, and it takes a finer, more luscent finish. Weights apparently range between 70 and 80 pounds per cubic foot.

The precisional markings of this wood result from its natural contexture. Therefore the narrow billets or logs were cut directly or obliquely across the grain, to produce oystered or marbled effects, or tangentially with the grain, when the lines produced in growth-ring figures also display a certain degree of correspondence. The former effects are found more often in British and Genoese cabinetwork than in productions executed by French *ébénistes*.

During the Georgian period, British cabinetmakers employed violetwood principally as a banding material. When it was again introduced as a principal surface veneer, at the beginning of the nineteenth century, it was more generally designated as kingwood, though it was still also known as violetwood, and as Guianawood.

According to *The London Cabinet-Makers' Union Book of Prices* (1811), the cost of veneering work in kingwood was to be calculated at the same rate as that figured for "yew-tree," a rate higher than that charged for veneering in rosewood. Later, *The Cabinet-Maker's Assistant* recorded the prices paid for these three woods as timbers. Just prior to 1853 "yew-tree" had sold for "about £20, £40," or even £60 per ton, and rosewood at £20 to £40 per ton for good "Rio wood." "King Wood" is recorded in this publication at a surprisingly low figure—"about £8 [*sic*] per ton."

Despite the limited dimensions of the timber, this is a most perplexing evaluation if it refers to true violetwood, one of the finest cabinet woods the world has ever known—unquestionably the most refined and the handsomest of the striped woods. That violetwood was a very costly timber during the days of its earlier vogues is indicated by its general restriction, as a principal surfacing veneer, to furniture produced by the most accomplished *ébénistes*, particularly those working in Paris during the reign of Louis XV, and by the most highly skilled cabinetmakers employed in the British Isles.

THE ILLUSTRATED EXAMPLES

The oystered parquetry patterns appearing in the cabinet presented here, and in the fall-front example shown under OLIVEWOOD, indicate the ingeniousness exercised in this type of veneering from the turn of the seventeenth century. As a decided contrast to this work, the moldings, turnings and other structural features of both pieces are virtually identical in their close adherence to established forms. A complemental use of cross-grained moldings and bandings is more noticeable in the violetwood cabinet, wherein, as an additional mark of

Fig. 151

153. A Louis XV inlaid violetwood *bureau plat*

154. A Louis XV violetwood parquetry commode

quality, some of these narrow traverses actually feature additional oystered effects.

In accordance with later nomenclature, the principal plain-sawed veneers of the sofa table, *circa* 1800, are designated as kingwood. Recalling the molding skills of a century earlier, the rounded, cross-grained edging of the sectional top is also of the same wood. The selection of yewwood as an inlay material is in agreement with the suggestions offered by *The London Cabinet-Makers' Union Book of Prices*, known elsewhere in the British Isles as *The London Book*.

Another production of *circa* 1760, the *bureau plat* with reverse diamond-matched drawer facings exhibits the light ground color that characterizes numerous examples of French furniture executed in violetwood. That it was possible for the *ébéniste* to make his selections from either light- or dark-toned timbers is manifest in the panels and contrasting surrounds of the following commode. Here the lighter, alternately matched veneers have been diagonally cut to achieve elongated oyster-shell effects. The high-wrought appliques are typical of this art as practiced in Paris *circa* 1760-1775— though similar work was performed outside of the capital city until about 1780.

107.

TROPICAL AMERICAN ROSEWOOD
BRAZILIAN ROSEWOOD
PALISANDER

Rosewood was formerly obtained from species of *Dalbergia* native to Brazil and the West Indies, and to a lesser extent from Honduras, where most of the present supplies originate. The most important of these species is *D. nigra*, found chiefly in Bahia and Rio de Janeiro. An alternative name for the Brazilian timber, jacaranda, has been confused with the *genus* of this name, embracing a large number of tropical American trees in an entirely different botanical family. Although the rosewood tree has been termed a "soverign" of Brazilian forests, it is tall but relatively slender. After a heavy sap ring, and outer defects of the heartwood have been removed, the logs seldom measure more than two feet in diameter, while even this remaining portion of the heartwood may contain a large amount of unsound or poorly colored wood.

Brazilian rosewood ranges in color from yellowish-tan, through orange and deeper red tones, to a very dark purplish hue. Brownish-black or black pigment figures are displayed most effectively when

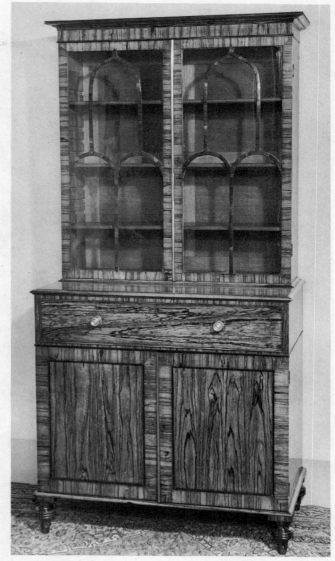

155. A Regency brass-inlaid Brazilian rosewood secretary Courtesy of A. Cook, London.

the irregularly shaped logs are sawed along planes paralleling the direction of the growth rings. The wood is hard, firm and medium-coarse in texture, displaying scattered vessel lines. In common with the other rosewoods, rays are not visible without magnification. Growth rings may be obscure or distinct. The grain is normally straight, but occasionally wavy. Weights range from 50 to 60 pounds per cubic foot.

Under a very broad classification, rosewood was known in Europe during the Renaissance period, probably through trading operations in tropical America. The first variety of these timbers to win special recognition was characterized by the darkest of the purplish colorings. Supplies of this description, designated as palisander, were shipped from

156. A George II Brazilian rosewood architectural bookcase Courtesy of Phillips of Hitchen.

Brazil (chiefly from Pernambuco), and from the Lesser Antilles. During the second half of the seventeenth century these supplies were utilized in Dutch cabinetwork, and from that country they were introduced into the principal furniture centres of northern Europe. As *bois de palissandre*, alternatively known as *bois de Sainte-Lucie*, the wood became popular in French *ébénesterie* of the Régence period.

Rosewood timbers of browner and less pronounced dark purple casts were not particularly favored during the greater part of the eighteenth century, although this type of wood may appear in work then executed in various port sections of western and northern Europe and Coxed and Woster, as well as Chippendale, are known to have employed it on occasion. With the great popularity of rosewood furniture in the British Isles during the later Sheraton period and the succeeding years, these timbers might be designated according to the areas from whence they were shipped, but without such knowledge it is likely that even tropical American and eastern varieties of rosewood could not be differentiated. This is apparent in confusions indicated by *The Cabinet-Maker's Assistant*, and, as late as 1875, by Laslett's apology that "Further in-

157. A George III inlaid rosewood sofa table

158. A Régence inlaid palisander commode

formation as to the Rosewood is much wanted.''

The former publication regarded rosewood as "likely to furnish a permanently fashionable material for drawing-room furniture," devoting considerable space to considerations of the tropical American timber: "The importations from Rio de Janeiro furnish the largest-sized and best figured wood, and bring a considerably higher price than those from Bahia, the other principal seaport, situated about 800 miles to the north of Rio de Janeiro. . . . The prices at present current are, for good *Rio* wood, in lots, about £20 per ton; and for *Bahia* wood, about £12 per ton. . . . An inferior kind is occasionally imported from Honduras, and sold at about £7 per ton; but it is so soft, porous, and ill coloured, as to be fit only for the manufacture of ordinary furniture."

To fill in the pores or vessel lines it was recommended that "after the surface has been finished by the cabinet-maker, rub it carefully in with plaster of Paris, coloured with rose-pink, which, after being *set*, is to be carefully papered off. This does not shrink like the size; and has the effect of preventing the oil used with the French polish from finding a hiding-place in the pores, whence it afterwards exudes on exposure to the air, and eats off the polish like rust on a metallic surface."

The lengthy account ends on a decorative note: "Besides being intrinsically beautiful, it [rosewood] contrasts admirable with the materials usually employed in drapery; whilst mahogany, maple, satinwood, and walnut, are apt to lose by comparison with the stuffs with which they are associated, or may have the effect of depriving these of their proper effect. We are not acquainted with any drapery material which can interfere with the beauty of rosewood, or any for which it does not present an appropriate foil, and setting."

(Honduras rosewood, referred to above, is obtained from a tree now designated as *D. stevensonii*. While the structural characteristics are similar to those of Brazilian rosewood, the timber is somewhat redder, and also heavier—weighing 60-63 pounds per cubic foot. Titmus rates it as "slightly ornamental," in comparison with Brazilian rosewood as "a first class, highly important decorative cabinet timber.")

THE ILLUSTRATED EXAMPLES

Fig. 156
Architectural pieces such as the break-front cabinet are usually considered by English experts to have been evolved under the influence of William Kent, (b. 1684, d. 1748). However, it is most un-

likely that such a large use of rosewood could have occurred during his lifetime. In 1743 Horace Walpole declared that this wood had been used for a much smaller cabinet with triangular pediment, made to contain his enamels and miniatures. Nevertheless it is apparent that he had been misled by his cabinetmaker or by his own judgement. The museum now in possession of this hanging cabinet describes the wood as mahogany, while enlargement of a very clear photograph reveals markings that are more characteristic of padauk than rosewood or mahogany.

Brazilian rosewood appears in the door frames, drawer surrounds and shelving of the present cabinet in which the wing units retain their original grilles. The drawers are faced with matched veneers which, in consideration of their color, graining and exceptionally fine texture, may very well be of lignum vitae, a wood that is also liable to develop the hairline cracks that are noticeable in the photograph. Mahogany was chosen as a more suitable material for the carved feet. Fig. 15

In the Sheraton sofa table of *circa* 1800 the drawer surfaces are richly and evenly colored, while the top is distinctively marked by eccentric reserves of unpigmented wood, harmonizing with the solid material of the legs. Fig. 15

According to *The Cabinet-Maker's Assistant*:

"*Colour* is of more importance than either size or soundness in rosewood. Much of it is to be found of a dull light brown colour, resembling nothing more than a dried peat; whereas in wood of good quality, the ground is of a clear sharp colour, varying in depth of shade from orange to dark red, having the graining or figure distinctly marked in black." In regard to *figure* it was recommended that rosewood planks "should be carefully selected for veneers, while the plainer pieces are reserved for chair wood, couch-feet and scrolls, table-pillars and claws, and solid work generally. In cutting up veneer planks, regard must be had to the form of the concentric circles, in order to bring out the best figure which the plank is capable of exhibiting; and this object will be best secured by making the saw-draughts run as nearly as possible parallel to the circles. . . . Rosewood, in this respect, presents a remarkable contrast to mahogany; for in it the finest figure is secured by causing the saw-draught to go right across the concentric rings, instead of parallel to them. The cause of this difference is, that in rosewood the medullary rays, or transverse septae, are hardly distinguishable; and hence, there is almost none of that lustre or transparency which lends the chief beauty to mahogany, maple, birch, and other woods, in which the medullary rays are large."

159. A Regency inlaid Brazilian rosewood cabinet Courtesy of Smith & Watson, Inc., New York City.

Fig. 159 The small open-shelf cabinet, *circa* 1810, is surfaced with quietly figured veneers of Brazilian rosewood. This piece is supported by turned front, and rear inset *pieds en toupie* similar to those appearing in the French *secrétaire à abattant* made of plum-pudding mahogany.

Fig. 155 A rare cutting of rosewood is represented in the veneers of the Regency writing cabinet. Resembling a cross between tulipwood and rosewood, the ground color is of a decided olive tone, while the blackish pigmentation is typical of this development as it takes place in Brazilian rosewood (rather than in varieties of zebrawood, calamander or other *Diospyros* species), although the figuring is quite unusual. In order to assure the accuracy of this identification the photograph of the cabinet was submitted to Mr. J. L. Stearns, who verified the olive color as of fairly common occurrence in Brazilian rosewood, and the figuring as more characteristic of this timber than any other.

Palisander is so dark in coloring that there are no particularly noticeable markings to recommend its use as a surfacing material, while amaranth, a still plainer but much finer and richer wood, has always been preferred as an inlay material. The weighty forms of late Renaissance and baroque furniture in which palisander was featured did little to add to its somber appearance. The present commode is typical of many others with *bombé* **Fig. 158** shapings, and elaborate, often grotesque mounts, which were executed during the first half of the eighteenth century in leading cities of southeastern France.

Although a number of these examples are stamped with the names of Parisian *ébénistes*, such as *Mondon* and *Criaerd*, native authorities have ascribed their origins to Tours, Dijon, and other cities located in the central provinces of France. Little determinative evidence is presented in the nondescript construction and outlines of the coarser pieces, or in their gilded bronze mounts. The more pronounced shapings appear to be more characteristic of work performed in southern France and northern Italy, while exactly matching appliqués were repeatedly cast, at least until 1760, in towns situated along the southern and eastern borders of France and in Switzerland.

108. EAST INDIAN ROSEWOOD

The East Indian blackwood tree, *Dalbergia latifolia*, native to India and Ceylon, produces a timber that is more generally known as Indian, or East Indian rosewood, or as blackwood, but which may also be called shisham or sissoo (*vide* SISSOO). Of an unusually slow growth habit, the tree attains a height of eighty feet, and a butt diameter of five feet—greater than that of the Brazilian rosewood.

This timber appears in medium or dark purplish-brown colors, and it is marked with denser black streaks produced by similar zones in the growth rings. Color effects may be somewhat similar to those of Brazilian rosewood, but as a rule contrasts are less pronounced. The wood is hard, moderately coarse, and uniform in texture, permitting a smooth, lustrous finish. A normally interlocked grain accounts for inconspicuous stripe figures that occur in radial surfaces. The oil content is not so high as in Brazilian rosewood, and an aromatic scent is less pronounced. Weights vary from 50 to 60 pounds per cubic foot.

Timbers of this description were distributed among other sections of the Orient before they were introduced in Europe, eventually becoming so common in southern China as to acquire the name of Chinese blackwood. Much of the so-called teak furniture (and smaller objects) produced in this area during the past hundred years is actually made of the finer, heavier, and darker East Indian rosewood.

Supplies received in England during the nineteenth century were described by *The Cabinet-Maker's Assistant* under the heading of *Sissoo*: "*Dalbergia latifolia* another and superior sort of sissoo, is a product of the Malabar coast. It is much darker than the former, (*D. sissoo*), being of a greenish black, with lighter coloured veins running in various directions, and takes a fine polish. This variety, called by the English: Indian rosewood, and black-wood tree, and by the natives, *sit sal*, is one of the largest trees in India, attaining a circumference of 15 feet. Both sorts possess the qualities of good cabinet-wood, in dimensions of timber, firmness of texture, and average appearance."

A later English notation on rosewood gives first place to India as a source of the *Dalbergia* timbers received in England during and after the sixteenth century. The account quoted here indicates a similar uncertainty regarding East Indian rosewood, even at a time when the popularity of Brazilian rosewood had reached great heights in England.

THE ILLUSTRATED EXAMPLE

The piece shown here was produced in China during the middle decades of the eighteenth cen-

Fig. 160

160. A Chinese carved East Indian rosewood secretary Courtesy of the Kunstindustrimuseet, Copenhagen.

tury, for visiting traders or their more permanently located representatives in that country. Prior to 1700 European trade with China was carried on principally in Canton, the port where shipping of the various East India Companies was confined during the early years of the following century. Of the northern areas engaged in this trade the British Isles, Denmark and Sweden were influenced to an extent by cultural developments in Holland, while the Scandinavians were also inspired by designing skills developed in the British Isles. It may therefore be assumed that the example of Sino-European furniture represented here was made in Canton, but it should not be presumed that all such examples were infallibly copied from English originals.

A Danish merchant is known to have acquired the elaborately carved secretary, along with several other pieces of furniture, upon a visit to Canton during the middle years of the eighteenth century. While the handling of the principal portions and the paw-foot base is strongly reminiscent of Dutch designs, and to a lesser degree of those executed in the Dutch East Indian and South African colonies, the pediment is cusped and scrolled in a manner especially favored by Danish and North German cabinetmakers. The interior fittings, especially in the curved and stepped sections of lower small drawers, are also typical of Dutch arrange-

ments which were repeated in neighboring areas of the Continent and in the British Isles. The handles and escutcheons are of tutenag, a white metal introduced in the manufacture of British fire grates, fenders, etc.

109. AMARANTH

Amaranth, or *bois d'amarante*, an especially handsome cabinet wood, is produced by at least two different species of trees in the genus *Peltogyne*, indigenous to the Guianas, Surinam, Trinidad, Brazil and the small neighboring island of Maranhao. The timber is mentioned in old English accounts as "Purple Wood," a name later changed to purpleheart. Despite statistics regarding the size of the Amaranth tree, given at more than one hundred and fifty feet in height, and four feet in the diameter of its trunk, timbers cut during the past were apparently of small or moderate dimensions, particularly in regard to breadth. Current supplies are available in widths of no more than twelve inches, although it is said that larger scantlings may be procured if specially ordered.

When freshly cut this timber displays dull brown hues, which soon change to bright purples, and, with continued exposure, tone to amaranthine or deep violet shades. Amaranth is hard, strong and elastic, fine and uniform in texture, and at

161. A Louis XV inlaid amaranth and tulipwood *bureau plat*

times presents exceedingly smooth, fairly lustrous, evenly colored surfaces. A certain proportion of the wood displays finished surfaces marked by distinct vessel lines, and by prominent light-toned parenchymatous deposits. Material of this nature may also appear in lighter and redder tints, as well as in the deeper violet shades. Growth rings are normally indistinct, with little effect on the appearance of the wood. The grain is generally straight, but it may be wavy or interlocked, producing reserved mottle figures. Fine rays are visible in the transverse sections. Weights vary from 55 to 65 pounds per cubic foot.

While amaranth received some favor in northern and central areas of the Continent, the rich appearance of this wood appealed more strongly to French *ébénistes*. *Bois d'amarante* may be found in their most elaborate productions of baroque, rococo and classic designs, selected for parquetry and marquetry decorations, to frame such panels or embellish their surrounding structural elements, or to serve as an entire surfacing material. In occasional specimens of antique furniture the superficial aspect of the wood had deteriorated to an unattractive greenish-brown color, apparently as a result of unsatisfactory finishing methods. For-

162. A Louis XV amaranth marquetry *table de dame* Collection of Mrs. Meyer Sasson Courtesy of Morton Lee, London.

163. A Louis XV amaranth *mueble d'entredeux* Courtesy of M. Gaston Bensimon, New York City.

tunately, the normal soft purple color remains directly beneath these deteriorated areas and may be revived through proper refinishing.

British cabinetmakers made use of this timber after its introduction elsewhere in Europe, principally as a marquetry or border material. Advices appearing in *The Cabinet-Maker's Assistant* are at variance, in certain respects, with current knowledge: "*Purple Wood*, called also Amaranthus, is a product of Brazil, and, like most other woods of small growth and irregular shape, is imported in the round state. In dimensions, it varies from 8 to 10 feet in length, and from 6 to 9 inches in diameter. In toughness and rigidity of fibre, it resembles rosewood, but is harder, much finer in texture, and heavier. It is wavy and irregular in grain, but has very little variety in figure, and is irregularly coloured in various shades of purple,

lighter near the outside, and gradually darker towards the centre.

"Purple wood is sometimes confounded with King wood and [*sic*] violet wood, but these are frequently figured, whereas purple wood is usually plain. It is used for buhl-work, for marquetry, and turning, and is sold by weight."

At the close of the eighteenth century "Purple Wood" was stocked by a very few cabinet shops in this country, but it is seldom found in American furniture of the period. The name "violetwood" has also been employed here to designate amaranth rather than as referring to the true violetwood of the eighteenth century, later known as kingwood.

THE ILLUSTRATED EXAMPLES

The small writing and dressing table is an Oeben Fig. 162

production of *circa* 1760-1770. Amaranth has been employed for the outer surfaces of the legs and the surrounds of the marquetry panels—in veneers displaying the light-toned hatchings mentioned above as consisting of parenchymatous deposits.

In 1754 Jean-François Oeben, a German by birth, was granted a *brevet de logement à la manufacture royale des Gobelins*. Six years later he commenced work on the world-famous *bureau du Roi* which he was not to finish, but which his foreman, Jean-Henri Riesener, completed and signed in 1769. Oeben's death is recorded by some authorities as occurring in 1763, while others give "28 Janvier, 1764" as the date of his acceptance in the Parisian corporation of *maître ébénistes*. In any case the marriage of his widow and foreman is known to have taken place in 1767, two years before the completion of his greatest masterpiece.

It is not generally recognized that Oeben's shop, apparently with the same staff of highly skilled artisans, continued in operation long after his death. Nor is it definitely known whether his widow, some other member of his family, or Riesener, supervised the running of this shop after 1769. Nevertheless a number of signed Oeben *meubles de luxe* that are exhibited in the most notable European collections are undoubtedly productions of 1770-1775 or of the Louis XVI period. This may be substantiated by the fact that some of these pieces incorporate working techniques that could not possibly have been evolved prior to 1772, while others feature outlines, marquetry patterns and *bronze doré* mounts that were developed between 1775 and 1780.

Fig. 163   In the large writing table with leather top, an example of *circa* 1770-1775, amaranth of a very smooth texture and an even, deep violet or purplish color has been employed to surround the drawer facings and panel inlays of the legs, which are of tulipwood, as are the inner surfaces of the legs. This same wood, in texture and coloring midway between these properties of the veneers appearing in the *bureau plat* and *table de dame*, is repre-

Fig. 161   sented in the *meuble d'entredeux* enhanced with highly wrought appliques. Here the vertical stiles, valanced front shaping, and handling of the relief ornament are indicative of work performed *circa* 1760-1765.

110. FUSTET

The Venetian sumac, *Cotinus coggygria*, alternatively known as the wig tree and the European smoke tree, supplies a timber of limited dimensions that was formerly employed as an inlay material of Continental furniture. This wood is recognized as fustet, young fustic, and *bois de fustet*. Structural properties are not given by the timber authorities consulted here, for the species is unimportant in modern commerce except in the production of yellow and orange dyes. Under a classification of *Rhus cotinus*, which is no longer recognized, Clouzot lists "Bois de Fustet" as a medium of eighteenth-century marquetry work in France, noting a "lively greenish-yellow color, veined in brown and greenish-brown tones."

111. EAGLEWOOD

Eaglewood, *Aquillaria agallocha*, is the *aloes* of Biblical times, known also as agalloch, calambac and paradisewood. This resinous wood, possessing a fragrant, aromatic, honeylike scent, is burned as a perfume in the Orient, where it is found in China, Indo-China and India.

Only the centermost portion of the oldest trees is suitable for cabinet purposes as the balance of the trunk is unusually soft and of a nondescript coloring. The usable wood is bicolored, appearing in various red and green hues. It is medium coarse in texture and normally straight in the grain, displaying decorative figures composed of pigment and growth-ring markings. Titmus records the weight at 20-30 pounds per cubic foot.

While this timber is now seldom procurable in world markets, it was formerly in great demand for inlaid work. It was introduced in Europe during the eighteenth century, when it was adopted as a medium of French marquetry work. In this use it was described by M. Clouzot as: "Aloès, bois d'aigle ou calambac (*Exocoecaria agallocha, aquilaria agallocha, aloexylon agallochum*), roussâtre et verdâtre, odeur aromatique."

112. LIGNUM VITAE

Lignum vitae, *Guaicum officinale* Linn. and *G. sanctum* Linn., is obtained in the West Indies and on the tropical American mainland. The tree matures with a short, usually crooked trunk, seldom attaining an extreme height of more than thirty feet, or a butt diameter in excess of twelve inches. Timbers of larger girths were available in the past, particularly in Cuba and Santo Domingo, when some logs measured as much as twenty inches in diameter.

The bright yellow sapwood of this tree, some-

164. Lignum vitae wassail bowls Collection of Mr. and Mrs. Edward H. Pinto, Oxhey Drive, Middlesex.

165. A Late Stuart lignum vitae parquetry cabinet on matching stand Courtesy of Ronald A. Lee, Ham Common, Surrey.

times comprising more than half of the trunk, is of a quality equal to that of the heartwood. In this portion of the trunk, brown, green or blackish ground colors develop, and the wood is usually marked by heavy black streaks. Greenish pigment streaks are present in much of the browner timber, erratically following the direction of the grain.

When freshly cut, lignum vitae is soft enough to be worked without excessive difficulty. After drying out it becomes so hard, and remains so oily that at present it is no longer cut into veneers. The texture is very fine and uniform, the grain remarkable for its unusual alternating spiral development. While growth rings are frequently indistinct, or even invisible, figures resulting from their formation are common in finished surfaces. Lignum vitae possesses a very high oil content, a distinctive pleasant scent, and a bitter taste. Weights range from 73 pounds to a high of 89 pounds per cubic foot.

When this timber was first imported into England, during the early years of the sixteenth century, it was especially valued for the medicinal properties of its resin, known as guaiacum and used as a remedy for gout, rheumatism and other ailments. During the following century the wood was employed by cabinetmakers working in Holland and the British Isles, and by turners who supplied the wassailing vessels of the period. Some furniture was completely or partially made of the solid wood, and in other instances it was utilized as a veneer. The smaller timbers were cut transversely or obliquely across the grain, when the resulting oyster pieces were used to form parquetry panels in which portions of the yellow sapwood were allowed to remain as a decorative feature of this work. As *bois de gaïac* the wood is also recorded as a medium of French marquetry work.

THE ILLUSTRATED EXAMPLES

Fig. 164. The uneven graining developed in lignum vitae, and the contrasting tones of the heartwood and sapwood, are evidenced in the three wassail bowls.

Fig. 165 Similar contrasts are featured in the veneered and turned work of the late seventeenth-century cabinet. Here the doors and side panels are surfaced with parquetry in which the light sapwood has been made to serve as a ground for setting off the dark, concentrically ringed oyster or heartwood portions of the veneer pieces. Matching but flat-cut veneers have been utilized for the frieze of the stand, and for the stretcher, while the solid turned supports are so unevenly colored that they appear to have been partially painted or ebonized. A lively decorative effect has been achieved without the *bizarrerie* that might easily have resulted through a lesser understanding of this intractable but highly interesting material.

113. GREEN EBONY
ÉBÈNE VERTE

Green ebony is obtained from several varieties of true ebony in which greenish colorings have developed. Most species of ebony do not produce a heartwood that is solidly black, or that is distinguished by a jet-black color. The sapwood is always quite pale, appearing in gray, yellow, or pinkish hues, and the entire trunk may remain light in color until the tree is many years old. When the mutation does occur, greenish or brownish as well as gray or blackish tones may develop in the heartwood. The blacker colorings frequently die away and reappear in different portions of the stem, decreasing to a considerable extent toward the head of the tree. In these processes a certain percentage of ebony timbers take on wide areas of the greenish colorings. *Diospyros melanoxylon* in particular is noted as a source of this true green ebony, at the same time being of equal importance in the supply of black ebony.

Several other tropical timbers that have come to be known as green ebonies bear no relationship to the ebony family, just as in the case of European ash which has acquired a greenish pigmentation.

Of these exotics the West Indian granadilla tree, *Brya ebenus*, a source of cocuswood, also yields one of the best so-called green ebonies of commerce. *The Cabinet-Maker's Assistant* recognized this timber without knowing its correct botanical designation, describing it under the heading of true ebony: "*Green Ebony* is a product of the West Indies generally, and is imported chiefly from the island of Jamaica, in pieces from 3 to 6 feet in length. The tree is smoother and thinner in the bark than the principal variety of Cocus, which it resembles in grain, and also somewhat in colour. The heart wood is of a brownish green, and is highly resinous, like rosewood; and, like black ebony, it is straight-grained, and cleaves easily. It is used in turnery and marquetry, and also for rulers, as it stands well."

Ébène verte, as employed by French cabinetmakers of the eighteenth century, displays an olive-brown or light bronze-brown color, with veinings of brighter and greener tones. The origin of this wood has not been determined specifically, but it was probably obtained along with other timbers shipped to France from South America. Laslett recorded two such woods as products of French Guiana: "*Ébène*. This wood is greenish in colour, very hard, heavy, strong, plain and even in the grain, solid, and good in quality. The sapwood is about 1½ inch thick. It would be useful in turnery, or for any of the purposes to which the common or Ceylon Ebony is applied." "*Ébène verte*. This wood is dark green in colour, very hard, heavy, close in the grain, solid, and of good quality. Like No. 3 (*Ébène*), it has about 1½ inch of sapwood. The dimensions of the logs varied from 14 to 16 inches square, and were about 14 feet in length. It would be chiefly used in cabinet work and turnery."

During the seventeenth century and later, green ebony was highly valued as providing a salient note in the inlaid decorations of European furniture. In regard to the varieties of tropical, non-*Diospyros* timbers, which usually present dull greenish or greenish brown tones, it may be quite impossible to make any discriminations. However, they may at least be distinguished from true green ebonies, for these woods generally display silkier textures, and clearer. but fairly deep and soft, sea- or sage-green colorings.

When areas of green pigmentation occurred in true ebonies, selected for their predominance of the more usual black wood, these areas were stained to produce evenly colored surfaces. This recourse may be observed in old furniture when an edge of a split or broken banding reveals a natural green coloring in the wood immediately beneath a black-stained and polished surface. In certain instances other portions of these bandings have been examined and found to contain blackish wood. Some strips removed from damaged furniture have indicated the possibility that green ebony was sometimes stained to provide the more popular black bandings of the late eighteenth century.

114. CALAMANDER

Calamander, known also as coromandelwood, is a product of several species of trees that are indigenous to Cylon and southern India. These species are members of the genus *Diospyros*, containing all of the true black ebonies, their woods being partially marked in the usual shades of black, but also streaked in brown or red hazel tones. The major species is now generally recognized as *D. quaesita*, with some doubt cast upon the accuracy of the designation *D. hirsuta* (*vide* MARBLEWOOD), given by Linnaeus. Webster's authority gives the latter species as a principal source of calamander, the opinion of Linnaeus also being upheld by Holtzapffel, a botanist of the nineteenth century who apparently was drawn upon in the account of calamander appearing in *The Cabinet-Maker's Assistant*:

166. A Regency inlaid calamander sofa table Courtesy of Arthur S. Vernay, Inc., New York City.

Generally expressed, its appearance is something between rosewood and zebrawood, with a red hazel or chocolate brown ground, figured with black stripes and marks. The darkest kind of wood is that most seen in this country, and is known as Calamander; a lighter coloured variety, somewhat striped, is called Calemberri; and a third kind, almost as light in shade as English yew, but possessing a ruddier hue, and partially veined and marked with darker tints, is called Omander.

All these timbers, whether the produce of different trees, or of the same tree in different states, are very hard, but still they are easily cut by the veneer saw, and as easily wrought upon the lathe, for which, indeed, they are peculiarly well adapted; and all of them form very elegant furniture woods.

The duramen or heart-wood of the Calamander, like all other woods, is surrounded by a thick sap wood, which, in this timber, has a light yellow colour, and is of equal hardness with the heart, but has a coarser, opener fibre.

It is imported in small logs of about 3 feet long, and 3 to 6 inches diameter, though some logs, at times, are to be met with having a diameter of 9 inches. It is irregularly shaped in the log, but sound, and not subject to rend while seasoning. Being in considerable request in ornamental turnery, and frequently scarce in the market, its price fluctuates, but, generally speaking, it sells from 8d. to 1s. per lb.

References to a "striped" appearance are not quite accurately descriptive of calamander. This wood is *irregularly streaked*, with areas of black-toned wood substance, interrupted by other areas of light, to fairly dark hazel colorings. It is very fine and even in texture, affording an equally smooth finish. Ornamentation occurs solely in the varied development of color patterns, for no discernible effects are produced through the structural elements. The weight is 70-75 pounds per cubic foot.

Calamander was introduced in British furniture at about the same time that Sheraton brought out his first designs in the pure Regency style. Veneers of this wood are seldom found in the more generous breadths quoted above, in fact those appearing in large surfaces of Regency cabinet pieces frequently measure only an inch and a half, to three inches in width. Prior to this introduction, however, it is said that calamander was employed in producing furniture for Dutch residents of the East Indian colonies. It would seem that a less decorative Ceylonese wood was used in this work, possibly obtained from certain of the *D. quaesita* timbers. In 1875 Laslett mentioned this species as "the Calamander wood . . . now getting scarce; it is one of the most valuable ornamental woods of

167. A Regency inlaid calamander sofa table At Marlborough House. Reproduced by gracious permission of Her Majesty Queen Mary. Copyright *Country Life*.

168. A Regency inlaid calamander sofa table Courtesy of Richard Grose, Ltd., London.

Ceylon and South India."

THE ILLUSTRATED EXAMPLES

The esteem in which this decorative cabinet wood was held during the Regency period is manifest in the finished execution of the three sofa tables veneered with the darkly colored material. *Coromandel* was the term used in contemporary price lists, but *calamander* is preferred here as it has come into more general use, and the other name may possibly be confused with coromandel ebony, *vide D. melanoxylon.* Another expression current during the Regency years, *taper pointed panels,* refer to inlays such as those appearing in the unbraced bridge feet of the plainer sofa table, *circa* 1810. The scrolled underframing of the following example, of about the same date, would be less suited to a plain top, but here in an original treatment this surface has been accordantly shaped on the one side, where it projects to provide greater than usual serviceability when the table is placed in front of a sofa.

In the table from Marlborough House the conventionalized inlays are of brass, though they con-

Fig. 166

Fig. 168

Fig. 167

form with the usual figures in holly, ebony and other woods, as illustrated in the 1811 edition of *The London Cabinet-Makers' Union Book of Prices.* Beneath the top are two extending leaves connected by a mechanism so contrived that when one leaf is drawn out the other is propelled in the opposite direction.

115. MACASSAR EBONY

Macassar ebony has been classed as a coromandelwood, but while it bears a close resemblance to this other *Diospyros* timber it has been authoritatively designated as a product of the species *D. macassar,* native to the East Indies, mainly to the Celebes. The timber is cut into logs measuring up to sixteen feet in length and thirty inches in diameter, which are often defective in character. The wood is of a blackish or very dark brown color, with pronounced streaks and figures in gray and yellowish-red or yellowish-brown tones. These markings are displayed in irregular and often strikingly bizarre patterns when the timber has been cut along tangential planes. With radial sawing narrow, uniform bands of contrasting light and dark color tones are

169. A Late Regency inlaid macassar ebony display cabinet Courtesy of H. Blairman & Sons Ltd., London.

revealed. On coming upon chance supplies of this wood former cabinetmakers would be prone to follow the former method, but in modern use the timber is always quartered. A dense structure, in which most of the fine vessels are plugged with gum, permits a very smooth surface finish. Weights of this ebony range from 61 to 78 pounds per cubic foot.

Other decoratively marked ebonies, known as marblewood, are obtained from the species *D. kurzii*, *D. marmorata* and *D. oocarpa*, indigenous to the Andaman Islands, Ceylon and other parts of the East Indies. These bicolored timbers appear in blackish tones mixed with creamy-white, yellowish or russet areas. Marbled effects may be rather subtle and nebulous in contrast to those obtained in calamander and Macassar ebony.

THE ILLUSTRATED EXAMPLE

Fig. 169   The display cabinet attests a rare use of Macassar

ebony during the early part of the nineteenth century. Some indication of the manner in which true black ebonies may be penetrated by areas of lighter-colored wood substance can be derived from the appearance of the drawer facings. More strikingly bizarre, zebralike markings in the flanking door panels outmatch those of zebrawood itself. These veneers, and those of the upper door frames, inlaid pediments, etc., have been plain-sawed, in contrast to the modern cutting method mentioned above.

116. ÉBÈNE DE PORTUGAL

The exact origin of *ébène de Portugal*, a timber that was received in France during the eighteenth century, has not been authoritatively determined. It is believed that these supplies were obtained on the island of Mauritius, formerly known as the Île de France. The properties of the wood indicate it to be the product of a *Diospyros* species, possibly *D. tesselaria* or a closely related island growth.

As it is found in marquetry decorations of old French furniture, the ebony-black coloring of the wood is interrupted by whitish specks or larger spottings. It is an extremely hard wood, with minute, invisible pores, and an exceedingly fine texture—accounting for the high luster of polished surfaces.

117. PALMYRAWOOD

Palmyrawood has been widely used as a decorative veneer, principally as an inlay material contrasting with the better known, lighter- or more brilliantly-colored cabinet woods. In old European furniture it is found chiefly among the inlaid decorations of examples produced at Tunbridge Wells during and after the turn of the eighteenth century.

This wood is obtained from the Palmyra palm, *Borassus flabelliformis*, native to India, Burma, Ceylon and Africa, the only species of the genus with large rounded fan-shaped leaves. The usable portion of the tall stem develops near the perimeter, seldom reaching a depth of more than four inches.

The characteristic structural formation of an endogen is unmistakable in Palmyrawood, just as in porcupinewood—in fact it is also referred to by this other name because of its quill-like markings. In coloring, however, it is much darker than this other wood, appearing with a medium-brown tone in the ground tissues, which are penetrated, in the direction of the grain, by interrupted linear veinings filled with jet-black deposits. Palmyrawood possesses a considerable degree of hardness. It can be worked to a fairly smooth surface in which the medium-coarse texture of the ground contrasts with a relative smoothness in the profusely distributed black veinings. The weight is about 50 pounds per cubic foot.

118. EBONY

Ebony is produced by various species of *Diospyros*[31] native to tropical Asia and Africa. The tree is of moderate size in relation to other important hardwood timbers, attaining a height of about seventy feet and a diameter of about thirty inches in the bole. A uniform jet-black color characterizes the most highly prized wood, found in only a certain proportion of the trees. Frequently this material must be extracted from the balance of the heartwood, where it may be formed in irregular though fairly large masses, sometimes interspersed with streaks or splotches of a lighter tone or coloring. Other timbers are distinguished by grayish, brownish or greenish casts, rather than a pronounced black of full and rich intensity.

One of the finest jet-black ebonies is obtained from the species *D. ebenus*, indigenous to Ceylon but also found in southern India. Two other black ebonies, produced by the species *D. melanoxylon* and *D. tomentosa*, are of greater importance in India, and additional timbers of this description have been shipped from Africa, principally from the Guinea coast region where *D. crassiflora* provides one of the finest varieties.

Ebony, or *ébène*, *ebbenhout* and *Ebenholz* in French, Dutch and German, is extremely fine and even in texture, with a straight or slightly irregular grain, in rare instances presenting a delicate, subdued stripe figure in radial sections. No other structural characteristics are visible in ordinary examinations. The wood is very hard and brittle, frequently developing fine splits or surface checks in drying. To facilitate this process the trees are often girdled two years before felling. Ebony is exceptionally difficult to work, but it finishes smoothly and takes an excellent polish. Weights range from 70 to 80 pounds per cubic foot.

When *The Cabinet-Maker's Assistant* was published, nine different varieties of ebony were known in England, of which only timbers designated as Mauritius ebony or East Indian ebony were referred to as black. African Ebony, received from the Cape of Good Hope in billets of small dimensions, was considered "inferior to the two former in colour and grain," and used in making "mathematical and philosophical instruments."

This work reported that "The Mauritius variety (the *Diospyros Ebenus*) is the finest in the grain, the hardest as well as the blackest and the most beautiful of the three, and also the most costly. The best specimens of this kind of ebony vary from 6 to 8 inches in diameter; in this size the colour is more uniformly and intensely black, and the wood more sound. When it rises to from 16 to 18 inches diameter, blemishes abound, and the colour is a dark steel gray. Ebony is uncommonly apt to split on exposure to sunlight or rapid seasoning. . . . The Mauritius ebony, when first cut, is usually quite sound, and, with a view to its preservation, it is immersed in water for many months; and when taken out, the two ends are secured from splitting by iron rings and wedges. . . . It is sold at from £16 to £20 per ton.

"East Indian Ebony (*Diospyros ebenaster*), which

170. A Louis XVI ebony and bronze
doré table à écrire

grows in continental India, Ceylon, and the Indian islands, has greater range in the dimensions of its timber than the former. It varies from 6 to 20 inches, and even to 28 inches, in diameter; that from the continent of India is imported chiefly from Madras and Bombay. In grain, colour, and figure, the Indian ebony is inferior to Mauritian, but it is less liable to split in seasoning, and more free from interior blemishes. Besides the *Diospyros ebenaster*, there are other Indian species which yield ebony, namely, the *Diospyros tomentosa* and the *Diospyros Roylei*.... Ceylon or East Indian ebony sells at from £9 to £10 per ton."

It is believed that the first appearance of ebony in Chinese furniture dates from the middle or early years of the Ming dynasty. That there was little difference in time between this introductory use in the Far East, and a similar use in the West, is attested by contemporary records establishing the fact that the wood was so employed in southern Europe during the first half of the sixteenth century. Later, *bois d'ébène* became a most highly valued medium of French furniture, favored by the most outstanding *huchiers-menuisiers*, who, through working in this wood, eventually came to be known as *ébénistes*. However, *ébène* had been employed for various purposes in the construction of French (and Netherlandish) Renaissance and

baroque seat furniture and cabinetwork before establishment of the Communauté des Maîtres Menuisiers et Ébénistes in Paris, and similar guilds in other cities of France.

Primarily, ebony was employed in the solid, for entire pieces, for separate panels set off by native woods, for sculptured and turned effects, moldings, etc. It was also cut into small pieces of a moderate thickness, and, usually in combination with similar pieces of contrasting woods, set into the solid surfaces of chairs, tables, cabinets, etc., to form intarsia patterns. Decorations of this latter type were popular throughout the Continent during the sixteenth and seventeenth centuries, and in English work of the Elizabethan and Stuart periods.

With the institution of veneering techniques ebony still continued to serve as well in various purposes where the solid wood was necessary or preferred. The new surfacing method entailed sawing the wood in thinner sections than those adequate for intarsia work, a difficult procedure with hand tools, and indeed even with the advanced equipment of modern shops.

In parquetry and marquetry work, and as a banding or border material, the blackness of the wood provided a suitable foil for many of the designs and techniques advanced throughout Europe during the eighteenth century. However, it was not entirely suited to the lighter and more

171. A Louis XVI ebony and burl yewwood *secrétaire à abattant* Courtesy of French & Co.,
New York City.

172. An Indian carved ebony cabinet-on-stand Courtesy of the
Kunstindustrimuseet, Copenhagen.

refined designs of the rococo period and a greater appreciation was withheld until after the first wave of classicism. At that time ebony was again featured as a single or predominant surface wood in the more restrained French compositions of the era, a system also followed during the widespread vogue of Empire designs.

THE ILLUSTRATED EXAMPLES

Fig. 170
The small writing table is one of those unsigned Parisian masterpieces that are frequently, on the very scant evidence offered by the conventionalized forms developed toward the close of the eighteenth century, attributed to Jean-Henri Riesener—although numbers of his compeers executed similarly stylized designs featuring extrinsic work supplied by the *fondeur ciseleur*. Despite an equal lack of individuality in the ornamental openwork and figural plaques of *bronze doré*, this type of applied ornamentation is usually ascribed to Gouthière or Thomire—as these names, too, have become more popularly known than those of other currently practicing artists in bronze.

Fig. 171
Ebony has been employed for the principal panel surrounds and borders of the extraordinary French cabinet with *bronze doré* mounts. Executed about 1780 by the renowned Parisian *ébéniste*, Philippe Pasquier, this piece has a most redoubtable history including ownership by Mme du Barry, and later inclusion in the Hamilton Palace Collection. The gouache paintings are all protected under glass. One of the most remarkable features was passed over in a description published by Molinier, apparently as the famous French authority was unable to identify the veneers displaying handsome marbled effects. These veneers were obtained from an unusually contorted growth of yew in which vermiculate bands of light-toned sapwood became imbedded within the trunk of a tree that developed under exceptional growing conditions and attained a great age.

Fig. 172
The Indian cabinet is carved with a profusion of lotus scrolls and blossoms, motifs that are repeated in the smaller of the silver mounts and in the central lock plate *repoussé* with figures of Buddhas emerging from lotus stems. Together with a bedstead, a settee and several chairs, all of the same wood and with the same type of carving, this cabinet was made in India during the latter part of the seventeenth century and "sent back to" Denmark where it is now included in the furnishings of Brahetrollegorg Castle. Similarly fashioned and elaborated furniture of Europeo-Asiatic designs also originated in Ceylon, and at Batavia in Java, a principal Dutch trading point. The present example is of a typically Oriental design above the torsed supports, while Dutch techniques are represented in these filleted turnings and in the angular stretcher of the stand.

APPENDIX

1. *Timber* is a term employed here in reference to a tree or trees, or to wood suitable for manufacture, whether a part of the standing tree, cut into logs, slabbed into squares, cut into boards, or dressed in any other way for use in joinery or cabinetwork.

2. *Pith* is the loose, spongy tissue in the center of a dicotyledonous tree, which, as the trunk grows, loses its vital function. It also appears in the tree's branches as they grow out of the lengthening trunk, centered among the growth rings which are accordingly diverted with the development of these limbs.

3. The hard and tough *heartwood* of dicotyledonous trees consists of dead tissues compacted by the growth of tyloses. It is rendered darker in color by infiltrations or depositions of tannins, gums, resins and other substances.

4. *Parenchyma* or soft tissue consists of thin-walled cells which may surround vessels, run as fine lines tangentially to the annual rings and at right angles to the rays, or as fine lines bounding annual rings. In the latter instance these lines are developed at the end of a growing season to store food for the start of another, and often serve to distinguish the growth layers of ring-porous woods as they are lighter in color than the surrounding wood substance. In an extended sense *parenchyma* also includes other living tissues such as wood rays.

5. *Cambium* is the soft formative tissue in dicotyledonous and gymnospermous trees; it may be seen and felt as the sticky substance uncovered when bark is peeled from a forest tree stem or branch. It develops immediately under the inner bark in a ring of cells

which grow and divide, producing new wood on the inside, and new bark on the outside of the tissue.

6. *Tracheids* are water-conducting cells that serve also for support, being especially characteristic of coniferous trees, in which they may comprise as much as ninety-five per cent of the wood substance. They appear in some hardwoods, where they are much smaller than the vessels and hardly distinguishable from *parenchyma.*

7. *Tyloses* are intrusive growths or cells forming obstructions in the vessels of hardwoods, and in the tracheids of softwoods. They develop during the transformation from sapwood to heartwood.

8. Technical notes often credit *fibers* with producing various grains and figures. *Fiber* is also accepted as synonymous with *grain*, which is defined as "the fiber which forms the substance of wood." However, all of the vital elements are involved in these different configurations, and not only the fibers; for the sake of clarity, therefore, a preference is given to the inclusive term *elements*, in the following descriptions.

9. The identification of woods through printed technical descriptions of cellular structures requires a specialized knowledge such as few experts in commercial timbers possess. A less demanding approach to this form of determination has been supplied during recent years through microphotography. For those interested in carrying out this type of inspection in a simplified approach a lens of ten diameters magnification will serve. The various cell patterns revealed through this aid can then be compared with such identifying photomicrographs as may be found in the publication by Alexander L. Howard, *Studies of the Identification of Timbers,* and in works by other authorities on world, European or American timbers.

10. Wood or nut oils, and seed oils, were used in the finishing of old furniture, both types being known as drying oils, i.e., convertible into solids by absorbing oxygen when exposed to the air in thin films. The seeds of flax plants, commonly cultivated over the centuries, yield linseed oil, which provides a principal base of dressings employed to fill the pores and grain of cabinet woods. Drying properties are often increased by heating or boiling these oils.

11. For centuries varnishes have been used in artificial forms differing from the natural varnishes of China and Japan. *Oil varnishes* are essentially solutions of resins, solid or semisolid organic substances chiefly of vegetable origin, or of asphalt in drying oils, especially linseed oil and tung oil. *Spirit varnishes* are solutions of resins, etc. in volatile solvents such as alcohol or spirits of turpentine. A solution of *shellac* in alcohol is one of the more common types of wood filling and varnishing agents, shellac being a purified lac resin. *Lac* is a resinous substance secreted by a scale insect which lives on the twigs of certain trees, these insects

being extensively cultivated in northern India. The substance in its natural state, incrusting the insects and small twigs, is known as *stick-lac.* When crushed and washed it becomes granular and is then known as *seed-lac.* This is melted, further purified by straining and the resin (*lac resin*) is solidified into various forms, particularly as the thin layers or flakes of the familiar *shellac* still used in most furniture shops. The impure residue left from straining is called *refuse lac. Seed-lac* and *shell-lac*[14] are referred to in seventeenth-century accounts of finishing methods, while refuse lac was also used from this time on as a filling agent, beneath coatings of the refined product.

12. Stains are made up in preparations which are thinner than paint and are consequently absorbed by wood pores without forming a coating. They were often used with spirit or oil bases in former times, as today. Colors were introduced in mineral or vegetable tinctures such as ochers, umbers, alkanet, dragon's blood, gamboge, benjamin, etc.

13. *Tan*, as this color is defined by Webster, is red-yellow in hue, of high saturation and medium brilliance. While timber experts prefer various qualifications of *brown* in descriptions of wood colors, it is believed that such terms are often less descriptive and more prone to confusion than the use here of *tan.* This word limits to some extent the large number of shades which may be interpreted under the term *light brown.* It is employed here synonymously with *tawny* —as a tawny lion, or a tawny but not too darkly tanned skin. It also permits a better understanding of qualifications such as *reddish-brown*, since hickory, for example, has been described elsewhere as having a "reddish-brown" heartwood, which to the neophyte may indicate a tone equal to that appearing in a much darker, but nevertheless "reddish-brown" San Domingo mahogany.

14. Stalker's *Treatise of Japanning and Varnishing*, published in 1688, describes the finest "Seed-Lacc-varnish" then used as "of a reddish tawny colour, which did not keep the true natural, and genuine colour of the wood." This work employs the term *Shell-Lacc-varnish* to indicate an inferior agent with "greater body than Seed-Lacc," recommending that "Venice-turpentine" be added to harden it and provide a more satisfactory finish for furniture or parts of furniture made in solid wood.

15. Species with botanical names followed by the abbreviation "Linn." were so classified by the famous Swedish botanist, Carolus Linnaeus or Carl von Linné, 1707-1778. Linnaeus first announced his system of plant classification in 1735, and it was published in greater detail in 1753. Joseph Pitton de Tournefort, 1656-1708, the first notable student of economic botany, and the Swedish scientist are considered the fathers of modern systematic botany.

16. Shrubs retain all of their lateral shoots, so that their heavier branches are formed near the ground. On the contrary, trees soon lose their lower lateral branches and develop in a principal stem or trunk which bears a crown of branches and twigs.

17. From the second half of the seventeenth century through the Victorian period workshops in Tunbridge Wells, Kent, continuously produced decorative articles, turnery and furniture from an unusually large repertory of native and exotic woods. Around the close of the eighteenth century Tunbridge wares were frequently inlaid in geometric patterns displaying specimen veneers of exotic woods or the more unusual varieties of native timbers. Later objects were largely inlaid with mosaic effects, obtained in veneers cut from blocks which were formed by gluing together strips of variously contrasting woods; a method recalling that employed in producing millefiore glass.

Woods used in Tunbridge wares include:

holly	plane tree
laurel	yew
green ebony	plum
(green ash)	laburnum
birch	zebrawood
bird's-eye maple	walnut
orange tree	acacia
sycamore	snakewood
barberry	baywood
lilac	mahogany
furze	tulipwood
canary	beefwood
fustic	red ebony
box	partridgewood
broom	rubywood
chestnut	kingwood
green oak	rosewood
evergreen oak	purplewood
bog oak	green ebony
amboina	calamander
mulberry	palmyra
apple	madagascar
beech	black ebony
pear	

18. *Pollarding* has been practiced in Europe and the British Isles for centuries, and is said to have originated in England when many sturdy oaks were cut down to prevent use of these valuable shipbuilding timbers by invaders. It is effected by removing the crown of a tree down to the principal section of the trunk or closer to the ground, and also by cutting the branches close to the trunk. After such treatment the vitality of a tree is concentrated in the remaining portion of the trunk, with veneers later yielded from this section displaying more concentrated or intensified markings than would appear had the tree developed normally. Branches that have been formed at the summit of a pollarded tree trunk often produce a thick mass of burlwood, while at the same time the trunk thickens and produces numerous shoots, frequently in clusters that produce additional burls. Ash, elm and oak trees were pollarded in England, and in some French provinces the practice was extended to walnut trees. *Coppicing* varies from pollarding in that the tree trunk is cut off near the ground, to produce shoots in the stump.

19. This advertisement has been previously quoted in conjunction with a Boston cabinet executed in bird's-eye maple, a selection of material which of course has nothing to do with either *knurlwood* or *burlwood*, and which would not have been in demand until a much later date than that of the announced requirement.

20. Chippendale, Haig & Co. in 1772 supplied David Garrick with "a very large Inlaid Case of Fustick & fine black Rosewood with Sundry other ornaments curiously Inlaid with various fine woods, the middle part to hold a Bed, the Ends for Shelves, Cloakpins, Night Tables etc. enclosed with Doors, very neat Shap'd Doors with Carv'd ornaments hung with pin hinges on Sliding parts, Glaz'd with Looking Glass & back'd with mahogany, very neat carv'd Cornice Japan'd to match the Fustick Wood etc." In the same year this firm altered a "Japan Cabinet" for Garrick, "new veneering the Top with Yellow wood."

21. "The grain of the wood of *Quer. sessiliflora* is generally less varied and of a more uniform and deeper colour than that of *Quer. pendunculata*, and with less of the laminated appearance which is called a *flash* or silver grain; and it is now ascertained that the timbers found in old houses, and other ancient buildings in different parts of the kingdom, and which were long considered to be formed of the wood of the sweet chestnut, are, in reality, composed of oak, and mostly of the sessile-fruited kind. We are only surprised how such a belief ever obtained credit, considering that the chestnut does not appear to be of indigenous growth, that at no period has it prevailed in Britain as a forest tree, and indeed does not even appear to have grown at any time in many districts where house timbers of this description have been found."—Prideaux John Selby, *A History of British Forest-Trees*.

22. In 1701 the trunk of a fallen oak in Yorkshire measured one hundred and twenty feet in length, thirty-six feet in circumference at the butt end, thirty feet at the middle, and eighteen feet at the smaller end where the trunk had been broken off. A tree in Dorsetshire, measured in 1755, was sixty-eight feet in circumference. The Boddington Oak, in Gloucestershire, the remains of which were burned down in 1790, was fifty-four feet in circumference at the base. Other standing oaks are recorded by Selby as possessing circumferences as great as seventy-eight feet.

23. Material cut from oak burls, of naturally developed or pollarded trees, displays a typical arrangement of twisted graining surrounding the eyes or tiny

"knots." In keeping with the handling of other burl-woods, these growths were generally utilized as veneers, laid upon cores of less refractory nature.

24. The firm of Gillows, under various partnerships, existed during the greater part of the eighteenth century, continuing to manufacture furniture at Lancaster throughout the Victorian period. In addition to regular shipments made to London from the middle years of the former era, their furniture is also recorded as being exported to the West Indies. R. S. Clouston, *English Furniture and Furniture Makers*, 1906, credits Robert Gillow with a certain independence in his attitude when dealing with "the most exalted personages," citing an instance which bears repeating for the benefit of those interested in the buying and selling of fine furniture: "He was one day showing a table, priced at eighty guineas, to a nobleman: 'It's a devil of a price,' said his lordship. 'It's a devil of a table," replied the independent salesman, and the deal was concluded there and then."

25. In *girdling* a tree is cut into as far as the heartwood, at a point near the ground and extending completely round the trunk, thus killing the tree and causing the trunk to dry out naturally prior to the time for felling and further handling.

26. During the early days of the British East India Company candle auctions were especially important as a means through which timbers, spices, dyes, silks and other commodities were disposed of after their reception from "The Indies," through regular trading activities or privateering. Much of the traffic handled by the company was dispersed at these sales after advertisement in public notices displayed at the Royal Exchange. Sales were conducted with an inch of lighted candle on a desk, each lot going at the highest bid received before the light flickered out.

27. Contrary to the usual tendency toward applying earlier dates to stories of old furniture as they are repeated, though with similar possibilities for misinterpretation, the opposite effect has taken place in recountings of circumstances surrounding the production of a candlebox for one Dr. William Gibbons. Supposedly representing "the first use to which mahogany was applied in England," the date of this incident has been roughly indicated, in an account of 1821, by reference to the physician who, "at the latter end of the seventeenth century, had a brother. . . . Soon after . . . etc. *The Cabinet-Maker's Assistant* mentioned the incident as occurring "nearly a century later" than 1596. More recently dates of 1720 and 1724 have been given for this "first use" of Mahogany in England.

28. Vernacular terms associated with the Australian "oaks" and beefwoods have resulted in a rather involved nomenclature, accompanied by numerous conflicting analyses of the various woods classified under these names. She-Oaks, with *Casuarina suberosa* as a principal species, are widely noted as possessing broad and lengthy rays—such as appear in Botany Bay oak. The she-oak has also been mentioned in reference to the beefwoods, although the he-oak is more often associated with timbers of this classification. She-oaks are also known as forest oaks and river oaks, while *C. suberosa* has been designated as a swamp oak.

Beefwoods include several species of *Casuarina*, and three timbers belonging to the family Proteaceae: *Stenocarpus salignus* and *Grevillea striata* of New South Wales, and *Banksia integrifolia*, the honeysuckle oak of Queensland. *G. striata* was singled out by Laslett as "the Beef-wood, so called from the resemblance of the worked timber to raw beef." Some of these species and others belonging to their genera have been described with, and without mention of strong rayed figures, including timbers that are alternatively known as silky oaks, a term usually denoting the presence of pronounced rays. The one casuarinawood that is generally agreed upon as a beefwood, without contradiction, and with no mention of rays, is that of *C. equisetifolia*; which may appear in some listings as a bull oak or a swamp oak.

29. Laslett listed three woods under Bahama timbers: sabicu, *Lysiloma sabicu*, braziletto, *Caesalpinia crista* and *C. brasiliensis*, and horseflesh, "An allied species of *Caesalpinia*." In the family Caesalpiniaceae, rather than the genus *Caesalpinia*, Webster gives *Peltophorum adnatum* as a second West Indian timber that is now recognized as sabicu, and "also its dark-red or purplish mahoganylike wood." Sabicu and horseflesh are accepted by Webster as synonymous.

30. Coco was spelled *cocoa* first in Johnson's dictionary, probably through error, and later this became the more common spelling, though *coco* is now preferred. Porcupinewood is at times known as cocowood, or, less correctly, as cocoawood.

31. The genus *Diospyros* contains all of the species known as true black ebonies, with these or other species of the same genus also producing timbers described here under calamander, macassar ebony, green ebony, etc. The diversity of these woods will be indicated more readily by consulting the botanic listings in the index. Other timbers rivaling true ebony in blackness, but not in texture or hardness, are now obtained from various trees belonging to the genus *Maba* of the ebony family, particularly *M. ebenus*, yielding a wood that has been considered worthy of classification as an ebony. Among the *Diospyros* species not important in the present consideration is *D. virginiana*, the only North American member of the ebony family, supplying persimmonwood, which until quite recently was valued only for its sapwood.

BIBLIOGRAPHY

John Evelyn, *Sylva—or a Discourse of Forest Trees*, reprint of the fourth edition issued in 1706.

The London Cabinet-Makers' Union Book of Prices, London, 1811.

Prideaux John Selby, *A History of British Forest-Trees, Indigenous and Introduced*, London, 1842.

The Cabinet-Maker's Assistant, London, 1853.

Thomas Laslett, *Timber and Timber Trees*, London, 1875, revised by H. M. Ward in 1893.

William Noyes, *Wood and Forest*, Peoria, Ill., 1912.

Samuel J. Record, *Identification of the Economic Woods of the United States*, New York, 1914.

———, *Timbers of Tropical America*, New Haven, Conn., 1924.

Henri Clouzot, *Les Meubles du XVIIIe Siècle*, Paris, 1922.

Arthur Koehler, *The Identification of Furniture Woods*, Washington, D.C., 1926.

Chalk and Rendle, *British Hardwoods, Their Structure and Identification*, London, 1929.

Phillips A. Hayward, *Wood, Lumber and Timbers*, New York, 1930.

William Macpherson Horner, Jr., *Philadelphia Furniture*, Philadelphia, 1935.

Malcolm H. Sherwood, *From Forest to Furniture*, New York, 1936.

Dr. V. I. van de Wall, *Het Hollandsche Koloniale Barokmeubel*, Antwerp, 1939.

Forest Products Research Laboratory, *A Handbook of Home-Grown Timbers*, London, 1939.

Alexander L. Howard, *Studies of the Identification of Timbers*, London, 1942, with supplement of 1943.

William Bullock, *Timber, From the Forest to its Use in Commerce*, London, 1945.

Forest Products Research Laboratory, *Empire Timbers*, London, 1945.

Alexander L. Howard, *A Manual of the Timbers of the World*, London, 1948.

F. H. Titmuss, *A Concise Encyclopedia of World Timbers*, London, 1948.

L. J. F. Brimble, *Trees in Britain*, London, 1948.

Harold T. Eyres, *Introducing Wood*, London, 1950.

C. W. Bond, *Colonial Timbers*, London, 1950.

George N. Lamb–Mahogany Association, Inc., *The Mahogany Book*, Chicago, 1951.

Alfred Schwankl, *Welches Holz Ist Das?*, Stuttgart, 1951.

G. & C. Merriam Company, *Webster's New International Dictionary of the English Language*, Springfield, Mass. (A source of information that is generally unacknowledged, but one which has offered the most valuable aid in regard to the names, botanical designations and brief descriptions of present-day timbers, and some that are no longer available.)

INDEX

Italic page numbers refer to illustrations.

Acacia, 103-104, *104*
  false, 65
  ironbark, 143
Acacia stenophylla, 143
Acajou, *126*, *131*, 132
  bois d', 46
  mouché, *126*, 133, 138
  noix d', 132
  satiné, 132
Acaju, 132
Acapu, 152
Acer campestre, 29
Acer platanoides, 29
Acer pseudo-platanus, 38
Acer saccharinum, 30
Acle, 142
Adenanthera pavonina, 118
Aesculus hippocastanum, 19
African Cherry, 117

Agalloch, 168
Ahorn, 29
Aigle, bois d', 168
Akeake, 143
Alder, 11, 60-62, *61*, *62*
Alisier, bois d', 20
Almond, 99
Alnus glutinosa, 60
Alnus incana, 60
Aloes, 168
Amandier, bois d', 99
Amarante, bois d', 46, 165, 166
Amaranth, *28*, 47, *100*, *102*, 103, 163, 165-168, *165*, *166*, *167*
Amaranthus, 167
Amarello, *p'ao*, 53, 54
Amarilla, 53
Amarillo, 3, 53-55, *55*
  palo, 53

  vinhatica, 54
Amboina, 15, 43, 47, *52*, 53, 77-79, *77*, *78*, 91, 139, 140, 144
Amboine, bois d', 78
Amourette mouché, bois d', 116
Amyris, 57
Amyris balsamifera, 57
Andira americana, 152
Andira inermis, 152, 154
"Angelim," 153, 154
Angelin, 152
Apple, 21, 79-80, 87, 93
  common, 79
  crab, 79
  wild, 79
Aquillaria agollocha, 168
Argan tree, 142
Ariba, 53
Artocarpus integra, 142

Ash, 12, 13, 15, 16, 17, 18, 22-26, *24*, *25*, *61*, 67
  American black, 23, 25
  American white, 23
  basket, 23
  black, *25*, 26, *31*, *34*, 35
  brown, 23
  burl, 22, 23, *24*, 25, *26*, 30, 68, 79
  Canadian white, 23
  curly, 23
  European, 22, 23
  "Green ebony," 22
  hoop, 23
  Hungarian, 23, *25*, 26
  mountain, 79
  northern brown, 23
  oriental, 23, 26
  red, *25*

white, 23
Aspidosperma vargasii, 53
Assagai, 62
Assegaihout, 62
Astronium fraxinifolium, 150, 151
Aubépine, 88
Aubour, bois d', 95
Aune, bois d', 61
Australian Beefwood, 143-144
Avodire, 3, *47,* 55

Balata, 144
Bamboo, 10, 37-38, *38,* 81
Bambusa arundinaria, 37
Barberry, 40
Bay, 128
  laurel, 21
  tree, 21
Beech, 11, 13, 17, 38, 80-81, *80, 81,* 84, 133
  cape, 56
Beefwood, Australian, 143-144
Beefwood, South American, 144
Berberis vulgaris, 40
Bermuda Cedar, 117-118
Betula alba, 27
Betula excelsa, 27
Betula lenta, 27
Betula lutea, 28
Betula nigra, 27, 28
Betula pubescens, 27
Bilsted, 58
Birch, 3, 11, 12, 13, 15, 17, 18, 26-28, *28,* 46, 54, 55, 162
  American, 26, 27, 54
  black, 27, 28
  Canadian, 28
  Canadian silkywood, 28
  Canadian yellow, 28
  cherry, 27
  common, 27
  curled, 27, *28*
  European, 26, 27, 46, 61
  gray, 28
  Karelian, 27
  mahogany, 27
  (mountain mahogany), 27
  Quebec, 28
  red, 28
  river, 28
  silver, 27
  sweet, 27, 28
  yellow, 27
  white, 27
Bitter Orange, 37
Black ash, American, 23, 25
Blackthorn, 87
Blackwood, 163, 164
  African, 144
  Chinese, 164
  East Indian, 113, 163
Bloodwood, 143
  ironbark, 143
  red, 143
Boca, 154
Borassus flabelliformis, 175
Botany Bay, 144
  oak, 144-145
  olive, 143
  wood, 144
Bouleau, bois de, 45
Boxwood, 20, 45-46, *59,* 60, 100
  false, 62
Brasilete, 115
Brasiletto, 115, 146
Brazaletto, 115
Brazilete, 115
Braziletto, 115
Brazilienholz, 53
Brazilwood, 114, 115-116, 146
Breakax, 143
Brésil, bois de, 115, 116
Brésillet, 115
Brézil, 114
Broom, 64-65, *64*
  common, 64

dyers, 64
  Irish, 64
  Scotch, 64
  Spanish, 64
Brosimum paraense, 141
Brown ebony, 151
Brya ebenus, 151, 170
Buis, bois de, 45
Buchenavia capitata, 151
Bumelia languginosa, 143
Bumelia tenax, 143
Burapinima, 99
Butternut, 65-66
Buttonwood, 82, 84
Buxus sempervirens, 45

Cabbage bark, 152, 153, 154
Cabbage wood, 152, 153, 154
Caesalpinia sp., 146
  brasiliensis, 115
  crista, 115
  echinata, 114, 115
  granadillo, 151
  sappan, 114
  vesicaria, 115
Caju, 132
Calamander, 65, 98, 163, 171-173, *171, 172, 173*
Calambac, 168
Calemberri, 172
Caliatous, bois de, 118
Campeachy, 114
Campeche, 114-115
Campêche, bois de, 115
Campechea wood, 115
Camphorwood, 63-64, *63*
  East African, 63
  East Indian, *63,* 64
Canadian silkywood, 28
Canalete, 113-114
Canary (an amarillo), 54, 55
  yellow wood, 44
Canarywood, 55-56
Candlewood, 57
Canella batalha, 55
Cangelim, 154
Canoewood, 44
Cape beech, 56
Carpinus betulus, 19
Carpinus caroliniana, 143
Carya sp., 21
Cashew tree, 132
Cassia siamea, 143
Castanea dentata, 66
Castanea pumila, 66
Castanea sativa, 66
Casuarina equistifolia, 144
Casuarina sp., 143
Casuarinaceae, 144
Casuarinales, 144
Cedar, 23, 37, 90, 117
  bastard Barbados, 116
  Bermuda, 117-118
  cigar box, 116
  Havanna, 116, 117
  Himalayan, 62
  Indian, 62
  pencil, 86
  red, 86-87, 116
  Spanish, 54, 116-117, 132
  swamp, 116
  West Indian, 116
Ceddar, red, 116
Cedrela odorata, 116-117
Cedrelas, 116
Cedrus sp., 87
  deodara, 62
Cerisier, 86
Charme, bois de, 19
Chatâignier, 66
Chene, bois de, 70
Cherry, 18, *31, 34,* 35, 80, 84-86, *85,* 117
  African, 117
  American black, 86
  American wild, 86
  Austrian, 85

black, 85, 86
  cultivated, 86
  European wild, 84, 85, 86
  St. Lucie, 85
Chestnut, 13, 16, 18, 19, 54, 66-67, *67*
  American, 66, 67
  dwarf, 66
  European, 19, 66
  Horse, 11, 19, 44
  rose, 142
  Spanish, 66
  sweet, 66
Chinese blackwood, 164
Chinquapin, 66
Chittamwood, 143
Chlorophora tinctoria, 53
Chloroxylon swietenia, 52
Cinnamonum camphora, 63
Cinnamonum zeylanicum, 63
Citharexylum quadrangulare, 37
Citroenhout, 53
Citronnier (citronwood), 3, *28,* 46-47, *46,* 48, 93
Citrus sp., 46
  aurantium, 37
City wood, see Mahogany, Cuba
Clairembourg, 53
Cliftonia monophylla, 143
"Cocoa Wood," 151
Cocobolo, 152
Coconut palm, 151
Cocus nucifera, 151
Cocuswood, 151, 170
Colima, 143
Colubrina ferruginosa, 143
Connarus guianensis, 98
Corail, bois de, 118
Coralwood, 3, 118
Cordia gerascanthus, 113
Cormier, bois de, 79
Cornel, 62
Cornus florida, 62
Cornus sanguinea, 62
Coromandel, 144, 171, 173
Corylus avellana, 44
Côtelet, bois, 37
Cotinus coggygria, 168
Coudrier, bois de, 44
Courbaril, 114, 150
  plum, 114
Crataegus oxyacantha, 87
Cuba wood (fustic), 53
  (mahogany), 127, 128
Cucumber magnolia, 45
  tree, 45
  wood, 44
Cunonia capensis, 116
Cupressus funebris, 100
Cupressus sempervirens, 99
Cupressus torulosa, 100
Curtisia faginea, 62
Cypress, American, 99
Cypress, Chinese, 100
Cypress, European, 99-100
Cypress, Himalayan, 100
Cypress, weeping, 100
Cyrilla racemiflora, 143
Cytisus laburnum, 95
Cytisus scoparius, 64

Dalbergia sp., 100, 101, 103, 114. 157, 175
  cearensis, 157
  granadillo, 152
  hypoleuca, 152
  latifolia, 163, 164
  melanoxylon, 144
  nigra, 159
  retusa, 151, 152
  sissoo, 113, 164
  stevensonii, 162
  tesselaria, 175
Damson, 99
Deodar, 62-63
Dialium divarcatum, 143
Dimorphandra mora, 141

Diospyros, 103, 142, 163, 171, 173, 175, 176
  ebenaster, 175
  hirsuta, 171
  kurzii, 174
  macassar, 173
  De Marmorata, 174
  melanoxylon, 170, 173
  oocarpa, 174
  quaesita, 175
  Roylei, 176
  tomentosa, 175, 176
Dodonaea viscosa, 143
Dogwood, 62-63
  American, 62
Dyers broom, 64
Dyers mulberry, 53

Eaglewood, 168
East Indian Rosewood, 103, 163-165, *164*
East Indian Satinwood, 47, 52-53, 54, 77, 79
Ebbenhout, 175
Ebbone, 115
Ébène, bois d', 175, 176
Ebene de Portugal, 174-175
Ebenholz, 175
Ebenhout, 175
"Ebene Rouge," 114, 150-151
Ebene Verte, 170-171
Ebony, 35, 43, 44, *75,* 76, *82,* 88, 93, 100, 103, 154, 170, 173, 175-179, *176, 177, 178*
  African, 175
  black, 169, 171, 175
  brown, 151
  East Indian, 175, 176
  green, 151, 170-171
  Macassar, 173-174, *174*
  Mauritius, 175
  red, 150-151
Elaeodendron croceum, 56
Elder, 40
Elm, 11, 12, 13, 15, 18, 67-69, *68*
  American, 69
  burl, 30, 68, 69, 79
  Canadian, 69
  common, 67, 68
  Dutch, 68
  European, 67
  Irish, 67
  mountain, 67
  Scotch, 67
  Spanish, 69
  wych-, 67, 68
Els, Red, 116
Epi de blé, 154
Erable, bois d', 31
Erable, broussin d', 31
Erable moucheté, 31
Eucalypts, The, 143
Eucalyptus corymbosa, 143
Eucalyptus fergusoni, 143
Eucalyptus marginata, 143
Eucalyptus microcorys, 143
Eucalyptus paniculata, 143
Eucalyptus rostrata, 143
Eugenia buxifolia, 143
Eugenia confusa, 143
Eugenia rhombea, 143
Euonymus europea, 20
European Cypress, 99-100
Euxylophora paraensis, 54
Exothea paniculata, 143

Fabaceae, 152
Fagus sylvatica, 80
False acacia, 65
False boxwood, 62
False logwood, 143
Faux acacia, bois de, 65
Faux ebenier, 95
Fer, bois, 143
Ferolia guianensis, 141
Ferréol, 143
Fiddlewood, 37

Fistulina hepatica, 66
Forestiera sp., 143
Fraxinus americana, 23
Fraxinus excelsior, 22
Fraxinus mandshurica, 23
Fraxinus nigra, 23
Fusain, bois de, 20
Fustet, 168
 bois de, 168
Fustic, 53, 54
 young, 168
Fustick, old, 53
Fustoc, 53
Fustock, bois de, 53

Gaiac, bois de, 170
Gardenia rothmannia, 142
Genip, 143
Genista tinctoria, 64
Gleditsia triacanthos, 65
Goldwood, *see* amarillos
Goncalo Alves, 151
Goncalo de para, 99
Granadilla, 151, 170
 tree, 151
Green Ebony, 170-171
Grenadille, 151
Guaicum officinale, 168
Guaicum sanctum, 143, 168
Guiana wood, 157
Gum, 58-59, *58*
 black, 58
 blood, 143
 figured red, 13
 locust, 114
 plain, 58
 red, *5,* 58, 143
 sour, 58
 swamp, 58
 sweet, 58
 tree, 148
 tupelo, 58
 white, 58

Haemotoxylon brasiletto, 115
Haemotoxylon campechianum, 115
Hard pear, 117
Harewood, 38, 50
Hawthorn, 87
Havanna, 117
Havannah, 117
Hazel, 11, 44
Heisteria coccinea, 154
Hetre, bois de, 81
Hickory, 17, 21-22, *21,* 23
Hicoria alba, 21
Hicoria glabra, 21
Hicoria ovata, 21
Hippomane mancinella, 60
Holly, 3, 11, *20,* 21, 28, 45, 46, *49, 50, 88,* 100, 173
 American, 20
 European, 19
Hoop ash, 23
Hornbeam, 11, 19-20, 28, 143
 hop, 143
Horse Chestnut, 11, 19, 44
Horseflesh mahogany, *145, 146*
Houx, bois de, 20
Hungarian ash, 23
Hymenaea courbaril, 114
Hypernic, 115
Hypelate trifoliata, 143

If, bois d', 92
If, racine d', 92, 93
Ilex aquifolia, 19
Ilex opaca, 20
Indes, bois des, 154
Inga sp., 142
Ironbark, 143
 acacia, 143
 bloodwood, 143
Iron tree, 142
Ironwood, 142
 bastard, 143

black, 143
white, 143

Jacaranda, 159
Jacaranda, 159
Jackwood, 142
"Jamaicawood," 124
Jamaikaholz, 53
Jarrah, 143
Jaune, bois, 53
Joewood, 143
Juglans cinerea, 65
Juglans nigra, 66, 107, 108, 113
Juglans regia, 104
Juniper, 56-57, *56*
 Bermuda, 87
 Carolina, 87
 Swedish, 57
Juniperus bermudiana, 117
Juniperus communis, 56
Juniperus virginiana, 86, 117

Karelian burl, 27
Khaya ivorensis, 129
Khaya senegalensis, 129
Kingswood, Brazilian, 150
Kingwood, 37, 144, *156,* 157, 167
 see violetwood
"Kingwood," 154
 violet, 157
Ko-yen-ta-ka-ah-ta, 44
Krugiodendron ferreum, 143

Laburnum, 64, 84, 93, 95-98, *96, 97*
 Alpine, 95, 96
 alpinum, 95, 96
 anagyroides, 95
Lacewood, 84
Lafoensia puncifolia, 53
Larch, 41-42, *42*
Larix decidua, 41
Larix europea, 41
Laurel, 21
 bay, 21, 45
 magnolia, 45
Laurier, bois de, 21
Laurus nobilis, 21
Leatherwood, 143
Lemon tree, 100
Leopardwood, 116
Letterwood, 116, 143
Lettres, bois de, 116
Lettres de Chine, bois de, 116
Lezard, bois de, 116
Lignum vitae, 116, 162, 168-170, *169*
 bastard, 143
Lilac, 57-58
Lime, 40-41, *41,* 44
Linden, 19, 40-41
Lingo tree, *see* amboinawood
Lingoum indicum, 77
Liquidambar styraciflum, 58
Liriodendron tulipifera, 44
Locust, *65,* 93, 114
 American, 114
 black, 65
 honey, 65
 South American, 114
 West Indian, 114, 150
 yellow, 65
Logwood, 115, 154
 false, 143
London Plane, 82-84, *83*
Lythraceae, 100
Lyonothamnus floribundus, 143
Lysiloma sabicu, 145

Macassar Ebony, 173-174, *174*
Madagascar, 103
 Rosewood, 103
Madeira, 55-56, 143
 mahogany, 55
Maderah, 55
Magnolia, 44, 45
 acuminata, 45
 cucumber, 21, 45

evergreen, 45
grandiflora, 45
laurel, 45
mountain, 45
virginiana, 45
Mahaleb, *see* European cherry
Mahogany, 3, 6, 11, 12, 13, 14, 18, *20,* 25, 27, 31, 47, 48, *49, 50, 51,* 52, 53, 54, 55, 56, 58, 69, 75, 92, 93, 100, 103, *106,* 109, 111, 115, 116, 117, 118-138, *119, 120, 121, 122, 123, 124, 125, 126, 127, 128, 129, 130, 131, 132, 133, 134, 135, 136, 138, 140, 141,* 142, 143, 145, 148, 150, 162, *163*
 African, 128, 130
 American, 4
 birch, 27
 blond, 54
 Brazilian, 54
 cherry, 117
 cigar box, 116
 Cuban, 117, 124, 127, 141
 forest, 143
 Honduras, 85, 117, 124, 125, 128, 153
 horseflesh, 145, 146
 Jamaica, 124, 125
 Madeira, 56
 mountain, 27
 Nassau, *see* West Indian cedar
 Puerto Rico, 124
 red, 143
 Santo Domingo, 124, 125, 126, 127
 Spanish, 53, 118, 124, 125, 127, 128, 141
 Tropical American, *4*
 Western Australian, 143
 West Indian, 15, 85, 121, 124, 125, 126, 127, 128
 yellow, 53
Malus pumila, 79
Malus sylvestris, 79
Manchenille, 60
Manchineel, 60
Manillawood, 53, 144
Mansanille, 60
Makore, 117
Manscin, 29
Maple, 13, 14, 17, 18, 23, 29-36, *31, 32, 33, 34, 35, 36,* 46, 58, 59, 93, 95, 100, 162
 American, 15, 29
 bird's-eye, 11, 15, *25,* 26, 29, *31, 32, 34,* 35
 burl, 29, 31
 buttwood, *5,* 29, 30, 95
 Canadian, 30
 common, 29
 curly, 29, 30, *31, 32*
 European, 15, 29
 field, 29
 French, 29
 knurlwood, *5,* 23, 29, 30, 31, *34, 35, 36, 61,* 95
 Norwegian, 29
 rock, 30
 sugar, *4,* 29, 30
Marblewood, 171, 174
Marinheiro, 132
Marronnier de l'Inde, 19
Masar, 29
Mazer, 29
Melaleuca genistifolia, 143
Meleze, bois de, 42
Meliaceae, 52
Memecylon edule, 143
Merisier, 86
Mesquite, 143
Metrosideros vera, 142
Millettia sp., 142
Mimusops globosa, 144
Mimusops heckeli, 117
"Mohogany," 131
"Mohogony," 130

Molave, 53
Moluchia tomentosa, 64
Mopane, 142
Mora, 53, 141-142
 amarilla, 53
 excelsa, 141
Moraceae, 116
Morus alba, 93
Morus nigra, 93
Morus tinctoria, 53
Mösurr, 29
Mountain ash, 79
Mulberry, 30, *36,* 53, 93-95, *94,* 141
 dyers, 53
Murier, bois de, see Mulberry
Myrtaceae, 143
Myrtle, ridge, 143
Myrtus gonoclada, 143

Nania vera, 143
Narra, 3, 118
 amarilla, 53, 118
 blanca, 118
 encarnada, 118
Nicaraguawood, 115
Noisetier, bois de, 44
Northea seychellana, 142
Notelaea sp., 143
Noyer, bois de, 44, 108
Nussholz, 44
Nutwood, 44
Nyssa aquatica, 58
Nyssa sylvatica, 58

Oak, 3, 6, 11, 12, 13, 16, 22, 38, 42, 54, 66, 67, 69-75, *72, 73, 74, 85,* 86, 87, 111, 115, 134, 135
 American, *121,* 134
 American red, 70, 71
 American white, *4,* 70, 71
 Australian, 11, 144
 Austrian, 69
 Baltic, 69
 black, *5,* 70
 bog, *5,* 70, *108,* 111
 Botany Bay, 3, 144
 British, 69, 70
 British brown, 70
 British red, 70
 brown, 66
 burl, 71
 cork, 70
 Danzig, 69
 Dutch, 70
 European, 69
 evergreen, 70
 forest, 144
 Franconian, 70
 French, 70
 he-, 144
 holly, 70
 holm, 70
 Irish, 70, 71
 Italian, 70
 North American, 70
 pollard, 71, *73,* 74
 Portuguese, 70
 Prussian, 69
 Rhenish, 69
 Russian, 69
 she-, 144
 Spanish, 70
 tropical American, 4
 Turkish, 70
Octea bullata, 102
Oeil-de-Perdrix, 154
Olea, sp., 143
 capensis, 142
 europaea, 59
 paniculata, 143
Olive, 59-60, *59,* 143, 157
 Botany Bay, 143
 wild, 60
Olneya tesota, 143
Omander, 172

Omphalobium lamberti, 98, 99
Orange, Bitter, 37
Orange, bois d', 53
Oranger, bois de', 37
Orangewood, 48
Orme, bois d', 69
Orme, loupe d', 69
Ostrya virginica, 143
Ozier, bois d', 44

Padauk, 3, 9, 92, 101, 118, 148-150, *148, 149, 150*, 151, 162
  Andaman, 148, 149
  Burmese, 148, 149
Palisander, 100, 159-163
Palissandre, bois de, 160
Palm, 10, 37, 50, 151, 154
  (arecaceae), 10
  coconut, 151, 152
  Palmyra, 175
Palmetto, 117
Palmyrawood, 152, 175
Palo amarillo, 53
P'ao amarello, 53, 54
Paradisewood, 168
Parrotia persica, 142
Partridgewood, 151, 152-154, *153, 154*
  black, 153
  brown, 153
  red, 153
  sweet, 153
Pau amarello, 54
Pear, 81-82, *82*, 87
  hard, 117
Peltogyne, sp., 165
Peltophorum adnatum, 146
Pepperidge, 58
Perdrix, bois de, 154
Pernambouc, bois de, 115
Pernambucowood, 115
Persea, sp., 56
  canariensis, 55
  indica, 55
Persian tree, 142
Petowood, 141, 142
Pheasantwood, 153, 154
Physocalymma floribundum, 100
Physocalymma scabberimum, 100
Pipe tree, 57
Piratinera guianensis, 116
Pithecolobium vinhatica, 54
Plane, London, 82, 84
Plane, occidental, 82, 84
Plane, oriental, 82, 84
Plane Tree, 18, 82-84, *83*
Planta genista, 64
Platanus acerifolia, 82
Platanus occidentalis, 82
Platanus orientalis, 82
Platanus foliolosa, 54
Platanus reticulata, 54
Plum, 87, 88-90, *89*, 93, 99, 114
  Courbaril, 114
Podocarpus elongata, 37
Podocarpus thunbergia, 37
Poirier, bois de, 82
Pommier, bois de, 80
Poplar, 11, 15, 43
  "American," 12, 39, 44-45, 46, 50, 58
  burl, *43*, 78
  English, 43
  European, 19, 44
  Italian, 43
  New England, *44*
  yellow, 44
Popple, 44
Populus alba, 43
Populus canescens, 43
Populus serotina, 43
Porcupinewood, 151-152, 175
Prima vera, 54
Princewood, 113-114, 156
Princeswood, 156
Prosopis glandulosa, 143
Prosopis juliflora, 143

Provedencewood, 131
Prune de damas, 99
Prunier, bois de, 88
Prunillier, 88
Prunus amygdalus, 99
Prunus avium, 84
Prunus domestica, 88, 99
Prunus institia, 99
Prunus mahaleb, 85
Prunus serotina, 86
Prunus spinosa, 87
Pterocarpus dalbergioides, 118, 148
Pterocarpus indicus, 118
Pterocarpus macrocarpus, 148
Pterocarpus santalinus, 152
Pterocarpus vidalianus, 118
Puriri, 143
Purpleheart, 165
Purplewood, 144, 165, 167
Pyrus, 79
  communis, 81

Quebracho, 143
Quercus alba, 71
Quercus cerris, 70
Quercus ilex, 70
Quercus pendunculata, 69
Quercus robur, 69, 70
Quercus sessiliflora, 69, 70
Quercus suber, 70

Racine d' if, 92
Rapanea melaophloeos, 56
Red cedar, 86-87, 116
Red els, 116
Red sandalwood, 152
Red sanders, 152
Red stopper, 143
Rhodes, Bois de, 57
Rhodeswood, 57
Rhus cotinus, 168
Ridge myrtle, 143
"Rio wood," 157
Robinia prouasensis, 154
Robinia pseudacacia, 65
Rood els, 116
Roi, bois du, 155
Rose, bois de, 100
Rosewood, 13, 31, *36*, 50, *52*, 53, 65, 69, 79, *83*, 84, 92, 98, 100, 103, *104*, 114, 128, 141, 142, 144, 148, 151, 154, 157, 159, 160, *161*, 162, 163, 164, 170, 172
  Bahia, 159, 162
  Brazilian, *78*, 103, 151, 159-163, *159, 160, 161, 163*, 164
  East Indian, 103, 163-165, *164*
  Honduras, 162, 164
  Indian, 113, 164
  Jamaica, 57
  Madagascar, 101, 103
  Rio, 162
  Rio de Janeiro, 159, 162
  Tropical American, 159-163, *159, 160, 161, 163*
Rowan tree, 79
Rubywood, 152

Sabicu, 3, *49*, 101, 145-148, *145, 146, 147*
Saffronwood, 56
Sainte-Lucie, bois de, 160
Sal, 77
Salix alba, 43
Salix babylonica, 44
Salix coerulea, 43
Salix triandra, 43
Sambucus nigra, 40
Sandalwood, 57
  Australian, 57
  red, 118, 152
  Venezuelan, 57
  West Indian, 57
Sandarac tree, 138, 139
Sanders, red, 118

Santal, 152
  rouge, bois de, 57, 152
Santalum album, 57
Sapan, bois de, 114
Sapanwood, 114
Satiné, 50
  jaune, 53
  Rouge, 141
  rubane, 141
Satin walnut, 58
Satinwood, 3, 18, 20, 27, 28, 35, 46, 47, 48, 53, 54, 55, 56, 92, 93, 100, 103, 117, 140, 144, 162
  African, 47
  Brazilian, 54, *55*
  East Indian, 47, 52-53, *52*, 54, 77, 79
  San Domingan, 54
  West Indian, 2, 3, 18, 46, 47-51, *49, 50, 51*, 52, 53, 54, 94, *133*, 137, 138, *140*
Sattin wood, 48, 53, 54
Savannawood, 37
Savanna wattle, 37
"Sedar," red, 16
Service Tree, Wild, 79
Servicewood, 79
Shisham, 163
Shorea robusta, 77
Sideroxylon sp., 142
Silkywood, Canadian, 28
Silver tree, 143
Sissoo, 113, 163
Sloanea jamaicensis, 143
Smoke tree, 57
  European, 168
Snakebark, 37, 143
Snakewood, 37, 116, 144
Sorbier, bois de, 79
Sorbus acuparia, 79
Sorbus aria, 20
Sorbus torminalis, 79
South African Yellowwood, 37
Spanish Cedar, 54, 116-117, 132
Spanish elm, 69
Spanish stopper, 143
Spartium junceum, 64
Speckledwood, 116
Spindle Tree, 20, 95
Spruce, 41
Stadmannia oppositifolia, 142
Stavewood, 142
Stinkhout, 104
Stinkwood, 104
Stringybark, 143
Sureau, bois de, 40
Swamp cedar, 116
Swartzia tomentosa, 143
Swietenia macrophylla, 118, 128
Swietenia mahogani, 118
Sycamore, 11, 13, 18, 38-39, *39*, 84, 100
  European, 38
Sycomore, bois de, 38
Syringa vulgaris, 57

Tallowwood, 143
Tamo, 23
Tarrietia actinophylla, 142
Tarrietia argyrondendron, 143
Taxodium distichum, 99
Taxus baccata, 90
Teak, 75-76, *75, 76*, 164
Tectona grandis, 75
Terminalia obovata, 53
Tetraclinis articulata, 138
Thorn, 87-88, *87, 88*
Thuja, 15, *49*, 50, 78, 91, 138-141, *139, 140, 141*
Thuya, bois de, 138
Thyine tree, 138
Tilia europea, 40
Tipuana sp., 100
Titi, 143
Toddalia lanceolata, 142
Tortoiseshellwood, 116

Trichilia hirta, 143
Tropical American Rosewood, 12
Tulipwood, *49*, 50, 90, 99, 100-103, *100, 101, 102*, 144, 163, *165*, 168
  See "American Poplar"
  Brazilian, 26, 100-103, *100, 101, 102*
  East Indian, 100, 101
  French, 101
Tupelo gum, 58
Turraenthus africana, 47

Ulmus Americana, 69
Ulmus campestris, 67
Ulmus glabra, 67
Ulmus hollandica major, 67
Ulmus procera, 68

Vinhatico, 54
Violet, Bois de, 46, 154-159, *155, 156, 158*
"Violet Kingwood," 157
Violetwood, 90, 100, 115, 154-159, *155, 156, 158*, 167
  Brazilian, 100
Vitex parviflora, 53
Vouacapoua americana, 152

Walnut, 3, 6, 7, 13, 14, 15, 18, 23, *25*, 27, 31, 38, 58, 65, 81, *83, 84, 90*, 93, 102, 104-113, *105, 106, 107, 108, 109, 110, 111, 112, 113*, 131, *133, 134, 135*, 162
  American, 92, 107, 108
  American (light brown), 107, 110
  Ancona, 106
  black, 66, 107, 108
  black Virginia, 107
  Circassian, 13, 104, 106
  English, 104, 105, 107, 108, 112
  European, 105
  French, 104, 106, 108
  Irish, 112, 113
  Italian, 104, 105, 106
  Persian, 104
  Rhenish, 104, 106
  satin, 58
  Spanish, 104, 106
  Turkish, 104
  Virginia, 3, 9, 22, 107, 108, 110, *111*, 113
  white, 65, 66
Wamara, 143
Wattle, 103
White ash, American, 23
White ash, Canadian, 23
White tree, 20, 21, 44
White Walnut, 65, 66
Whitebeam, 20
Whitehorn, 79
Wig tree, 168
Wild Service Tree, 79
Willow, 11, 19, 43, 44
  weeping, 44

Ximenia americana, 151
Xylia xylocarpa, 142

Yava, 154
Yellow mahogany, 53
Yellowwood, 46, 47, 48, 53, 54, 55
  Brazilian, 54, *55*
  South African, 37
Yellow wood, Canary, 44
Yew, 9, 15, 37, *55*, 64, 77, 86, 90-93, *90, 91, 92*, 144, *156*, 157, 159, 172, 179
  burl, *177*

Zanthoxylum, sp., 46, 47
  elephantiasis, 151
  flavum, 47, 48
Zebrawood, 26, 37, 65, 98-99, *98*, 144, 151, 163, 172, 174